READING NATIVE AMERICAN LITERATURE

Native American literature explores divides between public and private cultures, ethnicities and experience. In this volume, Joseph Coulombe argues that Native American writers use diverse narrative strategies to engage with readers and are "writing for connection" with both Native and non-Native audiences.

Beginning with a historical overview of Native American Literature, this book presents focused readings of key texts including:

- N. Scott Momaday's *House Made of Dawn*
- Leslie Marmon Silko's *Ceremony*
- Gerald Vizenor's *Bearheart*
- James Welch's *Fool's Crow*
- Sherman Alexie's *The Lone Ranger and Tonto Fistfight in Heaven*
- Linda Hogan's *Power*.

Suggesting new ways towards a sensitive engagement with tribal cultures, this book provides not only a comprehensive introduction to Native American Literature but also a critical framework through which it may be read.

Joseph L. Coulombe is Associate Professor of English at Rowan University, US. He is the author of *Mark Twain and the American West* (2003) and has published articles on Mark Twain, Edith Wharton, Walt Whitman, Sherman Alexie, James Welch, and Emerson Bennett.

READING NATIVE AMERICAN LITERATURE

Joseph L. Coulombe

Routledge
Taylor & Francis Group

LONDON AND NEW YORK

First edition published 2011
by Routledge
2 Park Square, Milton Park, Abingdon, Oxon, OX14 4RN

Simultaneously published in the USA and Canada by Routledge
270 Madison Avenue, New York, NY 10016

Routledge is an imprint of the Taylor & Francis Group, an informa business

© 2011 Joseph L. Coulombe
The right of Joseph L. Coulombe to be identified as author of this work has been
asserted by him in accordance with sections 77 and 78 of the Copyright, Designs and
Patents Act 1988.

Typeset in Joanna and ScalaSans by Taylor & Francis Books
Printed and bound in Great Britain by CPI Rowe Ltd, Chippenham, Wiltshire

British Library Cataloguing in Publication Data
A catalogue record for this book is available from the British Library

Library of Congress Cataloging in Publication Data
Coulombe, Joseph L., 1966-
Reading Native American literature / Joseph L. Coulombe. – 1st ed.
p. cm.
Includes bibliographical references and index.
1. American literature – Indian authors – History and criticism. 2. Indians
of North America – Intellectual life. 3. Indians in literature. I. Title.
PS153.I52C59 2011
810.9'897 – dc22
2010029326

ISBN 13: 978-0-415-57942-1 (hbk)
ISBN 13: 978-0-415-57943-8 (pbk)
ISBN 13: 978-0-203-83290-5 (ebk)

For my children,
Miles, Jeremy, and Trevor.

And for their generation.

CONTENTS

ACKNOWLEDGEMENTS

I want to thank the National Endowment for the Humanities for funding my participation in the 2003 Summer Institute, "Working from Community: American Indian Art and Literature in a Historical and Cultural Context" at Evergreen State University in Washington state. The reading list and itinerary (arranged by Gail Tremblay) as well as the formal and informal discussions helped me develop my critical reading strategies for Native literature. Every participant earned my gratitude and respect during the six-week institute.

I also want to thank Dr. Kimberly Roppolo (University of Oklahoma) for reading the completed manuscript and offering constructive feedback.

I am particularly grateful to my colleague, Dr. Cathy Parrish, who agreed to serve another term as Chair of the English Department at Rowan University, allowing me to finish this project. In addition, I want to thank all my colleagues at Rowan who continually challenge me – with their excellent examples – to become a better teacher and scholar. My students over the years have also earned my gratitude by serving as a sounding board for the ideas in this book. Finally, thanks to Rowan University for funding the Adjusted Workload Program, which gave me the time to focus on scholarship as well as teaching.

I especially want to thank to my wife, Michele, who encouraged me to keep writing when I became frustrated, and whose genuine love of reading is an inspiration.

Finally, thanks to all the Native writers mentioned in these pages – and those not mentioned – who chose to share their artistry and ideas.

PERMISSIONS

The author and publishers are grateful for permission to reproduce the following texts:

"Writing for Connection: Cross-Cultural Understanding in James Welch's Historical Fiction." *Studies in American Indian Literatures.* 20: 3 (Fall 2008): 1–28. Reprinted in its entirety in Harold Bloom's *Modern Critical Series, Native American Writers* (New York: Chelsea House Publishers, 2010: 229–250). Reprinted with permission of the University of Nebraska Press.

"The Approximate Size of His Favorite Humor: Sherman Alexie's Comic Connections and Disconnections in *The Lone Ranger and Tonto Fistfight in Heaven.*" *American Indian Quarterly* 26:1 (Winter 2002): 94–115. Reprinted in its entirety in Harold Bloom's *Modern Critical Series, Native American Writers* (New York: Chelsea House Publishers, 2010: 93–114). Reprinted in part within *Approaching Literature in the 21st Century*, Second Edition, Eds. Peter Schakel and Jack Ridl. New York: Bedford/St. Martin's, 2008: 278–279. Reprinted with permission of the Unviversity of Nebraska Press.

Every effort has been made to trace and contact copyright holders. The publishers would be pleased to hear from any copyright holders not acknowledged here, so that this acknowledgement page may be amended at the earliest opportunity.

INTRODUCTION

NATIVE AMERICAN LITERARY OUTREACH
AND THE NON-NATIVE READER

In *The Man Made of Words*, N. Scott Momaday discusses one of his favorite stories, "The Arrowmaker." In the story, the arrowmaker and his wife are working inside their tepee when the man glimpses a stranger lurking outside. Calmly using his own language, he first alerts his wife to the potential danger. Then the arrowmaker addresses the stranger – still speaking in his native tongue – and, upon receiving no answer, concludes that the man is an enemy. While ostensibly checking the straightness of his arrows, he shoots the stranger outside the teepee through the heart. Momaday values this story for its combination of surface simplicity and deep profundity, and he focuses particularly on its evocative treatment of language as a method of self-definition that contains explicit dangers. The arrowmaker uses words to express and determine his relation to a potentially menacing stranger. To Momaday, language is simultaneously a means of self-protection and a calculated risk. Words allow people to create and define themselves, often by communicating to others, who may or may not be receptive in positive ways.

The story serves also as a lesson to those – metaphorically speaking – outside the tepee. Many readers of Native American fiction are non-Native. To indigenous authors, they are unknown entities, comparable to the lurking stranger in Momaday's "The Arrowmaker." Contemporary Native authors address them in their own language – sometimes literally, more often culturally. The experiences and philosophies that they share with readers are expressions of self-definition and outreach, and they risk much, as all efforts at authorship do, but more particularly considering the history of Native/white relations. For non-Indian readers, Native-authored publications represent both an invitation and a test. Remaining silent – by refusing to respond or failing to try – suggests that readers represent a type of enemy. According to "The Arrowmaker," silence signifies sinister intent.

In "The Toll Road," also from *The Man Made of Words*, Momaday retells the experience of a runner who takes a daily jog on a dirt track through some foothills. Every day somebody places an obstacle – a bundle of branches – in the middle of the road, which the runner removes, but which reappears on subsequent runs. Eventually, the runner leaves payment (a bottle of wine) for the unknown person putting the branches in the road, and he does not encounter them again. Momaday describes the wine as a sign of respect that "acknowledged the old man's possession of the land" (190). In effect, the bundle of branches initiates a dialogue with a trespasser, and such an assertion requires a response. To ignore the bundle would be to dismiss not only another's right of possession but also the gift of access.

This book is my response to an initiation for dialogue, my recognition of another's possession, and my appreciation of the gift. My goal is to read and interpret contemporary Native American fiction as a way to understand what indigenous authors want to communicate to those of us "outside the tepee." In this spirit, I approach texts written by Natives from the position of student rather than from a presumption of expertise. The authors are the experts – each in their own way (and, of course, without representing a monopoly upon pan-Indian or tribal opinion) – and they create and publish stories to educate readers about their perspectives and experiences. My role is to be a responsible reader, listener, and learner, rather than remain a silent lurker on the periphery. I hope this book contributes to a general "upbuilding" – to use Jace Weaver's term (*American* 6) – of Native ideas, experiences, and communities in all their varied manifestations. Teachers and critics can help further the literary successes of Native writers as well as the attendant cultural, political, and legal advancements that result from greater awareness and knowledge. Too often indigenous peoples have been treated as "vanishing." Responding to their proffered dialogue is one way to combat this particular falsehood. Ignoring Native publications – either by refusing to include them in courses or by failing to engage them in critical writing – would be a mistake.

Engaging community

Prominent Native critics agree, despite some confusion on the topic. Recent calls for American Indian literary nationalism and/or separatism have been misinterpreted by some as an effort to silence white critics. It is true that some Native American scholars have encouraged indigenous critics to interpret Native-authored texts using an Indian or specifically tribal intellectual approach – as Craig Womack's title *Red on Red* succinctly puts it – and they have also advocated for the privileging of Native ideas and experiences in criticism about Native literature. Yet no one is excluded. Jace Weaver writes, "I have never said, nor have I ever heard any responsible Native scholar say, that non-Natives should not do Native American Studies, much less the study of Native American literature, any more than Natives should prescind from bringing their own insights to literature by anyone else" (*American* 11). Craig Womack writes, "I have never said non-Indian critics cannot or should not participate in the criticism of Native literature – no such statement appears in a book or publication of mine, and I have never suggested anything like this in public or even in private" (Weaver, *American* 103). Likewise, Robert Warrior writes, "[L]et me say as clearly as possible that not only do I agree with my coauthors [Weaver and Womack] that anyone can write about American Indian issues, but I also share their hope that more people of every background will do so" (Weaver, *American* 197).

Nevertheless, non-Native teachers and critics should operate with care when approaching Native American literature. Despite centuries of efforts by Indian intellectuals to assert Native autonomy and sovereignty, white pundits and politicians have often concocted their own self-serving narratives. There exists a long and sordid history of Euro-Americans defining indigenous art and cultures in ways that distort and destroy. As a result, academic approaches to Native texts should exercise caution, particularly when shifting focus from the published text to a tribally specific cultural context, since tribal cultures are often deeply informed by religious and spiritual beliefs.[1] William Weahkee, executive director of the Five Sandoval Indians Pueblos, comments upon non-Native mis-use of tribal images: "These things are tied in with song. They're tied in with the ritual. They're tied in with things that we cannot divulge, because what happens when we divulge something like that [is that] it's always exploited at our expense. Nothing comes back to the tribes" (in Brown, *Who Owns Native Culture?* 82). To turn someone's sacred beliefs into an academic study, then, seems presumptuous and intrusive. In the case of Indian/white relations, it threatens to replay the cultural misappropriation and dispossession that has taken place over the past five centuries. Although Native critics are increasingly calling for a critical approach that privileges tribal epistemologies, traditions, and belief systems, such an approach should probably come from Native intellectuals, as Lisa Brooks contends: "I would argue that this knowledge cannot be gained through traditional methods of scholarship, but is only fully accessible through interaction within the multi-faceted indigenous networks to which we [Native scholars] belong" ("Digging" 258–59).

Historically, white Americans have been quick to claim knowledge and control of Indian cultures, and examples of cultural colonialism are pervasive – from federal laws that outlawed religious practices (such as the Sun Dance and Ghost Dance, among others) to phony shamans and wannabee-Indian-grandmother-princesses. Only as recently as 1978 was the American Indian Religious Freedom Act passed, which protects the rights of Natives to worship in their own way without outside interference. Not until 1990 was the Native American Graves Protection and Repatriation Act passed, which finally led to the return of many items sacred to tribes, including the remains of the dead.

Despite these small steps forward, many indigenous people are understandably reticent when outsiders attempt to study and opine about traditional beliefs and sacred traditions. In the opening paragraph of Linda Tuhiwai Smith's *Decolonizing Methodologies*, she writes, "[T]he term 'research' is inextricably linked to European imperialism and colonialism. The word itself, 'research,' is probably one of the dirtiest words in the indigenous world's vocabulary … It galls us that Western researchers and intellectuals can assume to know all that it is possible to know of us, on the basis of their brief encounters with some of us" (1). This concern appears repeatedly in Native American writings. For instance, Linda Hogan writes in "Workday":

I go to the university
And out for lunch
And listen to the higher ups
Tell me all they have read
About Indians
And how to analyze this poem.
They know us
Better than we know ourselves.

(in Coltelli, *Winged Words* 85)

Warning academics against intellectual arrogance, Hogan asserts that certain types of knowledge are gained only through lived experience. Similarly, Thomas Darko, the vernacular narrator of Geary Hobson's *The Last of the Ofos*, states: "A Indian person jist ain't born a Indian – like a Ofo, or a Tunica, or a Choctaw – and let it go at that. That person need to learn to be a Ofo, or a Tunica, and such like, and it is that learning makes them Ofos and such-like. It's learning comes through the community" (17–18).

In the summer of 2003, I attended a National Endowment for the Humanities (NEH) Summer Institute, "Working from Community: American Indian Art and Literature in a Historical and Cultural Context," facilitated by artist, poet, and scholar Gail Tremblay in Olympia, Washington. The approximately 25 participants were a fairly eclectic group of Native and non-Native academics, teachers, artists, and writers from across the country. For six weeks we maintained a lively discussion about indigenous art, literature, and criticism, invigorated further by visits and presentations from Leslie Marmon Silko, Linda Hogan, LeAnne Howe, Laura Tohe, and Ophelia Zepeda, among many others. (James Welch was scheduled to come but illness prevented him.) In addition, we met local artists and tribal leaders during a three-day field trip to the Makah Reservation and a half-day visit to the Skokomish Reservation.

For these visits, Gail counseled all the NEH participants regarding protocol. We were being invited to hear clan songs and stories, to observe traditional and contemporary art, and to learn about tribal history and current legal battles. We were being welcomed into community centers as well as private homes. Gail reinforced my initial scholarly reticence by advising us to avoid asking questions that probe into private areas of tribal ceremony and belief. She indicated that tribal leaders would refuse to answer certain questions, and they did – always politely but firmly. (I should also point out that rarely did questions seem intentionally invasive; rather, some questions inadvertently crossed a line for our hosts.) In short, some tribal people chose to share certain parts of their culture with us, but access was necessarily limited. Greg Sarris details this same concern for privacy in his discussion of Mabel McKay, Cache Creek Pomo medicine woman and basket maker: "[F]or Mabel the questions about her basketry appear repetitive, most often inappropriate, no less so than the questions about 'Pomo life' or about her Dreams and doctoring. [...] Mabel cannot separate a discussion about the material aspects of her basketry from a discussion about Dreams, doctoring, prophecy, and the ancient basket-weaving rules, since for Mabel these things cannot be talked about or understood separately" (*Keeping Slug Woman Alive* 51). In light of all that I cannot know, for me to pose as an expert on Native cultures and beliefs – either in the classroom or in my criticism – would be arrogant as well as (very likely) erroneous. A major effect of the NEH Institute was to augment my sense that significant parts of tribal belief and ritual are meant only for people within that specific culture and not for others.[2] I will always remain outside tribal cultures, and no number of books, institutes, conversations, or visits to tribal centers will change that status.

Textual parameters for readers

A more appropriate response – in my opinion – is to position myself as a student in relation to published texts by Native authors. Rather than attempt to "read" or interpret an entire culture (or several cultures) that might inform a given novel, poem, or short story, I focus on what Native authors have chosen to share with readers textually. These published statements are a form of literary outreach to a diverse and inclusive audience.[3] They encourage thoughtful responses by introducing and directing readers to the issues and ideas important within them. Likewise, they steer readers away from other beliefs and traditions. Sherman Alexie has said: "We shouldn't be writing about our traditions, we shouldn't be writing about our spiritual practices. [... Y]ou also have to be aware that it's going to be taken and used in ways that you never intended for it to be. I think it's dangerous, and that's really why I write about day-to-day life" (Purdy, "Crossroads" 15–16). Most Native authors refrain from inviting readers to investigate the inner workings of tribal beliefs and rituals beyond those already presented within the text. Instead, much contemporary Native fiction guides readers to new ways of thinking about the world and their roles in it. Significantly, Native writers provide general readers with the requisite information and context to understand. Catherine Rainwater writes, "Indeed, today's widened audience for Native American literature has partially resulted from deliberate efforts by authors to foster solidarity with a non-Indian audience without *necessarily* demanding extensive, extratextual detours" (*Dreams* 36). While Rainwater acknowledges that some interpretations might benefit from additional cultural knowledge, she also maintains that Native writers foster "solidarity bonds" (*Dreams* xv; 37) between different types of people that help steer readers toward positive responses to issues important to indigenous people. Contemporary narratives actively reach out to mold readers into better informed participants in a pluralistic world community.[4]

Such literary activism is a long-running effort, and Natives have often used writing as an educational tool.[5] Luther Standing Bear is explicit about his goal to teach white readers. In his preface to *My People the Sioux*, he describes his autobiography as "a message to the white race; to bring my people before their eyes in a true and authentic manner ... No one is able to understand the Indian race like an Indian. Therefore, I trust that in reading the contents of this book the public will come to a better understanding of us. I hope they will become better informed as to our principles, our knowledge, and our ability" (v). Native writers continue to view literature as an opportunity to shape their readers. In an interview from 1981, Gerald Vizenor states: "I'm still educating an audience. For example, about Indian identity I have a revolutionary fervor" (quoted in Owens, "Afterword" 250–51). Rita Joe, in her poem "I Lost My Talk," writes:

> So gently I offer my hand and ask,
> Let me find my talk
> So I can teach you about me.
>
> (quoted in Weaver *American* xxiv)

Simon Ortiz, in his essay, "Empowerment," which commemorates the twentieth anniversary of his call for Native American literary nationalism, writes: "By our acknowledgment and affirmation, we are empowered, basically and simply because knowledge shared with each other and gained from each other through communication is empowerment. *We communicate with others because we need to empower ourselves*, especially as Indigenous peoples" (113–14, emphasis added). By communicating with others, Native writers define themselves and shape the contours of the dialogue. Self-expression sustains pride and community. Moreover, as Ortiz makes clear, communication is not only internal (tribal or inter-tribal); it is also external.[6] Indigenous writers inform and influence a varied readership while empowering themselves in the process. Writing to teach is as natural as reading to learn. Great literary texts disseminate facts and opinions about history, philosophy, religion, art, politics, sociology, and psychology. According to Momaday, storytellers even define their audience: "He [the storyteller] creates his listener in the sense that he determines the listener's existence within, and in relation to, the story, and it is never the same" (*Man Made* 3). Readers are formed (or reformed) by their connection to the story and to the text, and as a result their relationship to the world is forever altered.

Reading to learn (not to profess)

Exploring the relationship of author to audience is an interpretive method that transfers from one time to another, from one text to another, and from one type of writer to another. My efforts to understand how writers position themselves in relation to their audiences led to my first book, *Mark Twain and the American West* (2003). Chapter 4 outlines Twain's use of common Euro-American definitions of Native Americans to create an early persona popular with white readers. Twain capitalized upon reductive stereotypes and racial biases to construct a public personality simultaneously comic and dangerous, inclusive for some and exclusive to others. As I researched white narratives of racial superiority, I became increasingly interested in exploring how indigenous Americans define themselves, realizing that, as Womack writes, "Even postcolonial approaches, with so much emphasis on how the settler culture views the other, largely miss an incredibly important point: how do Indians view Indians?" (*Red* 13).[7]

My desire to find answers to this vital question began practically from scratch. In over 25 years of academic training – from elementary school and high school through college and graduate school – I was never assigned a Native American author or text, a lamentable but familiar situation for students and teachers coming of age in the 1980s and 1990s. Womack states, "Like many of us who would go on to teach and write about Native literature, I would do so with no graduate classroom training in the field whatsoever" (Weaver, *American* 151). I had an obvious gap in my education – as an Americanist, but also as an American – that I wanted to correct. From graduate school, I knew that the best way to grow as a learner/ teacher was to include new texts and authors in existing courses. Eventually, I developed courses focusing entirely on Native-authored fiction, courses which (to my knowledge) had never been taught at The University of Tennessee at Martin or at Rowan University in New Jersey, the two institutions at which I have taught full-time. Kathryn Shanley accurately defines one of my roles as a teacher: "to offer to be an audience and then to amplify those voices barely heard, or not heard at all without a committed audience" ("Indians America Loves" 27). My goal is to bring Native voices and texts into the classroom in order to expand my students' awareness – as well as my own knowledge – of indigenous history, thought, and writing.

Despite my students' evident interest in and sympathy for American Indians, many tend not to think of Natives as contemporaries in the modern world. Instead, most of them think about Indians as a single group of people who long ago lost their claim to the land, then were tragically killed off by disease and war. Very few students had ever read Native writers. Despite the popularity in academic circles of writers like N. Scott Momaday, Leslie Marmon Silko, James Welch, Gerald Vizenor, Sherman Alexie, and Linda Hogan, they are unfamiliar to many of my students. Their successes and their stories compel recognition of issues and ideas important to contemporary Natives (and non-Natives), so I regularly include in my courses the "fab five" and the "noble nine", as Daniel Heath Justice terms these well-regarded writers.[8] Despite calls for expanding the "canon" of indigenous writers, and my own re-working of course materials, I return to these much-discussed authors for several reasons.[9] If I get one chance to introduce a group of New Jersey students to contemporary Native writing, I want them to read *Ceremony* – a novel that I consider a masterpiece on several levels – more than *The Surrounded* (as much as I admire D'Arcy McNickle's novel). Rather than Louis Owens' *Wolfsong*, I often assign Welch's *Fools Crow*, an imaginative recreation that re-frames U.S. history for many students. I realize that my courses might reinforce the current Native American "canon," but it is not a canon my students are familiar with. All teachers make similar choices in every course. For instance, I include *Huckleberry Finn* more than *Roughing It*, Frederick Douglass more than Harriet Beecher Stowe, Edith Wharton more than W. D. Howells, Zora Neale Hurston more than Richard Wright. My choices result from my own preferences as much as the critical discussion surrounding them.

We read, discuss, and interpret some texts and authors more than others because they teach us so much. If we can no longer learn from them, then we stop giving them critical attention. Recently some critics have called for a moratorium of sorts on specific Native writers in an effort to avoid cementing a rigid canon in place. This is understandable at one level. However, the attention given to novels like *House Made of Dawn* and *Bearheart* attests to their continued relevance. Few nineteenth-century scholars would suggest that enough has been written about Twain, Emily Dickinson, or Walt Whitman. Readers are still learning from them, working to understand them, and identifying with them in various ways. Individual critics continue to propose unique and informative readings.

Momaday has asserted the impossibility of exhausting certain literary works, and he refers to "The Arrowmaker" as an example, writing: "One does not come to the end of such a story. I have lived with the story of the arrowmaker for many years, and I am sure that I do not yet understand it in all of its consequent meanings. Nor do I expect to understand it so" (*Man Made* 9). Great literature is practically limitless in its ability to speak to readers. In *The Surrounded*, Archilde listens to the elder, Whitey, repeat the story about "The Thing that was to make life easy," and McKnickle writes: "Archilde heard that story also. He wondered at it. And the more he reflected on it the more wonderful it grew. A story like that, he realized, was full of meaning" (69). Some stories are both beautiful and inexhaustible, so we return to them in our research and in our classrooms. While I do not expect to escape criticism for focusing on a much-discussed set of texts, most readers can at least acknowledge their continued power and efficacy.

Moreover, the very popularity of some writers invites an examination of their strategies for engaging readers as well as a recognition of the limits and responsibilities imposed upon their audience. I focus on widely taught contemporary texts – *House Made of Dawn*, *Ceremony*, *Bearheart: The Heirship Chronicles*, *Fools Crow* and *The Heartsong of Charging Elk*, *The Lone Ranger and Tonto Fistfight in Heaven*, and *Power* – because they exert so much influence upon so many readers. Their large readership results, in part, from their ability to speak across cultures. *Reading Native American Literature* examines the narrative strategies developed within these acclaimed texts to create and sustain useful connections between ostensibly different peoples. Much of U.S. history involves Euro-Americans attempting to dictate to indigenous peoples, and the results have been disastrous. Over the past 40 years, Native authors have commanded a large and growing audience, and their publications self-consciously foster intersections of thought to educate a predominantly white audience regarding American Indian opinions and experiences. By engaging readers and establishing connections, they unite readers behind unique solutions to enduring social problems.

Individual methods and shared goals

Each author utilizes different strategies. Momaday's *House Made of Dawn*, despite a sometimes confrontational stance, outlines a universal – if abstract – method by which individuals can overcome the debilitating alienation pervasive in modern society. Throughout his Pulitzer-prize winning novel, Momaday repeatedly references "nothing in the absolute," a concept that evokes eternity and spiritual wholeness, rather than nihilistic meaninglessness (as argued by some critics). To see beyond the physical world is to gain awareness of divine essence, origin, and wholeness, a recognition which necessarily exists outside of cultural categories and remains available to everyone. Although Momaday also draws heavily upon tribal songs and traditions, he proposes this shared and transcendent concept via his depiction of Angela's revelation, Tosamah's sermon, and Abel's vision.

In *Ceremony*, Silko revitalizes the Pueblo concept of the single clan to compel readers to participate in an ambitious act of civic performativity. Silko inscribes the structure and language of a traditional prayer onto her narrative so that reading the novel itself constitutes a speech act with the potential to change the world. Providing textual clues to guide her readers, Silko involves readers in a refashioned ceremony that resulted in her public censure by some Native intellectuals. Because Silko proposes a solution to problems that threaten the entire human population, she expands the definition of the clan to include all people. *Ceremony* is a *tour de force* that re-envisions the novel as a ritual performance with the power to restore balance, wholeness, and connection.

Vizenor uses his challenging style and wit in *Bearheart* to demonstrate how imaginative individualism, paradoxically, creates an intellectual community that exists outside of commonly accepted cultural definitions. While his characters struggle to survive a post-apocalyptic pilgrimage, readers are asked to make sense of often bizarre, fantastical events. The narrative – with its abrupt shifts and contradictory philosophies – refuses easy explanation; every group and creed becomes the target of satire at some point. For Vizenor, self-definition via cultural, spiritual, tribal, or ethnic affiliation is merely subscribing to a "terminal creed" and so doomed to fail. Vizenor uses his postmodern fiction to foster a genuine intellectual connection among individuals – a shared intellectuality centered upon the imagination.

In *Fools Crow* and *The Heartsong of Charging Elk*, Welch invites readers into the largely unfamiliar tribal perspectives of the Blackfeet and Lakota to revise persistent misconceptions about United States' history while offering hope and reconciliation for the future. Within both novels, Welch initially defamiliarizes common objects and ideas for readers using Native expressions and near-translations before he reorients and re-educates his audience within the appropriate tribal context. His descriptions of specific cultural practices, his recounting of tribal stories, his broad use of humor, and his emphasis upon the importance of community all include readers within an Indian world while also emphasizing their shared human connection.

In *The Lone Ranger and Tonto Fistfight in Heaven*, Alexie highlights the various ways that humor can bring people together or push them apart, simultaneously validating and questioning the individual's desire to bridge cultural and personal differences. He uses humor – or his characters use humor – to reveal injustice, protect self-esteem, heal wounds, and foster bonds. The function of humor changes from scene to scene, shifting to serve these varied goals. Rather than a sign of his "hip" irreverence, as argued by some critics, Alexie's sophisticated use of humor unsettles conventional ways of thinking and compels re-evaluation and growth, ultimately allowing Indian characters to connect to their heritage in new ways and forcing non-Native readers to reconsider simplistic generalizations.

Hogan uses an adolescent narrator as both interpreter and witness in *Power* to lead readers on a hunt not only for environmental and human justice, but also for spiritual balance and connection in a world nearly destroyed by colonization. Omishto narrates in the present tense, and the resulting immediacy prompts readers to share her struggle to understand the radical choices of a respected Taiga woman, Ama, who kills an endangered panther sacred to the tribe. That the Taiga is a fictional tribe created by Hogan simultaneously limits critical response to the struggle and emphasizes a key distinction reiterated within *Power*: beliefs can divide, but knowledge connects all people. Omishto's search for knowledge compels readers to re-examine their own relationships to human communities as well as the natural world.

Each writer emphasizes – in his and her own unique way – unity and wholeness, rather than division and categorization, and readers are encouraged to explore a complex set of interconnections that detail a shared humanity and a common purpose. As LeAnne Howe writes, "The Native propensity for bringing things together, for making consensus, and for symbiotically connecting one thing to another becomes a theory about the way American Indians tell stories" ("Blind Bread" 330). Writing for connection seems organic to many indigenous writers, and their narrative strategies and philosophies invite universal applications. Womack writes, "Tribal literary nationalism, contrary to the stereotype, is not defined by isolation but by the way a microcosmic view of the world can lead to macrocosmic understandings and relations" (Weaver *American* 127).

However, none of these writers simplify cultural complexities or ignore conflict. They do not offer a vapid unity or a homogenous world. Old and new differences will always exist between (and within) peoples and cultures. Their purpose, I believe, is to create a balanced world, an informed citizenry, and a just future, a tall order certainly, but an objective that is demonstrated explicitly within their work. Christopher B. Teuton asserts that "criticism as a social practice has been embedded within these works. [... T]hey are committed to community with an activist intent" (198). By reaching out to readers, they help educate an expanding audience about Native American history, ideas, and experiences. As a result, the following chapters are probably best suited for teachers and students. They provide an accessible way for readers to engage Native ideas and cultures by focusing upon the writers' particular presentation of them.

Critical methodology

Rather than bring a specific theory to the text, I seek to understand the theory within the text. My goal is to articulate the strategies that authors use to engage and involve readers. Kimberly Blaeser defines this approach effectively: "I have been alert for critical methods and voices that seem to arise out of the literature itself (this as opposed to critical approaches applied from already established critical language or attempts to make the literature fit already established genres and categories of meaning)" ("Native" 3). Like Blaeser, I am primarily interested in the authority and capacity of the literary works themselves, rather than that of theorists or critics (although I have been guided by them). In my opinion, if a literary theory has useful applications for a text, then the text itself must already contain the theory within its own unique articulation. Readers should seek to understand the theories advanced organically within a text, an approach consistent with one of Womack's recent recommendations for Native critics: "Literary nationalists need to demonstrate more close reading strategies" (Weaver, *American* 172). An effective close reading can outline a theory (or theories) as well as prescribe a useful historical context. Interpreting textual cues and authorial choices can lead to theoretical formulations regarding the function of literature, the textual positioning of readers, the psychology of the individual, the social construction of a group, the mistakes of the past, the problems of the present, or all of these things (or something else entirely!). Good writers have a purpose, and good readers seek to understand it as best they can. The most useful literary theory is directed by the text and its author.[10]

Exploring the cross-cultural connections and disconnections established by Native authors within contemporary fiction can lead in different directions. Sometimes it is as straight-forward as noting the rejection of stale stereotypes, such as the bloodthirsty savage, the noble red man, the stoic warrior, the doe-eyed princess, the nature-based mystic, the drunken degenerate, or the vanishing American, among others. When writers deconstruct familiar caricatures and mythologies, they allow readers immediate access to their texts. The point of connection – even if radically redefined – brings readers into the narrative while also relating the text to the extra-literary world. In effect, readers re-interpret their worlds as they interpret a literary work.

However, Native authors do not write merely to combat misinformation. Many write to offer positive solutions to seemingly intractably problems by emphasizing intersections of thought and being. Such strategies, rather than being defensive, go on the offensive.[11] By emphasizing shared rights, human equality, cross-cultural beliefs, and universal goals, they prepare readers for arguments regarding tribal autonomy and sovereignty. Writing for connection is not a new strategy, and indigenous people have employed it with white Americans for many years. In 1822, Chief Petalesharo of the Skidi Pawnee delivered a speech to President James Monroe objecting to efforts to control his people and culture: "I will not tell a lie – I am going to tell the truth. You love your country – you love your people – you love the manner in which they live, and you think your people brave. – I am like you, my Great Father, I love my country – I love my people – I love the manner in which we live, and think myself and warriors brave" ("Speech" 574; emphasis added). Petalesharo emphasizes broad similarities to enlist audience empathy. He initially tells readers about their own preferences and attachments in positive terms. Then the short declarative statement – "I am like you" – effectively jars listeners/readers from potential complacency and forces them into a personal comparison with a man to whom many would (presumably) not link themselves. Furthermore, Petalesharo constructs a connection that not only compels readers to think from the perspective of an indigenous man, but that also maintains and emphasizes the cultural autonomy of his tribe: whites and Indians are similar only in that they both love their quite different cultures. The connection does not surrender uniqueness; it urges respect by prompting readers to use their own nationalism to understand another's.

Likewise, William Apess begins "An Indian's Looking-Glass for the White Man" by emphasizing the shared humanity and spirituality between his readers and himself: "Having a desire to place a few things before my fellow creatures who are traveling with me to the grave, and to that God who is the maker and preserver *both of the white man and the Indian, whose abilities are the same and who are to be judged by one God*, who will show no favor to outward appearances but will judge righteousness" (emphasis added, 483). A Methodist preacher, Apess uses his Christianity to highlight human equality and universality, which then becomes the foundation for his criticism of Euro-Americans' treatment of Indians. White readers are forced to acknowledge their equivalence – within a Christian context – to a much-maligned minority.

Sarah Winnemucca uses a similar strategy. Arguing that the federal government typically sends corrupt agents to deal with Natives, she writes, "The government does not take care to send the good men; there are a plenty who would take pains to see and understand the chiefs and learn their characters, and their good will to the whites. But the whites have not waited to find out how good the Indians were and what ideas they had of God, just like those of Jesus, who called him Father, *just as my people do*, and told men to do to others as they would be done by, *just as my people teach their children to do*" (emphasis added, *Life among the Piutes* 51). By comparing Christianity to Piaute beliefs and customs, Winnemucca dismantles barriers that prevent respect and erode sovereignty. The connection she offers is as tenuous as it is important to her argument. She is not modifying Piaute religion or illustrating some type of hybrid belief system. Rather, she is describing her religion and culture in terms that her readers can, hopefully, understand. She even manages to compliment some white men while criticizing those who came to swindle the Piautes. Like Apess and Petalesharo, Winnemucca creates a cultural connection to encourage mutual respect and to protect autonomous co-existence. These three Native intellectuals obviously write in different times and circumstances, but they illustrate the manner in which cultural connections serve tribal sovereignty.

The power of fiction

This book works from the assumption – one reinforced by contemporary Native authors – that literature and the study of literature can serve a greater good.[12] Contemporary indigenous writers have done a great deal to heighten public knowledge of social, political, and legal issues important to Indian communities. They use fiction to educate readers about the human relationships and connections that contributed to past failures and that will lead to future successes – for Natives and for all people. Devon Abbott

Mihesuah and Angela Cavender Wilson, who advocate appropriately for an activist agenda from writers and scholars, seem to view literature as a potentially damaging diversion from the important work waiting to be done: "Not enough is being written about tribal needs and concerns, but an inordinate amount of attention is focused on fiction" (*Indigenizing the Academy* 3). Mihesuah makes the case more pointedly: "[M]any fiction writers are apolitical and do not threaten readers; therefore, 'lit-critters' can make careers studying Natives without lifting a finger to help solve tribal problems" (ibid. 38). Rather than viewing critics as "studying Natives" – which implies objectification and false superiority – we might better understand so-called "lit-critters" as learning from Natives. More-over, as Lisa Brooks asserts, "[T]he beauty of poetic writing is as essential to our political health as anyone's direct action" ("Digging" 257). Litera-ture can change the world one person at a time, which is, practically, the only way to change the world. Daniel Heath Justice expresses it well: "Understanding art for life's sake aids all Indigenous peoples, including the literary scholars among us, to decolonize our world in mind as well as body, to dismantle the ideas and forces that tear us into pieces" ("Seeing (and Reading) Red" 118). Likewise, Weaver writes, "Literary criticism may not be able to prevent someone from dying, but it can participate in a process by which people think differently about indigenous peoples (as well as the wider community of other-than-human persons) and by which Natives think differently about themselves" (*American* 70).

As readers, teachers, critics, and students, we should continue to focus conscientiously on the literary expressions of Native writers. They teach us important lessons, which then inform our subsequent interactions with others. The web of influence that extends outward from popular fiction might, conceivably, assist an important court case in the future simply by virtue of the social contexts and opinions it helps to create. Such incre-mental change helped recently to elect the first African American president of the United States. We should work to expand the audience for Native writers, not limit their influence and dismiss them (and their promoters) as inconsequential.

By engaging in acts of literary outreach, writers like Momaday, Silko, Vizenor, Welch, Alexie, and Hogan help to remove some of the damaging barriers that divide ethnic and racial groups in America and around the world. Their internationally acclaimed publications represent powerful tools in an ongoing effort to foster equality, respect, and trust. As I worked on this book, I have kept in mind the self-admonition of Geary Hobson's well-intentioned character, Dr. Payne, in *The Last of the Ofos*: "Sometimes scientists and scholars kill the very things they love, don't they, Thomas?" (108). *Reading Native American Literature* springs from my genuine appreciation of the artistry and ideas of contemporary Native writers, and I hope my response is worthy of their accomplishments.

1

FOLLOWING THE TRACKS

HISTORY AND CONTEXT OF NATIVE WRITING

Native American literature did not appear suddenly from a void with the publication of Momaday's *House Made of Dawn*. Its 1969 Pulitzer Prize is simply the historical moment when white America – and others – began to acknowledge the great value of Native writing. For centuries, indigenous Americans have written to express themselves and defend their lands, cultures, and sovereignty. From Samson Occom in the seventeenth century to D'Arcy McNickle in the twentieth century, Native writers have voiced their opinions, shared their stories, and advocated for their rights with force and intelligence. Their sermons, essays, autobiographies, histories, poems, plays, and novels offer an extensive foreground and a vital context for the prose and poetry currently earning acclaim.

Written Native American literary history represents an impressive achievement of wide-ranging styles, opinions, and goals, particularly considering the fact that many Native writers were compelled to use English rather than their own languages. Joy Harjo and Gloria Bird emphasize the success and creativity of Native writers – as well as the particular challenges of writing in English – in the title of their anthology, *Reinventing the Enemy's Language* (1997). Over the centuries, Native writers have adopted and adapted a language that white Americans more often used as a tool of betrayal and dispossession. Treaties, agreements, and laws enacted by Euro-American officials regularly offered empty promises, and non-Native writers consistently distorted indigenous peoples in poetry, periodicals, and fiction.

As a result, the impact of a well-phrased argument was often lost in the barrage of meaningless verbiage. Yet despite white America's desire to obscure these voices, Indian writers succeeded in accommodating the language to their own needs. In *Tracks* (1988), Louise Erdrich comments upon the obscure legalese used to seize tribal land and its other effects. One of her narrators, Nanapush, complains that the Anishinaabe have become "a tribe of file cabinets and triplicates, a tribe of single-space documents, directives, policy. A tribe of pressed trees. A tribe of chicken-scratch that can be scattered by a wind, diminished to ashes by one struck match" (225). Nanapush is a story-teller profoundly connected to tribal oral tradition, and he distrusts the written documents and their promises. His apprehension is matched by Margaret, who avoids touching printed words because she "didn't want the tracks rubbing off on her skin" (47). In the end, however, Nanapush follows the "tracks" of his granddaughter Lulu through a forest of paperwork to free her from a prison-like boarding school. His success mirrors Erdrich's own achievement – as well as that of other Native writers – who create and follow "tracks" to the past to help liberate succeeding generations.

Native American publications provide a pathway leading readers to a more complete understanding of Native history, ideas, and rights. Indian writers help readers look backward to interpret not only the past, but also the present. For Natives, the use of the enemy's language is a powerful weapon in the fight for self-determination and sovereignty.

Invasion and loss

In 1492, the Americas contained approximately fifty million people (Taylor, *American* 40). In the area currently occupied by the United States and Canada, population estimates at first contact range to 18 million (Green, *British Museum Encyclopedia* 122). Thus, overstating the diversity of indigenous cultures and traditions is practically impossible. Today, in North America alone, nearly six hundred indigenous nations sustain a range of social structures and belief systems.[1] Karen Kilcup describes North America as "peopled by diverse groups of tribal cultures dazzling in the variety of their language, religion, social and political organization, and means of livelihood" ("Introduction"2). To generalize about American Indians is, almost necessarily, to be wrong.

Nonetheless, all Indigenous peoples and cultures were threatened – either directly or indirectly – by the arrival of Europeans. Diseases decimated indigenous populations. Many tribes endured multiple waves of illnesses, which made them more vulnerable to colonization. From 1617 to 1620, for instance, a pandemic – likely brought from Europe by fishing vessels stopping for water and supplies – killed 90 to 96 percent of the Native population in the New England region (Loewen, *Lies My Teacher Told Me* 80). The psychological and cultural trauma – multiplied generationally for all tribes – is immeasurable.

Communities weakened by disease were often further destroyed by warfare and slavery. An often overlooked fact of American history is the enslavement not only of Africans and African Americans, but also of Native Americans. A 1708 South Carolina census identifies 1,400 Native slaves, and a 1730 census from Rhode Island lists 223 Indian slaves (ibid. 106). American Indians captured during war by Euro-Americans were often sold into slavery in the West Indies. Warfare weakened and destroyed many Native communities and cultures. Battles over land occurred regularly, and some escalated to the level of full-scale war. Early wars include the Pequot War of 1636–37, King Philip's War in 1675 (involving the Wampanoag, Narragansett, Podunk, and Nipmuck), and the French and Indian War (part of the global Seven Years War), which ran from 1754 to 1763. In each case, tribal populations were ravaged, and their lands were taken by American colonists.

Other land grabs were orchestrated with no consideration for tribal sovereignty or peoples. After the American Revolution, the United States negotiated with other nations – not tribal governments – for tribal lands. The Louisiana Purchase of 1803, for instance, removed France as a colonial competitor for Native lands. No indigenous officials were consulted or paid, despite obvious tribal ownership and occupation of the territory. The purchase is often heralded as a world-class bargain, but the U.S. paid France for Indian land. Likewise, the 1848 Treaty of Guadalupe Hidalgo claimed extensive tribal lands from Mexico, including California, Nevada, Utah, Arizona, and parts of Colorado, Montana, and New Mexico. Again, indigenous peoples were not consulted or paid during these negotiations for their lands.

These political maneuvers, cultural threats, and apocalyptic events contribute to the historical context for understanding Native writing in English. Indigenous intellectuals often wrote with a mixture of anger, frustration, and sorrow at white treachery and their own dispossession, while their marginalized position in American society compelled them to strike a moderate middle-ground to define themselves and defend their rights.

Adapting to change, writing for change

Facing relentless physical and cultural assaults, many Native people incorporated elements of Christianity into their belief systems, or they converted outright. In the eighteenth century, an increase in missionary efforts by European colonists – particularly during the Christian revivalism of the 1730s and 1740s – sought to Westernize indigenous Americans. Mission schools and Indian "Praying Towns" were established by white reformers on tribal lands, and many Natives took the opportunity to learn to read and write in English.[2] Hundreds of Natives attended programs at Dartmouth, Harvard, Princeton, and the College of William and Mary during the 1660–70s (Peyer, "Introduction" 5).

Samson Occom – the first published Native American writer – converted to Christianity during this period. His *Sermon Preached at the Execution of Moses Paul* (1772) went through nineteen editions. At the time, it was valued primarily as a temperance tract denouncing the "sin of drunkenness" (Occom, *Collected* 192). However, Occom implicitly condemns the white culture that introduced alcohol to Native people, and he subtly equates Moses' execution with the crucifixion of Jesus Christ. In this way, he suggests the betrayal at the heart of white/Indian relations. Occom himself was betrayed personally by his employer, Eleazor Wheelock, who broke his promise to care for Occom's family while Occom lived in England for two years raising funds for Wheelock's Indian charity project. Moreover, the funds were used to establish Dartmouth University primarily for white people, rather than to educate indigenous Americans, as planned.

Although several Natives write within this early Christian tradition, including Joseph Johnson (Occom's son-in-law) and Hendrick Aupaumut, William Apess is the best known. An ordained Methodist minister, he directly addressed white Christian readers to decry the hypocrisy of their racism. Apess used biblical references to authorize his opinions and his anger, while defending the dignity and rights of Native people. His autobiography, *A Son of the Forest* (1829), was his first publication, and an expanded edition appeared within two years. Building upon his success, he published *The Experiences of Five Christian Indians of the Pequot Tribe* (1833), which extended the range and form of the spiritual autobiography to showcase indigenous Christians facing racism and removal. Its final chapter, "An

Indian's Looking-Glass for the White Man," is a forceful vindication of Native morality and intellectualism as well as a finely honed attack on white-generated stereotypes and prejudice.

Apess was writing at a particularly bleak period of Native American history. By the 1830s, a federal policy of separation and removal had replaced a policy of assimilation-via-Christianity. After U.S. independence from Britain, federal policy increasingly sought to isolate Indians by restricting them to ever-shrinking reservations or removing them entirely from traditional tribal lands. Written treaties became a central feature of this policy, which lasted for nearly a century. Between 1778 and 1870, nearly 400 treaties were ratified.[3] Many were thinly veiled efforts to legitimize land theft using duplicitous legalese and straw-man signatures. Many more were broken. Charles Eastman wrote: "Never was more ruthless fraud and graft practiced upon a defenseless people than upon these poor natives by the politicians! Never were there more worthless 'scraps of paper' anywhere in the world than many of the Indian treaties and Government documents" (*Deep Woods to Civilization* 99).

The history of broken treaties is not only another unfortunate testament to U.S. hypocrisy, greed, and racism, but it is also an essential backdrop and context for reading Native American literature. Even when not mentioned explicitly, the history is never far below the surface.

Trail of broken treaties

The first treaty was signed with the Delaware (Lenape) in 1778 during the American Revolution. Although the Delaware agreed to help the new nation against the British in exchange for statehood, the treaty was not upheld by the U.S. The Delaware signed 18 subsequent treaties that essentially took their land and relocated tribal members from the eastern seaboard to Canada and Oklahoma (Nabokov, *Native American Testimony* 119). Another representative example of such malfeasance occurred between 1800 and 1812, during which 15 treaties took present-day Illinois, Indiana, and parts of Ohio, Michigan, and Wisconsin from several different tribes.

After the War of 1812, the federal government expanded its policy of removal and aggressively pressured eastern tribes to relocate west of the Mississippi River to "Indian Territory" (which became the state of Oklahoma in 1907, further disenfranchising many Indians). Some tribes had allied themselves with Britain during the war – such as the Creeks and Shawnee – and U.S. officials sought to punish them. The Red Stick War (1813–14) against the Muskogee Creek left 80 percent of the tribe dead, and the resulting treaty took 14 million acres of land (Green, British Museum Encyclopedia 131).

Indian lands were valuable, and, significantly, some tribes were successful competitors within the American economy. The Cherokee, who, in fact, had allied with the U.S. against Britain, were targeted for removal along with the Chickasaws, Choctaws, Creeks, and Seminoles – the so-called "Five Civilized Tribes." They lobbied hard to preserve their remaining lands in present-day Georgia, Tennessee, and the Carolinas, an effort aided by the Cherokee syllabary completed by Sequoyah in 1821. To publicize tribal concerns, Elias Boudinot began publishing The Cherokee Phoenix in 1828 in both English and Cherokee.[4]

Boudinot toured the eastern states in 1826 raising funds and awareness. His published speech, "An Address to the Whites," specifically targeted white readers on behalf of Cherokee people, lands, and rights. It begins by highlighting the similarity between whites and Natives: "What is an Indian? Is he not formed of the same materials with yourself?" (69). Asserting that whites "differ from them [the Cherokee] chiefly in name" (72), he claims "the common liberties of America" (77–78) for all Natives. Boudinot details their accomplishments – including the syllabary, conversion to Christianity, and success as ranchers and farmers – in an attempt to nor-malize Native people to white readers. Amongst other evidence, he explains that Cherokee in Georgia own "22,000 cattle; 7,600 horses; 46,000 swine; 2,500 sheep; 762 looms; 2,488 spinning wheels; 172 wagons; 29 ploughs; 10 saw-mills; 31 grist-mills; 62 Blacksmith shops; 8 cotton machines; 18 schools; 18 ferries" (72).[5] Boudinot concludes his address by warning of Cherokee extinction, a very literal threat considering the treatment of indigenous peoples over the previous three hundred years.

Despite efforts, the Indian Removal Act was passed in 1830 with President Andrew Jackson's full support. The Cherokee fought it all the way to the Supreme Court but were left with few good options. Boudinot was one of approximately 100 Cherokee who signed the Treaty of New Echota in 1835, which ceded remaining tribal lands. Fifteen thousand Cherokee signed an official protest circulated by tribal council – but to no avail. What followed is known as the Trail of Tears. By 1838, nearly 17,000 Natives were forcibly marched – often at gunpoint – from their tribal lands to Oklahoma. Approximately 4,000 died. Boudinot was killed in 1839 by tribal members for his role in the removal, as were other leaders who signed the treaty. In her historical novel, Pushing the Bear (1996), Diane Glancy recounts the personal and cultural devastation caused by removal.

While eastern tribes were being forced west of the Mississippi River, western tribes were also facing ongoing encroachment and assault. Spanish invaders had entered the southwest as early as 1540 when Francisco Vásquez de Coronado led an army through present-day Arizona and New Mexico (ultimately reaching Kansas). Euro-Americans continued making imperialist incursions into tribal lands, establishing missionaries and trading posts throughout the west. In *Life Among the Piutes: Their Wrongs and Claims* (1883), Sarah Winnemucca Hopkins (aka Thocmetony) offers a personal and tribal history of the years between 1844 and 1883, which includes the 1878 Bannock War. She recounts her childhood fear and helplessness as whites brought disease and took land in Nevada, California, Idaho, and Oregon. She documents massacres, rapes, and other brutalities perpetrated upon the Piaute and other tribes. As a translator, Winnemucca was in a good position to witness and publicize events taking place in the west. As in the hundreds of lectures Winnemucca gave throughout the United States, *Life Among the Piutes* sharply criticizes the reservation agents who profited personally without helping Natives or upholding treaty rights, and she was an outspoken and controversial advocate of land rights and reform.

John Rollin Ridge (aka Yellow Bird) also wrote about land rights and abuses in the far west, but he used popular fiction as his vehicle. In 1854, Ridge published the first novel by a Native American, *Life and Legend of Joaquín Murieta: The Celebrated California Bandit*, which dramatizes the struggle of a Mexican man resisting American colonialism in the 1850s after the Mexican War. Forced off his land and treated like the "conquered subjects of the United States, having no rights which could stand before a haughtier and superior race" (9), Joaquín becomes an outlaw and "live[s] henceforth for revenge" (12). After much violence, banditry, and bravado, interspersed occasionally with episodes of sentiment and romance, Joaquín is killed, but the legend of the outlaw lives forever, not least because of Ridge's efforts.

Joaquín serves as a proxy for Native America: both had their land stolen, and both fought to assert their dignity. Ridge, however, failed to express much pan-Indian solidarity in *Life*, and his novel treats the Tejon Nation of California in condescending terms. His family history is the centerpiece of a posthumous work, *Poems, by a Cherokee Indian, with an Account of the Assassination of His Father, John Ridge* (1868), which may be the first book of poetry published by a Native writer (Ruoff, "Native American Writings" 149). The author's father and grandfather, John Ridge and Major Ridge, were killed – like Elias Boudinot – because they signed the treaty that precipitated Cherokee removal and the Trail of Tears.

While the Trail of Tears is perhaps the most infamous removal, many indigenous people experienced grief and trauma from military takeovers and outright massacres. The atrocities of nineteenth-century U.S. history are well-documented (although not always well-publicized), and they inform Native thought and writing in the past as well as the present. In the Sand Creek massacre of 1864, for instance, over 150 Arapaho and Cheyenne – primarily women, children, and elderly – were killed and mutilated by soldiers in southeastern Colorado, despite the fact that their leader, Black Kettle, served as a peace chief for the Cheyenne (Greene, *Washita* 21). Likewise, in 1870, a peaceful band of Blackfeet in Montana was attacked by federal troops. Although its leaders had signed a peace treaty, over 170 women, children, and infirm were massacred. The men were on a hunting expedition, and not a single federal soldier was killed. James Welch recounts the event – known as the Marias Massacre – in his novel *Fools Crow* (discussed in Chapter 5).

Such atrocities represent important historical touchstones, and many are reconstructed in fiction and poetry by Native writers. Luci Tapahonso, for instance, writes of Navajo removal – also called the "Long Walk" – an event central to Diné tribal history. Tapahonso prefaces her poem, "In 1864," with a factual account of the event, in which eight thousand Navajo were marched at gunpoint three hundred miles from their land in New Mexico to a military enclosure at Fort Sumner: "They were held for four years until the U.S. government declared the assimilation attempt a failure. More than 2,500 died of smallpox and other illnesses, depression, severe weather conditions, and starvation" (*Sáanii Dahataał* 7). Tapahonso's poem not only documents the atrocity and memorializes the dead, but it also asserts the timeless beauty of the Diné and their continuing cultural traditions.[6] Likewise, Janet Campbell Hale writes about historical outrages by honoring the past as well as the present. In "Return to Bear Paw," Hale highlights the personal connections that she develops with her grandmother and the Nez Perce as she traces the epic route of Chief Joseph's band through Idaho and Montana toward Canada while being pursued by federal troops.

Like Tapahonso and Hale, many Native writers construct narratives that not only portray the brutal reality of American history but also highlight the strength and resilience of tribal peoples past and present.

New policies, old problems

The period between 1870 and 1890 is often referred to as the "Indian Wars." During this time, tribes still in possession of valuable land were confronted with increasingly dire prospects. In 1871, a shift in U.S. policy occurred with the passage of the Indian Appropriations Act. It stipulated that tribes would no longer be considered separate sovereign nations, so they would not be formally negotiated with. The era of the treaties was essentially over.[7] Moreover, with the end of the Civil War, the U.S. increasingly turned its attention to western land and resources.

As a result, many tribes in the west faced impossible choices. Treaties restricted them to reservations; railroad companies (with military attachments) surveyed routes directly through tribal lands; and buffalo herds were hunted to near extinction. Some tribes, bands, clans, and individuals opted to accommodate white demands, while others forcefully resisted. Although federal troops had more guns and soldiers, Natives achieved some notable victories. The most celebrated is the Battle of Little Bighorn in 1876, during which the Lakota and Cheyenne defeated their over-confident attackers, General Armstrong Custer and the Seventh Cavalry. Sitting Bull and Crazy Horse were among the defenders. Black Elk provides a first-person account of the U.S. attack in *Black Elk Speaks* (1932); James Welch examines its historical treatment in *Killing Custer* (1994); and Sherman Alexie treats Little Bighorn briefly via his adolescent narrator in *Flight* (2007).

The victory prompted the U.S. military to shift its strategy, and federal troops began campaigning more in winter, when plains Indians typically divided into smaller groups and thus became more vulnerable. The Lakota epitomized the desperate situation faced by many tribes at this time as they defended their land and rights against U.S. colonial expansion. Located on an ever-shrinking reservation in South Dakota, the Lakota were less able to follow their traditional lifestyles. Buffalo and other game were mostly gone, and whites continued to intrude into their land searching for gold and other resources. Many Lakota were forced to depend upon insufficient agency handouts.

Adding to the cultural clash, some Lakota became adherents of the Ghost Dance religion established by Wovoka (also known as Jack Wilson), a Paiute from Nevada. Practitioners believed that, if they adhered to traditional ways and performed the Ghost Dance, then their ancestors would return from the dead and force Euro-Americans out of North America. This syncretic belief system held that a savior would facilitate the return of all tribal land and the rejuvenation of the buffalo herds. The Ghost Dance gained popularity throughout Native communities in the 1880s, a time when federal officials increasingly suppressed tribal religious practices. The Ghost Dance, in particular, made many white people nervous.

On December 29, 1890, the Seventh Cavalry killed nearly 300 unarmed men, women, and children – practitioners of the Ghost Dance and advocates of tribal sovereignty – on the Pine Ridge Reservation in South Dakota. Charles Eastman, a Lakota doctor with a medical degree from Boston University, went to the site the next day, and he wrote, "Fully three miles from the scene of the massacre we found the body of a woman completely covered with a blanket of snow, and from this point on we found them scattered along as they had been relentlessly hunted down and slaughtered while fleeing for their lives" (*Deep Woods to Civilization* 111). The event lives in infamy as the Wounded Knee Massacre. Two weeks earlier, Sitting Bull had been assassinated. For many, these events signaled the end of armed resistance by Native Americans, and to this day they epitomize a profoundly tragic historical legacy. In 1970, Dee Brown published *Bury My Heart At Wounded Knee*, a Native-centered perspective of nineteenth-century history. In 1973, activists from the American Indian Movement (AIM) took over the town of Wounded Knee on the Pine Ridge Reservation to demand an end to official corruption and judicial bias, resulting in a two-month armed stand-off with the FBI.

The situation in Indian country got worse after 1890. A time-bomb was ticking in the form of the General Allotment Act. Passed in 1887 – and sponsored by Senator Henry Dawes of Massachusetts – the Dawes Allotment Act (as it is also called) eliminated communal land ownership rights for most tribes, instead assigning up to 160 acres to each family (and less to individuals). The directive was intended, ostensibly, to encourage individual enterprise, but it was a disaster. After allotments were distributed, the remainder of reservation land was taken by the federal government and sold to whites. Furthermore, allotments were tax-exempt for only 25 years, so many people lost their land in 1912 (and after) when heavy property taxes came due. Altogether, the Allotment Act cost Native Americans a total of 86 million acres of land in 47 years, and many reservations were made into checkerboards of Indian/white ownership (Janke, "Population" 159–61). Louise Erdrich explores the external pressures and the internal divisions caused by the Allotment Act in her historical novel *Tracks*.

Allotment threatened to fracture tribal unity in myriad ways. The Act also stipulated that Indian children must attend off-reservation boarding schools (ibid. 162). Rations were withheld from parents who refused to send their children away. By 1920, 70 percent of Native children were attending boarding schools in 14 states (Peyer, "Introduction" 20). English was mandatory. Tribal languages, dress, and hairstyles were prohibited. Boys were generally taught farming and commercial skills, and girls were trained for domestic services. Richard Pratt, a former general and prison warden, who became the first superintendent of Carlisle Indian School in 1879, famously stated, "Kill the Indian in him, and save the man," a sentiment that broadcasts the destructive nature of the schools ("Indians with Whites" 260). In *No Parole Today* (1999), Laura Tohe begins her collection with a "Letter to General Pratt," which implicates him directly in "cultural genocide" (xii). She writes: "Assimilation made us feel ashamed for what we were, where we came from, how we spoke, our stories, our families, how we dressed, and for speaking our language" (x). Her poems simultaneously document the pain caused by the schools as well as the process of de-colonization that she and other Natives undergo as they re-claim their tribal heritage.

Many Native writers have documented their reactions to the boarding schools. Zitkala-Sa (also known as Gertrude Bonin) wrote in 1900 about her experiences at a boarding school, and she expresses anger at the lack of freedom and respect extended to pupils. Trapped "among a cold race whose hearts were frozen hard with prejudice" (*American Indian Stories* 76), she relates the story of a girl punished for playing in the snow, who is then beat more for refusing to answer "yes" when "no" is her only English word. Zitkala-Sa describes being taunted as a "squaw" during speech contests, several of which she won. Reflecting back, she writes, "Like a slender tree, I had been uprooted from my mother, nature, and God. I was shorn of my branches, which had waved in sympathy and love for home and friends" (ibid. 97).

Likewise, Luther Standing Bear wrote about his experiences at Carlisle Indian School in 1879, its inaugural year. Although he maintains a surprisingly positive tone in *My People the Sioux* (1928), he also describes sleeping on the bare floor, having "a white man's name" sewn to his shirt (137), and feeling an overwhelming sense of loneliness and dispossession. He writes, "All I could think of was my free life at home. How long would these people keep us here? When were we going home?" (139). He writes of the time when his father visited him at the school, and he had to ask permission to speak to his father – who knew no English – "in the Sioux tongue" (149). Most written accounts of boarding schools emphasize that tribal languages were prohibited and students left ill-prepared either to return to Indian communities or to succeed in white American society.

Laura Tohe writes that "[t]he most crippling legacy of boarding schools is the devastation of our native languages and culture. We are still trying to recover from the loss. Separation from home, land, and culture equals loss of identity and language" (*American Indian Stories* x).

Recovering from loss, and continuing the oral tradition

The loss of tribal languages remains a severe threat to indigenous cultures and beliefs throughout Native American communities. Tribal literatures, in particular, are in jeopardy, despite strong ongoing efforts to preserve them. Before 1492, approximately 300 languages existed within eight language groups (Fixico, *American Indians* 39–40). Today nearly 190 languages survive in the United States, but many have limited active speakers, and only 20 languages are currently taught to children by their parents as a first language (Johansen, *Praeger Handbook* 5). When a language is lost, an entire worldview and philosophy is endangered. Native experts have argued for "the necessity of maintaining their ancestral language because their culture, their ceremonies, and their spiritual history and values can only be transferred through the metaphors inherent in the language and through the cognitive imagery these metaphors invoke" (García, Axelrod, and Lachler, "English is the Dead Language" 100).

Efforts at language restoration have increased since the 1960s. In 1968, the Bilingual Education Act passed, and in 1990, the Native American Languages Act passed. By the 1990s, over 30 tribal colleges existed with language programs (Fixico, *American Indians* 52). Because language revitalization is usually community centered, tribes with large populations are having the most success. According to Donald Fixico, "The Navajo, Iroquois, Inuit (Eskimo), Tohono O'odham, Pima, Apache, and Lakota have the highest number of native speakers" (ibid. 40). Ofelia Zepeda's collection, *Ocean Power*, includes poems that appear only in Tohono O'odham, not English. Nevertheless, even the most robust languages are still endangered (García, Axelrod, and Lachler, "English is the Dead Language" 103).

Historically, tribal knowledge and beliefs are passed from generation to generation using indigenous languages and oral traditions. Tribal oral traditions include stories, songs, and histories as well as prayers, ceremonies, and rituals. They are usually related integrally to the spiritual belief systems of specific tribes, clans, and individuals. Much of the cultural knowledge and context necessary to understand the individual components of tribal oral traditions is available only to tribal members. Commenting upon a

Cherokee creation story, Christopher B. Teuton writes: "The creation of Elohi is not simply a material matter; it occurs within and through a complex social context that is structured by clear ethical codes," adding: "to interpret oral narratives as though they are equivalent to texts that are products of literacy is to confuse and obfuscate the methods and purposes of two very different forms of communication" ("Theorizing American Indian Literature"194–95).[8] For this reason, particularly considering the exploitative history of white/Native relations, assessments of tribal literatures and cultures by non-tribal people should be limited. Richard Erdoes and Alfonso Ortiz write, "[T]here are strict systems of beliefs about the effects of telling certain stories in certain ways or at specific times. Even Trickster stories told principally for entertainment must still be told strictly according to tradition ... In some tribes the narrator is forbidden to change or omit a single word in a legend, while others permit free embellishment and modification. Some stories are 'owned' by a certain family or even a particular person, and cannot be retold by outsiders" (Erdoes and Ortiz, "Introduction" xx).

Trickster is a notable presence and "cultural hero" in many tribal traditions (ibid. xiv), appearing variously in the form of Coyote, Raven, Rabbit, Spider, and others. Erdoes and Ortiz write, "We certainly see them, in classic Trickster style, being clever and foolish at the same time, smart-asses who outsmart themselves. But they are much more than that. Iktomi is a supernatural character with broad powers; Rabbit Boy stars in important creation myths, as the creator. Iktomi is powerful as well as powerless; he is a prophet, a liar who sometimes tricks by using the truth. He is a spider but transforms himself into a man, bigger than life and smaller than a pea. He is a clown, often with a serious message. Like Coyote and Veeho, he has a strong amorous streak and at times seems completely driven by sex" (ibid. xiv). Evoking similar complexity, Vizenor describes Naanabozho, the "compassionate woodland trickster" of the Anishinaabe, who "wanders in mythic time and transformational space between tribal experiences and dreams." Vizenor continues:

> The trickster is related to plants and animals and trees; he is a teacher and healer in various personalities who, as numerous stories reveal, explains the values of healing plants, wild rice, maple sugar, basswood, and birch bark to woodland tribal people. More than a magnanimous teacher and transformer, the trickster is capable of violence, deceptions, and cruelties; the realities of human imperfections. The woodland

trickster is an existential shaman in the comic mode, not an isolated and sentimental tragic hero in conflict with nature. The trickster is comic in the sense that he does not reclaim idealistic ethics, but survives as a part of the natural world; he represents a spiritual balance in a comic drama rather than the romantic elimination of human contradictions and evil.

(*The People* 3–4)

Tricksters and trickster-like figures appear throughout Native texts, and they represent an immense source of entertainment and knowledge. Their very changeableness seems to facilitate the successful translation into written English. Kimberly Roppolo argues that Indian writers "have colonized English as much as it [English] has colonized" indigenous peoples (Roppolo, "Samson" 303). Trickster can probably be considered central to this ongoing linguistic event. With Trickster ranging free within it, English is no longer only the "enemy's language." Writing by American Indians in the twentieth and twenty-first centuries demonstrates this fact.

Fiction, poetry, and self-definition

The first half of the twentieth century is generally considered a bleak time in Native American history. Restricted largely to reservations, Natives experienced poverty, racism, and dispossession while the U.S. became increasingly wealthy and powerful on their lands around them. American Indians were not even allowed U.S. citizenship until 1924.

Nonetheless, Natives also distinguished themselves in myriad ways during this time. Jim Thorpe won two gold medals in the 1912 Olympics in Sweden. Will Rogers became an enduring national celebrity. The Society of American Indians (SAI) was created to influence public attitudes and policy. Nearly 10,000 Natives served in the First World War, and 25,000 fought in the Second World War (Fixico, *American Indians* xv). In 1934, the Indian Reorganization Act – sometimes called the Indian New Deal – lessened the control of off-reservation boarding schools and shifted power from Washington, D.C. back to Indian communities, encouraging "tribal governments to create their own constitutions, membership, and laws" (ibid. xx). Although no panacea, it helped advance a continuing reclamation of political, economic, and cultural sovereignty. By 1944, tribal leaders created the National Congress of American Indians to coordinate political efforts and speak with a more unified, powerful voice.

Writers also began to gain recognition, publishing a range of novels, histories, poems, plays, and story collections. Many works published by Indian authors between 1890 and 1960 have gained academic, if not necessarily popular, accolades. Yet recovery and interpretive efforts are ongoing. The writings of E. Pauline Johnson, Alexander Posey, John Oskison, Simon Pokagon, Francis La Flesche, and Todd Downing, among others, are only beginning to receive widespread evaluation. Some others have received much more attention, and healthy debate continues regarding their meaning and merit.

The first novel published by an Indian woman is *Wynema: A Child of the Forest* (1891) by S. Alice Callahan. It uses sentimental romanticism to portray the change of its title character from a Muscogee woman into a Victorian lady amidst the radical transformations of Creek culture generally. Womack labels Callahan's novel "a document of Christian supremacism and assimilation," stating that "the utter lack of any Creek opinions renders invisible the tremendous acts of resistance against Oklahoma statehood that were going on both within the Creek Nation and in alliance with other tribes in Indian Territory" (*Red* 107–8). Others defend *Wynema* as a product of the times. Siobhan Senier, while conceding it "as a rather haphazardly constructed and even racist book" ("Allotment Protest" 423), argues that Callahan omitted Muscogee traditions intentionally to avoid prying eyes, instead creating characters "concerned with asking their interlocutors to look more closely at the conditions of power that structure Indian-white relations" (ibid. 424).

In 1912, Mourning Dove (aka Christine Quintasket) completed her novel, *Cogewea, the Half-Blood: A Depiction of the Great Montana Cattle Range* (1927), but it was not published until after her editor, L.V. McWhorter, made substantial revisions and additions, fragmenting the narrative and muddying its goals. The plot draws heavily upon the popular western melodramas that Mourning Dove reputedly enjoyed. The heroine's heart vacillates between a deceptive white intruder and a dependable mixed-blood man, and her Grandmother tells her the cautionary tribal story of Chipmunk and Owl Woman to sway her away from the white man. McWhorter's contributions to *Cogewea* typically step outside this narrative to criticize federal Indian policy, although he also altered her prose throughout. A subsequent collection, *Coyote Stories* (1933), in which McWhorter's thumbprint is less visible, earned strong reviews for documenting elements of Okanogan oral tradition and spirituality.

John Joseph Matthews initially gained recognition as the Oxford-educated writer of *Wah'Kon-Tah: The Osage and the White Man's Road*, the first

Book-of-the-Month Club selection from a University Press (Wilson, "John Joseph Matthews" 246). On its merits, he was asked to write a novel, and the result is Sundown (1934), the story of a mixed-blood man named Challenge whose experiences at a university and in the military foster self-hatred and bitterness toward his Osage heritage. Contextualized by Oklahoma oil wealth and eco-destruction, the final chapters of Sundown detail Challenge's lapses into drunkenness, his movement toward tribal religion, and, ultimately, his desire to enter law school. Robert Warrior argues that the narrative involves much more than an individual identity struggle: "Matthews evokes a historical period of intense importance for Osage people and communities and attempts to sort out how the political strategies of various groups of Osages played out and what possible future might exist" (Tribal Secrets 54). Matthews also published the histories, Talking to the Moon (1945) and The Osages: Children of the Middle Waters (1961).

D'Arcy McNickle's novel, The Surrounded (1936), is typically recognized as a literary achievement of the first order. It recounts the internal and external struggles of a mixed-blood man returning to the Flathead Indian Reservation from his city-life as a musician. Although intending merely to visit the reservation before traveling abroad, the protagonist, Archilde Leon, increasingly recognizes the importance of his heritage and reacts against the encroaching Euro-American culture, represented by local opportunists (including his Spanish father) and Christianity (which his mother also comes to reject). Innocent of the two murders of which he is accused, Archilde fights to define his own life rather than become a helpless victim. Although McNickle arranges the narrative chronologically, he uses tribal stories and flashbacks to ground Archilde's decisions within a Native history and context. Some of the basic plot elements of McNickle's novel reappear in Momaday's breakthrough work, House Made of Dawn, 30 years later. While The Surrounded was not a financial success, McNickle went on to an estimable career as a diplomat, professor, museum director, and writer. Among other publications, he wrote the histories, They Came Here First (1949) and The Indian Tribes of the United States (1962), as well a second novel, Wind from an Enemy Sky (1978), published posthumously.

Black Elk Speaks appeared first in 1932 to little response, but, when republished in 1961, the collaboration between Black Elk and John Neihardt gained a huge audience. Many readers responded strongly to Black Elk's vision and spirituality. Recently, the "as-told-to" format has rendered the work suspect, and Neihardt is regarded by some critics as an interloper who transformed Black Elk's spiritual vision and life-story into a Christian conversion narrative (Julian Rice, "Black Elk" 213). From another vantage, however, Black Elk uses Neihardt for his own purposes, documenting a strong sense of identity, history, and spirituality that over-powers his transcribers' efforts to memorialize Indians as vanishing Americans. Two works that appeared after Black Elk's death, The Sacred Pipe (1953) and The Sixth Grandfather (1984), both reinforce his commitment to Oglala culture and belief. Although Black Elk Speaks is certainly a more troubled work because of Neihardt's involvement, it also helped to prepare the path for the unalloyed successes of Momaday, Welch, and Silko among a world-wide audience.

A snapshot of contemporary Native America

The so-called Native American Renaissance (1968-present) springs from two centuries of writing in English and many more centuries of literary production in indigenous languages. It coincides with an era of social change fueled by the American Civil Rights movement of the 1950s and 1960s and the counter-culture reaction against the Vietnam War. Native activists fought policies of the so-called "termination era" (from 1954 to 1962), in which Congress sought "to end federal responsibility for Native Americans as stated in treaties and to end health programs and sovereignty" (Fixico, American Indians xxi), and Red Power groups – comparable to the Black Panthers and the Brown Berets – critiqued the relocation programs of the 1950s that encouraged Natives to move from reservations to cities. Indigenous leaders increasingly took their fight to the streets, nationally broadcasting their rights to equal legal justice and to federal treaty obligations. Activists took control of Alcatraz Island in San Francisco Bay from 1969 to 1971, as well as Wounded Knee on Pine Ridge Reservation in 1973. Both acts gained national attention, as did the 1972 occupation of the Department of the Interior building in Washington, D.C. Further publicity was garnered for Native issues with the televised appearance of Sacheen Littlefeather at the 1973 Academy Awards as a proxy for Marlon Brando, who refused his Oscar for The Godfather to protest civil rights abuses. Two decades later, after a great deal of political and legal work done by Native Americans and their allies, Winona LaDuke was nominated by the Green Party to run for vice president of the United States (with presidential candidate Ralph Nader) in the 1996 and the 2000 elections. Epitomizing the expansive possibilities of Native Americans, John Herrington became the first tribally enrolled astronaut to enter outer space in 2002.

Native writers and intellectuals have also soared high during the past 40-plus years, benefitting – like so many Americans – from increased access to U.S. colleges and universities and from the growing academic attention given to non-Anglo writers and thinkers. In 1969, Native American Studies programs were begun at the University of Minnesota, Twin Cities, and at the University of California, Berkeley (the latter housed in the Department of Ethnic Studies). Over the next 40 years, hundreds of degree programs were established.[9] Also in 1969, Vine Deloria published *Custer Died For Your Sins: An Indian Manifesto*, advancing a forceful academic tradition of indigenous intellectuals that continues today. Native American scholars are increasingly defining the terms of academic debate, calling for more attention to the political and economic threats to indigenous people, land, and sovereignty.

Despite many successes, great pride, and growing hope, Native communities still struggle with poverty and its attendant problems. Understanding the history of Native writing – and its relation to white colonialism – helps foster the cultural and legal climate that will serve to uplift and empower the over four million Native Americans living in the United States today (Snipp, "Population Size" 705). As always, the future hangs in the balance.

2

NOTHING BUT WORDS

FROM CONFRONTATION TO CONNECTION IN N. SCOTT MOMADAY'S *HOUSE MADE OF DAWN*

House Made of Dawn presents a fragmented world defined by isolation, violence, and racism, but Momaday also offers a multi-faceted solution to such quintessentially modern ailments. Critics have focused largely on the use of traditional songs and stories – particularly the Navajo Night Chant and Beautyway – to promote healing and wholeness.[1] Yet *House Made of Dawn* also operates outside tribal traditions to show how individuals of different backgrounds can confront the destabilizing forces within contemporary society, connect to a unifying principle without personal or cultural boundaries, and heal their fractured selves.

Momaday demonstrates that individuals who extend themselves beyond the physical world – who momentarily transcend material existence and recognize "nothing in the absolute" – can overcome the exclusive categories that dominate modern culture and infect its inhabitants. Within *House Made of Dawn*, the concept "nothing" suggests eternity and spiritual wholeness, rather than nihilistic meaninglessness (as argued by some critics). To see beyond the physical world, according to Momaday's novel, is to gain awareness of divine essence, origin, and wholeness, a recognition that necessarily exists outside of cultural categories and remains available to everyone. Until characters begin to perceive the absolute, they remain trapped and isolated, unable to overcome debilitating divisions or find healthy human connection.

The abstraction at the center of *House Made of Dawn* contributes to its purposeful ambiguity, and Momaday does little to lessen the intrinsic challenges of his novel for most readers. Despite his syncretic methods – i.e., his use of modernist literary strategies and the acknowledged influence of writers like William Faulkner, James Joyce, and D. H. Lawrence – Momaday constructs a narrative that keeps readers at a distance.[2] Readers remain largely outside the thought processes of the protagonist Abel, who, nevertheless, occupies a focal point of racial confrontation. Violence also appears without much explanatory context or comment, and Abel's struggle for meaning and wholeness is – to many critics – equivocal. At one level, *House Made of Dawn* seems intended as a direct challenge to readers, as it confronts them with racial antagonism, cultural exclusivity, and their own ignorance (since it draws upon tribal contexts that are probably unfamiliar to many readers). In this regard, *House Made of Dawn* – published in 1968 – represents an initial confrontation of the so-called Native American Renaissance, particularly to non-Native readers. Nonetheless, Momaday demonstrates that confrontation is, in effect, the beginning of constructive connection. Helping to create an audience primed for re-education regarding Native ideas and experiences, *House Made of Dawn* offers clear warnings as well as modest assurances. It simultaneously resists simple solutions to social fragmentation and proposes a method of healing and wholeness available to all people.

Observation versus experience

Some of the complications of *House Made of Dawn* result from the fact that Momaday targets an audience about which he is skeptical. One of Momaday's criticisms of – and challenges to – non-Native readers is that they are poor readers of tribal cultures, and they can never fully understand or appreciate Native American experiences or even the land they have usurped.[3] In *House Made of Dawn*, Euro-Americans are defined as interlopers and outsiders. For example, identifying the diverse animals indigenous to the American Southwest, Momaday distinguishes between native animals and "other, latecoming things[...] these have an alien and inferior aspect, a poverty of vision and instinct, by which they are estranged from the wild land" (52). The contrast highlights the alienation of Euro-Americans from the land, indigenous peoples, and even themselves. They are the colonizers who can never understand, much less acclimate, to the sacred truths of the mountains, valleys, or plains, as described within *House*: "For man, too, has tenure in the land; he dwelt upon the land twenty-five thousand years ago, and his gods before him" (52). The characterization defines white Americans in a way that should alert many readers to the inherent difficulty of their encounter with a text about a specifically Native experience, land, and culture: white people are outsiders and will not be readily welcomed into tribal worlds whose members have every reason to suspect their intentions and reactions. In his essay, "On Indian–White Relations: A Point of View," Momaday distinguishes between the different levels of knowledge resulting from "the thing experienced" versus "the thing observed" (*Man Made* 51). Non-Natives will always observe rather than experience tribal cultures. Momaday does not make this assertion in his essay as a criticism, but rather to emphasize the incapacity of non-Natives to understand tribal life and belief as fully as those within it.

In this spirit, *House Made of Dawn* downplays significant cultural connections between Native and non-Native, and Momaday uses his novel – at one level – to maintain distance between white readers and tribal experience. For instance, he advocates for the restoration of the pre-colonial past, and readers are told about the inevitable return of the "prehistoric civilization" when "everything would be restored to an older age, and time would have returned upon itself and a bad dream of invasion and change would have been dissolved in an hour before the dawn" (52). Euro-Americans are defined as "invaders" and "enemies" who have no place in the land and should leave or be forced out (52). Momaday is quite explicit here, and non-Native readers would be hard-pressed to imagine that he is writing about someone else. He is not merely decrying past imperialism; he is outing all non-Natives, however sympathetic and liberal-minded. Many proponents of Native literature – including literary critics – enjoy seeing themselves in solidarity with Indian writers and peoples, but Momaday disconnects one from the other. If you're here, he asserts, then you are a colonizer.[4]

On the other hand, Momaday describes in positive terms Native people who maintain traditional beliefs and lifestyles, even as they adopt and adapt others' ideas: "They do not hanker after progress and have never changed their essential way of life. Their invaders were a long time in conquering them ... They have assumed the names and gestures of their enemies, but have held on to their own, secret souls; and in this there is a resistance and an overcoming, a long outwaiting" (*House* 52–53). *House Made of Dawn* promotes the preservation of tribal cultures against white onslaught until the opportunity arises for triumph. In this regard, Momaday might appear to reject change. In an interview, however, he asserts that change itself is a traditional part of Native cultures: "I think you have to understand that stability is change – the only constant is change – and I think that virtually all Native Americans have a history of great change" (Isernhagen, *Momaday, Vizenor, Armstrong* 40). As an example, he describes the Kiowa migration to the plains, a dramatic historical adaptation that he also incorporates into *The Way to Rainy Mountain* and *House Made of Dawn*.[5] Nonetheless, change for Momaday should also involve a firm grounding in the past: "I think we are losing our connections to the past, and that we must not do. And one of the ways in which we can avoid that particular danger is by preserving what we have, say, of oral tradition" (Isernhagen, *Momaday, Vizenor, Armstrong* 41). Momaday argues that, by maintaining a secure connection to ancestral knowledge and customs, Natives will defeat the newcomers who are, by definition, disconnected from Native traditions and mere observers.

In *House Made of Dawn*, Momaday creates white characters who desire (vainly) to gain entry into the Native world and its philosophies. Although they think that they understand something vital about tribal life, their presumption is revealed as false. Father Olguin, for example, feels a "grave satisfaction" that he "had at last begun to sense the rhythm of life in the ancient town, and how it was that his own pulse should eventually conform to it" (60). Yet he deceives himself. His obsession with – and his personal similarity to – Fray Nicolás' life and diaries exposes his own self-absorption, small-mindedness, and officiousness. Similarly, as he travels to meet Angela, he thinks how "[t]he prospect of her envy pleased him" (63). Yet he appears to be mistaken on both counts. Not only does Angela herself reject him, laughing at his long-winded pretensions and mocking him with echoes of Roman Catholic phrasing – "Oh my God [...] I am heartily sorry ... for having offended Thee" (64) – but also the local Natives reject him. Momaday describes his entrance into the town during the festival in terms that accentuate their nightmarish quality to Olguin. The chaotic and grotesque images of his perception not only reveal a white man alienated within Indian culture, but also an outsider distanced from others by his own incomprehension and self-satisfaction (65).

In the final section of the novel, Olguin's words and actions reinforce the idea that white people cannot easily understand or access Native cultures. Rather than achieving "the thing experienced," he merely attains "the thing observed." Olguin remains self-focused and complacent, yet he also realizes that his achievement – if you can call it that – on the reservation is drastically qualified: "In the only way possible, perhaps, he had come to terms with the town, and that, after all, had been his aim. To be sure, there was the matter of some old and final cleavage, of certain exclusion, the whole and subtle politics of estrangement" (170). Olguin tries to fit in, and even believes he has achieved some level of acceptance, but, ultimately, he senses that it is futile, and his desire to belong renders him foolish. When Abel interrupts his sleep to bring him Francisco's body, Olguin initially appears annoyed and confused, but as Abel walks away he "peered out into the darkness. 'I can understand,' he said. 'I understand, do you hear?' And he began to shout. 'I understand! *Oh God! I understand – I understand!'*" (184). His sudden and insistent declaration is unconvincing, and his desperation in the face of Abel's disregard signals his insignificance and exclusion within the Native community. Olguin's greatest error – and the foundation for all others – is his inability to recognize and admit his failure, and Momaday suggests that such self-knowledge might serve as an initial step toward a more respectful cross-cultural relationship. In his own interpretation of Emily Dickinson's poem #1068, he states, "The poet looks as far as she can into the natural world, but what she sees at last is her isolation from that world. She perceives, that is, the limits of her own perception. But that, we reason, is enough" (*Man Made* 82). Perhaps in his novel, too, Momaday wants readers to learn from Olguin's failings – his unwillingness to recognize his limits – and then to use this observation to understand their own positioning toward cultures and beliefs not their own.

House Made of Dawn invites readers to acknowledge their limitations. The novel is most emphatically not an open invitation into Navajo, Pueblo, Kiowa, or Jemez cultures. The connection – such as it is – that Momaday offers readers exists within the text and its expressed ideas. He has gone on record stating that he provides enough information for readers to understand his works fully. He considers them self-contained: "I don't think it's necessary to read beyond what I have written because I have tried to provide the necessary information" (Isernhagen, *Momaday, Vizenor, Armstrong* 33). Although he recognizes that readers might benefit from a familiarity with tribal cultures, he does not require readers to become avid students of tribal beliefs and customs. In fact, non-Native efforts to study and "learn" American Indian cultures have more often been viewed as appropriation and violation, deepening rifts rather than fostering respect.

Angela and Abel: connection and disconnection

Angela offers an example of a white character who exhibits both negative and positive responses to the tribal world she observes. On the one hand, she tends to romanticize – even fetishize – Indian culture, and she apparently considers Natives as underlings fit only for manual labor and sexual adventure. She eroticizes Abel from a distance as he chops wood and then makes advances upon him, describing herself all the while as a "white woman."[6] Her efforts to connect with Natives appear superficial and prejudiced, and, like Olguin, she falls into a pattern that Momaday satirizes. In an interview, he said, "Angela is a sick person. There are such people in the world. She moved the book along in a positive way, I think. Her attitudes toward Abel represented a reality that is important in the novel" (Isernhagen, Momaday, Vizenor, Armstrong 61). Angela reflects many of the historical problems with white attitudes toward Indians, and her privileged position as a doctor's pampered wife makes her additionally unsympathetic. Few critics defend her or recognize her constructive contribution – the way, as Momaday states, she moves the book along in a positive way.[7]

Nevertheless, Angela has a revelation that changes her sense of self and her relationship to the world – including, of course, the Native world. Her success appears to be more philosophical than cultural, and it does not occur without some stereotypical missteps. Like all of Momaday's characters, Angela is somewhat enigmatic, particularly when she re-appears at Abel's hospital bed with her bear story, and critics have debated the sincerity of her visit and tale.[8] In the first section of the novel, however, she and Abel are remarkably similar, except for the fact that she discovers healing and wholeness for herself before him. For this reason, Angela might serve as a gloss for readers regarding not only Abel's trajectory in the novel but also for their own response to its ideas.

Both Abel and Angela are sick; both have lost their identity; both have fractured perspectives; both are filled with self-loathing. Their illnesses have to do with the physical: Angela "could think of nothing more vile and obscene than the raw flesh and blood of her body, the raveled veins and the gore upon her bones" (31). Abel's self-hatred manifests itself in his drinking and, more ambiguously, in his violence. Readers are told: "His body, like his mind, had turned on him; it was his enemy" (89). Like Angela, Abel must heal his body as well as his mind, but he must find a cure that extends himself beyond his physical battles. Violence against external enemies alone is ineffective because a more profound danger exists within.

Abel provides a case study of the alienated modern man, and racist stereotypes complicate the general social malaise in which he (and Angela) exist. He has been corrupted by a divisive and materialistic world dominated by whites. He is not whole; the war, particularly, has fractured him: "everything in advance of his going – he could remember whole and in detail. It was the recent past, the intervention of days and years without meaning, of awful calm and collision, time always immediate and confused, that he could not put together in his mind" (21). His experiences in the military – particularly the industrial violence of war – have traumatized him, damaging his relationship to his grandfather, his culture, and his land. Most damningly, Abel has been rendered inarticulate:

> [H]e had tried to pray, to sing, to enter into the old rhythm of the tongue, but he was no longer attuned to it ... Had he been able to say it, anything of his own language – even the commonplace formula of greeting "Where are you going?" – which had no being beyond sound, no visible substance, would once again have shown him whole to himself; but he was dumb. Not dumb – silence was the older and better part of custom still – but *inarticulate*.
>
> (53)

He has lost his language and thus his ability to define himself – to others as well as to himself – in a way consonant with tribal tradition, which here, not incidentally, points to the future as much as the past (i.e., "Where are you going?"). Much of the novel entails his uneven progress toward a personal and cultural reconciliation that exists beyond the modern material world, beyond "visible substance." Unlike Angela, however, his spiritual healing becomes grounded in tribal traditions and stories.

Abel's progress and Angela's revelation

Much of the debate surrounding House Made of Dawn centers upon questions of Abel's success or failure. Does he overcome the debilitating sickness and fragmentation of modern life? Does he learn to live constructively within a colonized land? Does he rediscover meaningful connections to tribal traditions? The answers to these questions remain elusive because readers rarely are privileged to the private thoughts of Abel, and few (presumably) enjoy a panoptic view of the Native cultures that contextualize his progress. Most readers remain outside, forced to speculate about the true nature of his alienation, his pain, and his cure. If the novel represents a Native journey toward a usable identity,[9] the process is kept somewhat obscure. Certainly scholars have worked to outline the tribal stories, songs, and beliefs that might inform Abel's development, and readers are alerted explicitly to the spiritual significance of Night Chant and Beautyway, but these components of Abel's life are not explained fully within the novel itself.[10]

The omission appears intentional. When asked about his reaction to Maori writers who create cultural barriers for readers, Momaday responded: "I like the idea of using a kind of special diction or information, and I am not quite sure that it needs to be understood, that one needs to track it down and find it out. I think it's nice that occasionally you come across something in writing that you don't understand" (Isernhagen, *Momaday, Vizenor, Armstrong* 33). His choices about what to include and exclude regarding tribal knowledge undoubtedly result from his artistic vision, but they probably also result from the fact that non-Natives – as a group – have not proven themselves trustworthy. Momaday is particularly concerned about cultural "betrayal," and he condemns those that "are disclosing aspects of the Indian world that are very private and secret. Anthropologists have been doing that for generations, as you know. And that, it seems to me, is a very serious matter, and a criminal matter" (Isernhagen, *Momaday, Vizenor, Armstrong* 50). His caution within *House Made of Dawn* is understandable, and it signals to readers that some barriers must be respected. Abel and his recovery remain largely abstruse, even if not entirely unknowable.

On the other hand, Momaday allows readers into Angela's thoughts and feelings, and her similarity to Abel allows comparative interpretation. After struggling with questions of her own identity in a broken world, she arrives at climactic new knowledge via her remembrance of the Cochiti corn dance. Her personal response to the ceremony offers crucial insight into a recurring theme of Momaday's novel. As she recalls the dancers, she asks: "What was it that they saw? Probably they saw nothing after all, nothing at all. But then that was the trick, wasn't it? *To see nothing at all, nothing in the absolute.* To see beyond the landscape, beyond every shape and shadow and color, *that* was to see nothing. That was to be free and finished, complete, spiritual" (33, emphasis added). Her perception lifts her above the fragmentation and sickness of the modern world, above the self-hatred that both she and Abel experience. Angela discovers a cure by transcending the physical and thus overcoming divisions to achieve wholeness and freedom – even if only momentarily.

Angela's healing is reinforced when the rain finally comes to the hot, dry summer. Rather than focus on Abel or Francisco, Momaday directs readers to her: "Angela stood transfixed in the open door and breathed deep into her lungs the purest electric scent of the air. She closed her eyes, and the clear aftervision of the rain, which she could still hear and feel so perfectly as to conceive of nothing else, obliterated all the mean and myriad fears that had laid hold of her in the past" (67). Momaday's symbolic treatment of the rain suggests renewal and regeneration – properties further associated with Angela because she is pregnant. She seems able to release the anxieties that prompted her antagonistic positioning toward Abel. Although using slightly different terminology – centering upon rain and the natural world – the description of her cure emphasizes "obliterating" the excess and simplifying to essentials, thus echoing "nothing in the absolute." Likewise, Francisco responds to the rain in a manner that indicates its symbolic value. He is glad "to see the return of weather, of trade and reunion upon the town" (68), and he thinks of the children: "For they, too, were a harvest, in some intractable sense the regeneration of his own bone and blood" (68). The rain – and Angela's response – signals that she is cured (at least in part) of the ailments that afflict her and Abel both.

Many critics have expressed skepticism regarding Angela's insight and cure, yet, even among the skeptics, there is disagreement and some apparent confusion. Lawrence Evers characterizes her recognition of "nothing in the absolute" as a "nihilistic vision" that "is finally a denial of the value of the landscape which the novel celebrates" ("Words and Place" 10). Likewise, Sean Kicummah Teuton contrasts "nihilistic 'nothingness'" with meaning grounded more positively in "self and tribe" (Red Land 60). Kenneth Lincoln interprets Angela's perspective as "spiritual emptiness" – a "divine trick" that she merely "fancies" (Native 119). In an apparent inconsistency, Lincoln describes the concept of "nothing" positively in his chapter comparing House Made of Dawn and Black Elk Speaks: "Lakota traditions place value in the spiritual openness, or positive 'Nothing,' inside material things. The ideal, through ceremonial sweat and visionary ritual, is to purify by cleaning out and becoming selfless" (Native 88). If this is the case, and plains cultures are related (as Lincoln contends), then Angela's vision would seem to be more than a cheap trick. Despite Lincoln's assertions about the indigenous philosophical basis of "nothing," Arnold Krupat insists that the concept of "nothing" itself is entirely foreign to tribal cultures: "this is hardly what Native American cultures have believed nor is it what Momaday's own practice reveals. Words have power; they may indeed be sacred. But they do not come from 'nothing'; 'nothing' is yet another category of the West whose Native American equivalents would be hard to specify" (Voice 187).

In response, Owens writes that Krupat is "seeming to accuse the Kiowa author of not writing like an Indian" (*Other Destinies* 109), and he defends Angela: "As Angela learns to see 'beyond,' to the interconnectedness of all things in the Indian world, she moves toward integration and health" (*Other Destinies* 107).

Angela's knowledge may begin with the ceremonial dance "in the Indian world," as Owens states, but, in my opinion, it necessarily extends beyond the Indian world. For starters, her familiarity with Native customs and beliefs is severely limited and demonstrably contorted. That she would suddenly see to the heart of a tribal truth is hard to believe or accept. And yet she becomes "free and finished, complete, spiritual" (*House* 33). While Angela's cure is prompted by her reflection upon Native dancers, her insight exists outside of culturally determined beliefs. Significantly, Momaday uses the concept of "nothing in the absolute" to offer a philosophical connection to readers that transcends cultural contexts. Although the dancers themselves are certainly engaged in a tribally specific religious act, she arrives at a perspective that transcends cultural specifics and that appears available to anyone. The "absolute" – and the wholeness and interconnectedness it implies – necessarily exists outside of cultural parameters and physical entities. Angela sees "nothing in the absolute," which is to say that she sees (even if only momentarily) everything in its entirety. She recognizes wholeness and her own inclusion.[11]

Moreover, it is worth noting that after her insight Angela is not compelled to participate in Native ceremonies or intrude herself into other tribal customs (as Olguin does). Rather, she comprehends that spiritual wholeness came to her via a transcendent knowledge existent beyond the physical world, and as a result she is able to move toward personal healing. Her physical and spiritual recuperation depends upon her recognition and appreciation of nothing in the absolute – "the last reality" (33) – available to anyone who can look past the categories and divisions of the human world (including Christianity). The positive power of "nothing" results from the fact that it is not exclusive to any tribe or society, even if most cultural groups find a unique manner of expressing it. In his essay, "The Morality of Indian Hating," Momaday discusses Tai-me, the "sacred Sun Dance doll"[12] acquired by the Kiowa as they journeyed from the mountains to the plains: "The Tai-me myth is not an entertainment, nor even the journal of an old salvation: it is infinitely more. It is an emotional reaction to the elemental experience of being, *the affirmation of an eternal reality behind all appearances; it is sacred*" (*Man Made* 64, emphasis added). According to Momaday,

Tai-me is a physical manifestation of a universal truth – a truth that exists within and beyond cultural categories and, as a result, one that offers the possibility of meaningful shared knowledge for everyone.

Momaday provides a similar glimpse of cross-cultural connection in his essay, "Revisiting Sacred Ground," in which he recounts visiting the Medicine Wheel in the Bighorn Mountains of Wyoming. While there, he befriended a Swiss "pilgrim" named Jurg who – along with Momaday and his friend Chuck – had "come together in recognition of the sacred" (*Man Made* 121): "He had touched us deeply with his trust, not unlike that of the wild animals we had seen, and with his generosity of spirit, his concern *to see beneath the surface of things*, his attitude of free, clear, direct, disinterested kindness" (*Man Made* 123, emphasis added). Jurg appears to be a journey-man-traveler who, rather than insisting upon specific cultural definitions, searches beyond exteriors for universal meanings. His apparent respect for others' traditions and his ability to appreciate shared truths compare to Angela's recognition of an all-encompassing spiritual absolute beyond the visible substance of the material world. Both provide a method for readers to comport themselves in relation to tribal cultures and within an interconnected world.

Nevertheless, Momaday likely has different goals for different readers. He is not necessarily advocating the same thing for everyone – particularly in terms of providing "answers" to societal ailments. James Ruppert, in his study of mediational techniques in Native texts, argues that the mythic elements of *House Made of Dawn* target Native readers while the psychological elements target non-Native readers, but ultimately the two story-lines affect both sets of readers: "When the mythic story displaces the psychological story at the end, both audiences are encouraged to examine their episte-mological frameworks for limitations, connections, and new insights" (*Mediation* 54). In other words, Momaday poses as many questions as answers, and both will vary among different readers. The concept of "nothing in the absolute" offers a possible answer to the confusion and fragmentation of the modern world without inviting every reader into a tribal belief system.

Words, language, and meaning

The philosophical and spiritual concept of "nothing" appears repeatedly in the novel. For instance, it echoes throughout the sermon of Tosamah, a Kiowa who practices a syncretic religion combining Christianity ("the gospel according to John") and Native spirituality (the peyote ceremony). In his sermon, he uses a non-Native origin myth (i.e., the Judeo-Christian story of Genesis) to emphasize the power of words and language. According to Tosamah, a single word, a single sound, began the creative process: "Nothing made it [the word], but it was there; and there was no one to hear it, but it was there. It was there, and there was nothing else" (81). At least two possible readings are here possible. First, "nothing" might be taken literally as an absence: something began within a void; meaning emerged from meaningless. Considering the Judeo-Christian origins of the story, however, this response seems insufficient. Instead, "nothing" suggests a spiritual entity or creative force. If "the word" – and hence all oral tradition and cultural knowledge – came from nothing, then the concept seems to indicate something other than emptiness or meaninglessness. Rather, to see "nothing in the absolute," according to Tosamah, is to recognize a divine source for all things and the resultant connections between them. In the novel, it directs readers to origins and essence, not absence or nihilism.

The search for primal knowledge might begin within a specific cultural framework, but ultimately it extends beyond human creations and into the absolute, as in Angela's case. If the knowledge is brought back into a cultural paradigm, Momaday implies, then the experience is likely to be corrupted, and its benefits diminished. Tosamah, for instance, complains that the apostle John in particular and white people in general allow their stories to become distorted with unnecessary words:

[O]ld John was a white man, and the white man has his ways. Oh gracious me, he has his ways. He talks about the Word. He talks through it and around it. He builds upon it with syllables, with prefixes and suffixes and hyphens and accents. He adds and divides and multiplies the Word. And in all of this he subtracts the Truth.

(83)

For Angela and apparently for Tosamah, the truth is realized by simplifying – by removing the nonessentials and embracing "nothing." Momaday demonstrates how Angela and Tosamah (despite their respective shortcomings) benefit from their realization – a realization that is repeated and supported throughout the novel – and he suggests that individuals with self-evident differences can arrive at an insight that might serve to repair divisions within the self and between people.

Violence, whiteness, and evil

Throughout much of the novel, Abel seems to be left out of the healing process. He remains isolated and distant from Francisco, Angela, and the reader. Furthermore, he kills the albino, a violent act which seems diametrically opposed to the spiritual wholeness – the nothing in the absolute – perceived by Angela and advocated by Tosamah. Nevertheless, by killing the albino, Abel initiates a form of renewal that is simultaneously antagonistic and regenerative, a paradox that is indicative of – and central to – the novel as a whole.

On the surface, Momaday's treatment of the albino is the strongest rejection of white society and people in the novel. The albino is described repeatedly as "the white man." He is "bloodless" and "hideous" and "unnatural" (39). Like Euro-American culture, he is both accomplished and destructive, and he demonstrates his skill at the feast of Santiago, where he wins the rooster pull and abuses Abel, simultaneously adopting and distorting Indian culture in a way reminiscent of white people past and present. Paula Gunn Allen writes, "Certainly, the albino in his death resembles the white man, the Church, and the unseen, nameless evil which Abel seeks to destroy or evade" ("Stranger" 12).[13] The albino is initially described as "[a] perfect commotion, full of symmetry and sound. And there was something out of place, some flaw in proportion or design, some unnatural thing" (39). Like Olguin, the albino lives among the Indians, but does not fit into Indian culture. He is a dangerous outsider occupying the region. Francisco senses "some alien presence" watching him while he tends his field, and the final lines of the section associate this presence with the albino: "Above the open mouth, the nearly sightless eyes followed the old man out of the cornfield, and the barren lids fluttered helplessly behind the colored glass" (60). Abel also senses the evil connected to the albino, and the fact that he kills him suggests a hostile or even militant stance in *House Made of Dawn* against the latecoming things – the white invaders – and the threat they represent.

On a more abstracted and symbolic level, the killing of the albino represents a confrontation with evil itself, rather than a localized reference to the murder of a "white person" (or the prejudicial treatment of an albino). The killing is described in terms suggestive of the ceremonial – emphasizing inevitability and recurrence – and the act is linked to Momaday's treatment of eagles and a snake. On the night of the killing, Abel and the albino speak confidentially to each other and agree to leave the bar together: "they were ready, the two of them" (73). Once outside, the albino "raised his arms, as if to embrace him, and came forward," and Abel "felt even the scales of the lips and the hot slippery point of the tongue, writhing" (73), which prompts him to stab the albino repeatedly. The snake-like attributes − as well as the sexualized undertones of the act − recall Abel's youthful vision of a snake killed by two mating eagles. When Tosamah later derides Abel for telling the court that he killed a snake, Abel is further associated with the eagles. Since eagles are described as "sacred" (51), Abel's act acquires meaning beyond the merely temporal or social.

The parallel between the actions of the eagles and of Abel suggests that the killing of the albino was part of some larger, recurring pattern. Abel killed the albino like the eagles killed the snake; each act is related. In fact, Momaday emphasizes interconnectedness when he describes eagles: "The eagle ranges far and wide over the land, farther than any other creature, and all things there are related simply by having existence in the perfect vision of a bird" (52). All things are connected: Abel is related to the albino, like he is related to evil, as all people are connected to each other as well as to evil.[14] Francisco recognizes his connection: "His acknowledgment of the unknown was nothing more than a dull intrinsic sadness, a vague desire to weep, for evil had long since found him out and knew who he was" (59–60). After the albino is killed, Francisco is again in his fields, but this time he "knew only that he was alone again" (76).

Abel's act has removed − at least temporarily − a danger that exists beyond racial and cultural categories. The albino is not evil *because* he is a white man; rather, he is symbolically representative of some distortion or corruption that infects the world. Like Angela's healing vision of nothing, evil also exists outside of specific cultural referents. In an interview, Momaday states, "I think of evil as something that is persistent in the world and unidentifiable. You can't say, 'This is the definition of evil' − surely if you do that, you exclude too much" (Isernhagen 37). To take the albino too literally as a white man would be comparable to reading him simply as an albino, as if Momaday was implying that albinos somehow represent a threat.[15] Evil, like goodness, transcends the physically defined world.

Three separate references during the killing state that the albino is looking intently into the distance, at what exactly is unclear. After Abel stabs the albino the first time, Momaday writes: "He seemed to look not at Abel but beyond, off into the darkness and the rain, the black infinity of sound and silence" (73). The "black infinity" recalls previous references to "nothing," particularly Angela's view of the absolute. When Abel stabs the albino a second time, readers learn: "The white hands still lay upon him as if in benediction, and the awful gaze of the head, still fixed upon something beyond and behind him" (73–74). The description of the gesture as a "benediction" alludes to the spiritual component of "nothing" that Tosamah recognizes. On the point of death, the albino seems to envision and even exemplify the absolute. The third time: "When [Abel] looked up, the white man still was standing there, still intent upon some vision in the near distance, waiting" (74). Literally waiting for death, he also seems to be out-waiting the immediate, and in fact he recurs – that is, evil appears again – in the form of the corrupt cop "culebra" (i.e., the snake).[16] None of these descriptions offer any conclusive facts regarding the role of "nothing in the absolute," but they are tantalizingly reminiscent of previous references in which the role of good and/or evil exists outside of specific cultural paradigms. Momaday again forces readers into conjecture mode, reminding us of what we do not – and, possibly, can not – know.

Despite the symbolic overtones, Abel himself rejects any responses to the killing that extend beyond the literal. During his trial, he describes what happened in blunt terms:

> He had killed the white man. It was not a complicated thing, after all; it was very simple. It was the most natural thing in the world ... They must know that he would kill the white man again, if he had the chance, that there could be no hesitation whatsoever. For he would know what the white man was, and he would kill him if he could. A man kills such an enemy if he can.
>
> (91)

Here, arguably, *House Made of Dawn* is at its most militant. The protagonist explains the murder of "the white man" in racial terms. Since the albino did not commit any offense beyond winning the rooster pull (and spying with seemingly sinister intent upon Francisco), Abel apparently defines the "enemy" in terms of his race and thus his status as an invader and colonizer. When Hartwig Isernhagen asked Momaday, "Can your texts then be read as endorsing violence?" he answered: "If you want to read them in that way, certainly" (*Momaday, Vizenor, Armstrong* 72). A characteristically elliptical answer, it implies that his novel does indeed advocate certain types of violence – perhaps even racially motivated violence – but that readers are ultimately in control of their own responses to his texts, an implication that surely qualifies the text's (and author's) possible endorsement of violence.

Confrontation and affirmation

The novel itself returns to the idea of confrontation in ways that resist simple responses and that refrain from the outright advocacy of violence. Abel's story exists in fragmented but thematically related strands within *House Made of Dawn*. During the description of the trial, for example, Momaday often shifts to Abel's suffering on the beach after he is brutally beaten and tortured by "culebra." While slipping into and out of consciousness, Abel has a vision of ceremonial runners who provide a nonviolent yet openly defiant example: "Evil was. Evil was abroad in the night; they must venture out to the confrontation; they must reckon dues and divide the world" (92). Perceiving the world in terms of good and evil (rather than simply white and Indian), they, like Abel, confront evil, but unlike Abel, their response seems far more affirmative and liberating: "They ran with great dignity and calm, not in the hope of anything, but hopelessly; neither in fear nor hatred nor despair of evil, but simply in recognition and with respect" (91–92). Although the act itself is undoubtedly significant culturally, and even evokes the ceremonial, their quest is universal; they recognize evil, acknowledge it, and confront it, realizing that evil will persist in myriad unassailable forms.

The runners offer a vision to Abel lying on the beach. Broken physically, he recognizes a constructive and traditional response to evil in the world:

> His skin crawled with excitement; he was overcome with longing and loneliness, for suddenly he saw the crucial sense in their going, of old men in white leggings running after evil in the night. They were whole and indispensable in what they did; everything in creation referred to them. Because of them, perspective, proportion, design in the universe.
>
> (91)

With this vision of the runners, Momaday reiterates a key idea that helps readers interpret Abel's sickness as well as his cure. Resisting fragmentation and division (quintessential evils of the modern world), the runners simultaneously represent wholeness and balance as well as strength and defiance. They provide order to the world – "perspective, proportion, design" – in the present and for the future. Rather than again confronting evil with violence, Abel reacts in a way that echoes the ideas underlying "nothing in the absolute." Both Angela's humanistic perspective and Abel's vision of the ceremonial runners reject fragmented views of the world that categorize and disconnect. Both emphasize essence and wholeness. Abel, however, is directed toward a traditional tribal reaction to a world beset by evil, disconnection, and racism. The action and the outlook simultaneously heal and defy.

Like the runners in Abel's vision, the novel itself performs a confrontational yet curative act. It resists and challenges readers with its multiple perspectives and shifting possibilities, while it also provides perspective and design. It is shaped in a way to prevent easy responses, but it still offers answers to readers, the same answers that Abel perceives: confront evil through constructive and expansive acts, not division or violence. In this way, readers are invited to enter the narrative (not tribal cultures), negotiate its divergent possibilities, and develop a coherent response to a broken world. Words, language, story, perspective – these have the power to change the world. That Momaday extends his invitation to everyone via publication is promising, yet his message suggests that much work needs to be done. Louis Owens underscores the challenge for readers; *House Made of Dawn*, he argues, has "serious responsibilities: to tell us who we are and where we come from, to make us whole and heal us, to integrate us fully within the world in which we live and make that world inhabitable, to compel order and reality" (*Other Desinies* 94). Owens' words apply to both Native and non-Native readers, but for the latter, as Momaday implies, the process is more of a challenge.

A timeless challenge and the reader

In *House Made of Dawn*, white people are separated from language, and words are cheap. Too often used as a weapon, language is destructive rather than constructive. For example, at Abel's trial, readers are told: "Word by word by word these men were disposing of him in language, their language, and they were making a bad job of it" (90). Likewise, Tosamah states: "The white man takes such things as words and literatures for granted, as indeed he must, for nothing in his world is so commonplace. On every side of him there are words by the millions … He is sated and insensitive; his regard for language – for the Word itself – as an instrument of creation has diminished nearly to the point of no return" (84–85). These words from Tosamah – a complicated, sometimes contradictory figure in the novel – seem to reflect Momaday's views as well. In an interview, Momaday states: "I think it's true that the Indian has a greater investment perhaps than other people in general in language ... In the oral tradition one cannot, one dare not use language carelessly, and there remains, I think, in the Indian world that sense of responsibility and that respect for language" (68–69).

Respect for language is further emphasized in House Made of Dawn when Tosamah focuses on his grandmother: "When she told me those old stories, something strange and powerful was going on. I was a child, and that old woman was asking me to come directly into the presence of her mind and spirit; she was taking hold of my imagination, giving me to share in the great fortune of her wonder and delight. She was asking me to go with her to the confrontation of something that was sacred and eternal. It was a timeless, timeless thing" (84). Stories here reveal the "mind and spirit" of the teller, inviting listeners to witness and participate in something "sacred and eternal." Tosamah was invited by his grandmother – as are readers via this novel – to a "confrontation." That the confrontation is "timeless" suggests again that it is transcendent and exists beyond racial and cultural categories. The implication is that words and language have the creative power to counter-balance the evil that persists in the world.

Benally is another character who utilizes words in a specific manner to help Abel. Several critics, including Lawrence Evers and Susan Scarberry-García, have detailed Benally's use of traditional songs to facilitate Abel's transformation and restoration before he returns to the reservation. Benally's belief in words and oral tradition helps Abel overcome his sickness and embrace a more expansive response to evil in the world. Although his words are directed at Abel primarily, Momaday uses Benally to target readers as well. In an interview Momaday agrees with the assessment of Benally as "a central interpreter figure in House Made of Dawn" (Isernhagen Momaday, Vizenor, Armstrong 47). Momaday reconstructs Benally's memories using the second-person pronoun and so his stories, in particular, convey a sense of inclusiveness. Addressing readers as "you," he allows readers to feel as if he is actually speaking of their experiences or sharing advice with them particularly. Readers are told, in effect, what they (i.e., "you") have experienced, and, in fact, they do experience – or, at least, observe – Benally's past vicariously via the narrative. Whereas Abel remains elusive and distant within the text, Benally offers a more personal point of intersection for readers.

Furthermore, Benally appears to be working out his own positioning toward modern society and Native traditions. Teaching Abel about "those old ways, the stories and the songs, Beautyway and Night Chant," he says, "I sang some of those things, and I told him what they meant, what I thought they were about" (129). Tellingly, Benally revises his stance toward the meaning of the Navajo songs from a position of certainty to that of personal interpretation. The shift may simply result from his modesty, but it also signals the difficulty of "knowing" with certainty any complex cultural system and its relation to spiritual absolutes. If it is difficult for Benally, who was raised by his grandfather within tribal traditions, then it must be nearly impossible for non-Natives to try to learn and live according to a tribal system.

Benally provides an example for readers by developing an individualized response, and he interprets and employs the songs in his own way (truncating the full song sequence, usually a nine-day ceremony, according to Scarberry-García). Yet they retain significant meaning for him. Benally is a reminder to readers that trying to define the complexities of a spiritual belief system is perhaps less important than allowing for their effect on individuals. For Abel, the songs – and Benally's interpretations – also have a positive influence: Abel returns to the reservation with a hopeful aura about him, and Benally's words – "the house made of dawn" – enter Abel's thoughts in the final lines of the novel.[17] Interestingly, readers are allowed a glimpse into his mind in these final lines, suggesting that cross-cultural openness and understanding is possible, but that it will not happen easily.

Scarberry-García argues "that healing takes place both inside and outside of Momaday's novel, that the power of the narrative extends to the reader" (*Landmarks of Healing* 2). According to Scarberry-García, though, the types of healing are quite different; the healing within the novel is done via a specific tribal belief system with sacred stories exerting a powerful influence, whereas the healing outside the novel is done through a reader's efforts to interpret a difficult text. She contends: "The novel forces the reader to think imaginatively, associatively, and holistically, and this push towards seeking relationships parallels the impetus for healing" (*Landmarks of Healing* 121). Readers do not heal because of their knowledge of tribal stories, according to Scarberry-García; they heal through the process of interpreting, which presumably will take various forms and operate outside of specific tribal belief systems. Momaday does not compel or even desire readers to accept tribal knowledge as their own truth. Rather he uses various strategies – including the concept of "nothing in the absolute" – to suggest healthy and inclusive choices without violating cultural privacy or inciting transgressions against it.

Eternity, nothing, and shared truths

Momaday returns to the idea of "nothing" subtly but insistently in the final section of the novel. In "The Dawn Runner," readers are privileged to Francisco's perspective and memories. Before dying, he remembers serving as a drummer in a ceremony and in a *"perfect act"* he *"crossed the stick to the heated drum and the heavy heated drum was in his hand and the old man turned – and nothing was lost, nothing; there had been nothing of time lost, no miss in the motion of the mind"* (181). Francisco maintains the rhythm while one drum is replaced by another; it is a successful act of transference. Since Abel is currently nursing his grandfather – their roles now reversed – an apparent transfer of knowledge and ritual occurs, particularly in regard to the race of the dead. That "nothing" is lost suggests that everything is maintained. The act points toward completeness, much like that implied by references to the absolute.

In addition, when Francisco dies, Momaday writes: "Abel was suddenly awake, wide awake and listening. The lamp had gone out. *Nothing had awakened him.* […] [H]e knew that the old man was dead. He looked around at the windowpanes, those coal-black squares of dim reflection. *There was nothing*" (emphasis added, 183). It is perhaps easy to read past these references as inconsequential, but considering the repeated emphasis placed on the concept of "nothing," Momaday seems to refer again to the "absolute" – a spiritual totality – associated often with death. He makes this clear, I believe, when Abel joins the runners. They gather in the dark valley and watch the ridge for the first sunlight: "But at the saddle there was nothing. There was only the clear pool of eternity" (185). Equating "nothing" with "eternity," Momaday implies that to see "nothing" is to find clarity and healing beyond human time. In *House Made of Dawn*, material, cultural, and personal realities are secondary to the transcendent truths available philosophically to everybody.

Abel finds a new beginning made possible by acting upon the vision of the runners, by the friendship and songs of Benally, and by the transference of tradition from his grandfather. Abel's renewal involves defiance and resistance. Like the dawn runners – the runners after evil – he also "venture[s] out to the confrontation" (92). He is not running away from anything. Instead his act recognizes, defies, and transcends evil in a materialistic, divisive world.

While Abel recovers his cultural place, readers are only invited so far. We are observers to his healing, but our healing will not likely involve running ceremonial races through specific southwestern landscapes, and it should probably entail more than interpreting a difficult novel (although that cannot hurt either). Momaday suggests that readers can help balance evil in the world by rejecting categorical worldviews, appreciating philosophical similarities between diverse people, and aspiring toward broad perspectives that encompass shared truths.

House Made of Dawn constructs a small but sturdy bridge between a Native author and non-Native readers, but the novel, like Abel, remains resistant and challenging. Nevertheless, it creates a philosophical and spiritual foundation for subsequent works by Native writers, particularly *Ceremony* by Leslie Marmon Silko, to be less confrontational and more inclusive, inviting all readers into a Native-centered world in order to help save it.

3

REVITALIZING THE ORIGINAL CLAN

PARTICIPANT READERS IN LESLIE MARMON SILKO'S *CEREMONY*

Leslie Marmon Silko's *Ceremony* is a radical revision of *House Made of Dawn*. In both, a Second World War veteran returns home fragmented and alienated, struggling to come to terms with a racist American society as well as his own Native community. Each character initially responds with alcohol and violence, but then finds some level of personal healing by rediscovering the spiritual power associated with tribal traditions.

Two key differences include the scope of the characters' healing as well as the authorial involvement of readers. Whereas *House Made of Dawn* is somewhat combative, *Ceremony* creates a constructive relationship with its audience, enlisting readers as active participants in a group effort to restore balance in the world. As the title makes clear, *Ceremony* serves as a civic ritual that re-unites individuals into a single group defined by mutual understanding and wholeness.[1] Silko attempts to repair a divided world by blending narrative fiction and tribal stories in a performative act that compels reader participation. Rather than simply advocating worthy ideals, *Ceremony* enacts and engenders human solidarity and universal healing via its own functionality. Readers "perform" the text as they read, making manifest – exponentially – the power of language and stories to change the world.

Ceremony's inclusiveness, optimism, and power result in large part from the Laguna Pueblo stories that Silko incorporates into her narrative. As is well documented, she has been criticized for publishing clan stories in *Ceremony* and thus sharing private knowledge with outsiders. Because of their sacred value to the Laguna, they have, historically, been reserved only for tribal members. Paula Gunn Allen and Jana Sequoya-Magdaleno argue that Silko violated custom by publishing the stories. Allen writes that Silko "is unaware of one small but essential bit of information: the information that telling the old story, revealing the old ways [to non-tribal members] can only lead to disaster" ("Problems" 384). Likewise, Sequoya-Magdaleno argues that Silko exploits "culture as commodity fetish" ("Telling the *dif-férence*" 102), adding that "the consequences of unsanctioned 'tellings' of the sacred stories is the cumulative loss of that power for the community" (103). Considering the centuries of appropriation and dispossession, they voice an understandable mistrust of non-Native responses to clan stories. On another level, however, excising the stories would reduce the transcendent purpose and performative effect of Silko's novel and, seemingly, the efficacy of the stories themselves. *Ceremony* links all readers together in a communal act of intellectual and emotional power that fosters respect for Native communities and combats the divisions that result in hatred and violence.

Clan stories and the reader

The central strategy of the novel is to extend the range and strength of the traditional stories. Silko's effort to combat violence, injustice, and war helps explain and justify her use of the clan stories. By sharing them with outsiders, Silko violates one custom in order to follow another; that is, her use of the stories corresponds to an oral tradition that embodies change and improvisation. In *Red on Red*, Craig Womack discusses the political and spiritual potential of tribal stories – with a particular focus on Creek tradition – and his ideas apply to Silko's re-framing of Laguna stories. He rejects the notion that Indian stories cannot be translated into another language and context without losing authenticity: "[T]he translation problem assumes that Native stories are problematic, that they should always remain the same, to deviate as little as possible from their correct original version. Stories have a correct cultural context and meaning, and translation always messes that up. The irony here is that stories supposedly retain their integrity by remaining authentically Indian, whereas in assimilation, the point is to erase Indianness" (*Red* 65). Womack argues that oral tradition is not "a static body of narratives" but is "a living literary tradition" (*Red* 66).[2]

Silko expands the cultural context for the Laguna stories by including them in *Ceremony*, where they remain authentic and powerful. In fact, they potentially gain power because Silko extends their influence beyond their previous audience. To use Womack's phrasing, Silko does not "erase Indianness" so much as she assimilates whites into an Indian cultural framework.[3] The appearance of the Laguna stories, in effect, creates and extends the parameters of the clan, inviting readers into an inclusive community that embodies the capacity to change the world in positive ways. David Rice writes, "As important as Native sovereignty is to contemporary Indian lives, Silko's main object in *Ceremony* is to expand the boundaries of Laguna culture and tradition in order to show its relevance on a multicultural and global scale" ("Witchery" 138). In an act of immense optimism and human solidarity, Silko shares tribal stories with all her readers, revitalizing the traditional Pueblo idea of a single clan (as expressed in the novel) and broadening the power of the stories.

Obviously – but worth stating explicitly – Silko's effort does not suggest a formal or legal affiliation. Silko's invocation of the original clan is strictly informal, operating upon readers at an intellectual, imaginative, and emotional level. It is an attempt to heal divisions in the world using language, not diminish tribal sovereignty or self-determination in a legal or cultural sense. Tribal independence and governmental autonomy need to be respected and advanced. As Sean Teuton states, "With Indigenous property of all sorts still under siege, however, the actual destruction of cultural and territorial borders is nothing less than disastrous for Native people. Borders are absolutely vital for the survival of colonized people" (*Red Land* 138). The danger of Silko's literary strategy is that some non-Natives may use it as a flimsy rationale for ignoring treaty rights or intruding themselves into tribal cultural affairs.

On the other hand, for Silko to exclude the stories would also involve risks. *Ceremony* affirms the relevance and power of the stories – as well as the responsibility and capacity of readers – to cure the ills of contemporary society, including those that threaten tribal sovereignty. Excluding the stories would not only fail to utilize fully their capacity for good, but it would also fail to harness the potential power of Silko's audience. Change comes from common people; as Linda Krumholz writes, "Silko's strategy begins with the assumption of a more equal power dynamic in the cultural, discursive, and spiritual realms" ("Native Designs" 67). Instead of waiting for the usual power-brokers to better the world, Silko involves readers in a newly reconstructed language ritual to eradicate divisive hierarchies and restore balance in the world.

Silko's choice to share clan stories with non-Native readers is comparable to Nicholas Black Elk's decision to tell his vision to John Neihardt and his largely white audience in 1932. Like Silko, Black Elk was criticized for revealing sacred information. Gregory Fields writes, "Black Elk has been derided by some for exposing the Lakota sacred rites outside their own tradition, thus making the rites, and the knowledge in which they are grounded, subject to misinterpretation and exploitation" ("Inipi" 172). R. Todd Wise also writes, "The sharing of sacred knowledge with an outsider was unprecedented and audacious, but not foreign to his character" ("Black Elk" 243). Black Elk's decision to share, however, was in keeping with the content of the sacred knowledge itself as well as its culturally prescribed implementation. Upholding a unified conception of the world and its inhabitants, he believed that his visions must be shared with and performed by the whole community. In *Black Elk Speaks*, he relates: "I was seeing in a sacred manner the shapes of all things in the spirit, and the shape of all shapes as they must live together like one being. *And I saw that the sacred hoop of my people was one of many hoops that made one circle*, wide as daylight and as starlight, and in the center grew one mighty flowering tree to shelter all the children of one mother and one father. And I saw that it was holy" (my emphasis, 33). Black Elk shared his spiritual beliefs with outsiders because – according to his vision – there are no outsiders; everyone (and everything) is within the sacred hoop. He used written words (and Neihardt) to extend the range and power of his visions: "There is so much to teach you. What I know was given to me for men and it is true and it is beautiful" (xxvii). His knowledge is important because it is pragmatic in the contemporary world. As Womack states, "Oral tradition then becomes a useful tool rather than an ethnographic artifact" (*Red* 60).

Black Elk's choice is simultaneously radical and self-evident. Because the problems exist beyond the Lakota world, the non-Lakota world must be included in the solution. Frances Kaye writes, "Black Elk's vision is not just for himself. It must be reenacted for the people in order to have power. Traditional spiritual power was not for the individual but for the group" ("Cultural Appropriation" 165). The risk for Black Elk (and the Lakota) is not only that his decision expands the definition of the group, but also that he uses an untested medium. Wise states, "Lakota shamans had never attempted to initiate individuals into secret and sacred knowledge through the medium of literature" ("Black Elk" 243). Unable to speak or read English, Black Elk trusted Neihardt and his readers to respond to the inherent power of his vision and act accordingly. Silko, on the other hand, wrote with great familiarity of diverse literary traditions, read widely as she developed her own considerable skills as a writer – studying Flannery O'Connor, William Faulkner, John Milton, and William Shakespeare, among others – and understood astutely how to harness her readers' potential. In addition, she avoided the problems intrinsic to an intermediary like Neihardt, and she carefully framed and constructed her narrative in a way to compel (and contain) reader involvement.

The performative power of language

Silko initiates the solution in the very first lines of Ceremony, which come from Thought-Woman. The lines (organized on the page in verse-like form) emphasize the performative power of words and language: "Ts'its'-tsi'nako, Thought-Woman, / is sitting in her room / and whatever she thinks about / appears. / ... [she] named things and / as she named them / they ['the Universe / this world / and the four worlds below'] appeared" (1). Silko begins her novel, quite literally, at the beginning. As Ts'its'tsi'-nako thinks and speaks the physical world into existence, readers witness the origin of a story/novel that creates/changes the world. As is common within many Native oral traditions (and, in fact, many types of religious language), words and stories have creative and transformative power. In his book, Performativity, James Loxley writes that certain types of speech-acts "are actions in themselves, actions of a distinctively linguistic kind. They are 'performed,' like other actions, or take place, like other worldly events, and thus make a difference in the world; it could be said that they produce a different world, even if only for a single speaker and a single addressee" (2). Speech-act theorists often use the examples of betting and marriage as illustrations of performative speech. To say "I bet you," or to assert "I do" during a marriage ceremony, is more than a simple declarative statement; it "accomplishes, in its very enunciation, an action that generates effects" (Parker and Sedgwick 3).

Silko takes this process to an entirely new level. With Ceremony she has created a full-length textual example of performative language. Not content merely to state that everyone should be part of a solution, Silko includes all readers actively within the performance of a modernized ceremony that holds the power, conceivably, to restore balance in a divided world.

Audience participation in Ceremony is first emphasized when the narrative shifts from Thought-Woman's creative process to the authorial persona (or narrative voice): "I'm telling you the story / she is thinking" (1). As

Thought-Woman thinks it, the narrator tells it (and Silko writes it); we hear it (or read it), and so we think it too, simultaneously engaging in a communal act of the imagination with the potential to reconstruct the world. In this way, Ceremony signals its own status as a collaborative performance, and it enlists readers to help shape the world both intellectually and physically. Louis Owens argues that the opening structure makes Ceremony as close to an authorless text as possible by drawing upon a "polyvocal oral tradition" (Other Destinies 169–70). On the other hand, the polyvocal component of the text is multiplied by the numbers of active readers, creating as many participants as there are readers.[4] According to J. L. Austin, a founder of speech-act theory, "to say something is to do something" (Miller Speech Acts 2). Silko extends this equation in Ceremony. Rather than serving as passive entertainment or even social advocacy, the narrative enlists readers in an intellectual and imaginative performance, making them all "authors" of change and healing. According to the novel itself, to read Ceremony is to do something positive in the world.

The novel describes, enacts, and prompts a healing ritual. Immediately following the verse-like words of Thought-Woman, the word "Sunrise" appears alone on an otherwise blank page. The final page of Ceremony also includes only these three lines: "Sunrise, / accept this offering, / Sunrise" (262). More than an allusion to new beginnings or an indicator of cyclical time, these framing words effect a functionality for the entire novel, and Silko provides a helpful gloss for readers within the novel. After Tayo meets Ts'eh, a spiritual being associated with rain and regeneration, he improvises a prayer from long ago: "Sunrise. He ended the prayer with 'sunrise' because he knew the Dawn people began and ended all their words with 'sunrise'" (182). His prayer provides information integral to the performative value of the novel. By framing the narrative with the words "sunrise," Silko structures her novel like a prayer – following the example of the Dawn people (and Tayo) – thus making it, in effect, an expansive transformative speech-act with distinctly spiritual undertones that directly involves readers.[5]

Furthermore, Tayo's prayer emphasizes improvisation and interconnectedness, thus highlighting vital characteristics of Ceremony that Silko borrows from oral tradition. When he prays, Tayo uses a deeply personal sense of recollection, letting the words come naturally rather than reciting specific memorized phrases: "He repeated the words as he remembered them, not sure if they were the right ones, but feeling they were right, feeling the instant of the dawn was an event which in a single moment gathered all things together – the last stars, the mountaintops, the clouds, and the winds – celebrating this coming" (182). Not adhering strictly to previous versions, he spontaneously recreates the words to suit his mood and goals. In addition, his feeling of connectedness and unity reflects the conception of time among traditionalists: "He knew then why the old-timers could only speak of yesterday and tomorrow in terms of the present moment ... This night is a single night; and there has never been any other" (192). Tayo perceives an eternal present and its implication of inter-connectedness. He embraces the belief system of his ancestors that, sig-nificantly, upholds change, unity, and connection rather than separation or categorization.

Like Tayo, Silko does not conform to invariant rules, and she improvises within a continually growing tradition by incorporating clan stories into her novel. In this way, she mirrors the traditional role of the story-teller. Owens writes that "Silko, like a traditional storyteller, is remaking the story, reforming it, molding it to fit new situations and times" (*Other Destinies* 170). By linking the tribal stories to modern stories, Silko remains true to the tradition of story-telling itself. Robert Bell writes: "each performance of the ritual celebrates all performances in the past and is timeless in its power to alter events in the future" ("Circular Design" 29). Even Paula Gunn Allen, in an article unrelated to her previously cited criticism of *Ceremony*, concedes the inevitability of interconnected stories: "A text exists in relation to other texts – particularly, as [Henry Louis] Gates [Jr.] has demonstrated, to mother texts, that is, the sacred stories that energize and shape human consciousness – rather than in splendid autocratic, narcissistic, and motherless isolation" ("Border" 39). Silko demonstrates her understanding of these inter-relationships, showing how Tayo's experiences – his story – relate to Laguna stories. Ku'oosh, a traditional medicine man, explains their interdependence: "no word exists alone, and the reason for choosing each word had to be explained with a story about why it must be said this certain way" (36). The stories which make up the world are like spider webs: inter-woven strands attached to other similarly interconnected strands. To separate them is to falsify.

Connection and context

No single story stands alone; each is a requisite part of the whole. Ku'oosh uses the stories to illustrate "the responsibility that went with being human [;] ... this demanded great patience and love" (36). Significantly, he does not focus solely on specific tribal circumstances. Instead he emphasizes the larger human challenge and obligation to respect the model provided by the stories – and their mixture of ideas, people, places, and cultures. In her essay, "Interior and Exterior Landscapes: The Pueblo Migration Stories," Silko writes, "The ancient Pueblo vision of the world was inclusive. The impulse was to leave nothing out. Pueblo oral tradition necessarily embraced all levels of human experience" (*Yellow* 31). In *Ceremony*, she remakes and recontextualizes the old stories within a contemporary narrative to include more people as participants in a new type of ceremonial performance. Julie Cruikshank, in her study of the contemporary oral tradition sustained by two Tlingit/Tagish women in Yukon Territory, asserts, "My contention is that to relegate them [oral stories] to the local and the particular is to oversimplify the very real work that stories do" ("Oral History" 6). Likewise, Silko's novel integrates the old with the new, the particular with the universal, and the oral with the written. The result augments the power of the traditional stories in the modern world, combating the divisive effects of the Destroyers' stories and creating a greater sense of community.

The authorial stance is necessarily invitational and inclusive, and the text itself provides much of the requisite information for readers unfamiliar with Laguna traditions. As John Purdy writes, "Silko has given her readers enough evidence to make crucial associations that will allow them to share in the event" ("The Transformation" 67). For instance, Silko signals a reader-friendly attitude by translating Laguna names into English. She identifies Ts'its'tsi'nako as Thought-Woman, a choice which helps clarify later references to spider, her webs, and the story-complex. Her approach is in sharp contrast to Momaday's *House Made of Dawn*, which begins and ends with the traditional Jemez words "dypaloh" and "qtsedaba" without translation or explanation.[6] In a 1977 interview, Silko states: "I would say that good literature has to be accessible. It's incredibly narcissistic to be otherwise. Artists can't work with a chip on their shoulders" (*Conversations* 26). Silko constructed *Ceremony* to include all readers within the narrative; she rejects confrontation in favor of collaboration. In a letter to poet James Wright in 1978, Silko explains that traditional Laguna stories seem lean in translation because they rely heavily on very minor references to specific places that contribute to the story. Her statement implies that *Ceremony* – published the previous year – was written for a largely non-Laguna audience, as she tells Wright that her current film project is forcing her "to wean myself from involved descriptions of the land" since on-screen visuals provide the necessary details. In other words, *Ceremony* includes detailed accounts of the land to help non-Laguna readers understand their implications. Wright understands her correctly: "I trust you are referring to your actual work on the scripts, and not at all to your descriptions of the landscape in your fiction." To Wright, the descriptions in *Ceremony* helped "create the audience which will share the knowledge of the story" (Wright *Delicacy and Strength* 25–26). Her target audience includes non-Pueblo readers unfamiliar with specific land formations and their tribal implications, so Silko forms the audience that her novel requires, instructing them and constructing them as informed readers and responsible participants. As James Ruppert writes, *Ceremony* is "a novel that teaches us how to read it and how to understand its special narrative structure" (*Mediation* 78).

Silko's sense of the relationship between story and audience results in part from her childhood involvement within a Laguna community filled with stories both contemporary and traditional. To Silko, the stories shaped the listeners:

> That's how you know, that's how you belong, that's how you know you belong, if the stories incorporate you into them. There have to be stories. It's stories that make this a community. People tell those stories about you and your family or about others and they begin to create your identity. In a sense you are told who you are, or you know who you are by the stories that are told about you.
>
> (*Conversations* 12)

The effect of local stories to define listeners is comparable to the ability of published works to create and shape their audience, a fact that she capitalizes upon in *Ceremony*. From the beginning, Silko includes readers within the narrative and demonstrates the ability – immediate and real – of words and stories to create and shape the physical world, a foundational belief that she reiterates in *Almanac of the Dead*: "Yoeme had believed power resides within certain stories; this power ensures the story to be retold, and with each retelling a slight but permanent shift took place" (581). As a performative text, *Ceremony* augments its power because each reader necessarily "re-tells" the story in his/her mind while reading. In effect, the new ceremony is performed by countless readers. Greg Sarris writes, "More and more scholars of oral literatures are looking to the broader contexts in which these literatures live. Specifically, they are considering what lies beyond the spoken word, beyond their perceptual range as listeners and readers" (39). To believe in the power of the stories is to agree that they must be included. For Silko, the balance of the world depends upon it.

Racial politics

Despite their inclusion, readers are also challenged by *Ceremony* to re-think conventional views of the world. Much like James Welch in *Fools Crow*, she creates a tribally defined world shaped by a revolutionary cosmology. Within *Ceremony*, white people are an aberrant byproduct of powerful Indian stories. Although this piece of information appears in verse form (like the traditional clan stories), Silko created it herself, and she ascribes the story to Betonie in the novel. He tells Tayo about a gathering of Pueblo, Navajo, Hopi, and Zuni witches at a story-telling contest, and how one witch created white people to cause destruction in the world. Like Thought-Woman's story (and Silko's novel), the story of this witch embodies the performative power to enact change in the world: "*as I tell the story / it will begin to happen. / Set in motion now / set in motion by our witchery / to work for us*" (135). Readers learn about the creation and emergence of "*white skin people*" that lose connection with the earth and objectify all life: "*They fear / They fear the world. / They destroy what they fear. / They fear themselves*" (135). Clearly a dangerous force, white people, nevertheless, do not arrive from outside; they are created from inside. In other words, they are part of the Native world, not separate.

Since Native stories set in motion a destructive element, they must also contain and balance the destruction. Silko wrote *Ceremony* to help fulfill this responsibility. Recontextualizing traditional clan stories – within the novel as well as within a modern pluralistic society – she seeks to counter-balance the evil created by the witches. White people are not the primary problem, according to *Ceremony*; the destructive story of the witch is the focus, an assertion that shifts attention away from racial/ethnic categories. In a 1976 interview, Silko states, "It's just that in recent years we've gotten into the habit of talking about black and white and good and bad. But back when, it was force or counter force. It may seem corny, but it is the idea of balance, an idea that the world was created this way. I try to take it beyond any particular culture or continent because that's such a bullshit thing. It's all Whitey's fault, that's too simplistic, mind-less" (*Conversations* 19). Accent-uating race and division, according to Silko, deepens the problem rather than advances a solution. In *Yellow Woman*, she writes, "In this universe,

there is no absolute good or absolute bad; there are only balances and har-
monies that ebb and flow" (64). To help restore equilibrium, Silko uses the
power of ceremony and story throughout her novel.

She also demonstrates the disruptive effects of categorical thinking upon
her characters. Tayo does not initially accept his connection to others or
even value the power of the ceremonies. He epitomizes both the dis-
possessed American Indian, detached from his own tribal culture by racist
teachings and practices, and (in keeping with the expansive goal of the
novel) the alienated modern individual, disaffected from the larger society
by dehumanizing and divisive conflicts. Like Abel in Momaday's *House Made
of Dawn*, Tayo feels isolated and confused in a fragmented world defined by
prejudice, violence, and fear. Silko uses his own doubts and missteps to
acknowledge and (hopefully) eliminate readers' possible misgivings about
their prescribed role in the novel. The medicine man Betonie states: "The
people nowadays have an idea about the ceremonies. They think the ceremonies must be performed exactly as they have always been done ... But
long ago when the people were given these ceremonies, the changing
began, if only in the aging of the yellow gourd rattle or the shrinking of the
skin around the eagle's claw, if only in the different voices from generation
to generation, singing the chants" (126). Betonie defines change as an
inherent and inevitable part of tribal tradition. Since the sounds of the
rattles and singers vary over the years – thus altering the ceremonies in
subtle ways – he argues that the ceremonies can change in more dramatic
ways as well. To Betonie, adapting ancient customs to respond to modern
challenges sustains, rather than diminishes, their integrity. He tells Tayo:
"At one time, the ceremonies as they had been performed were enough for
the way the world was then. But after the white people came, elements in
this world began to shift; and it became necessary to create new ceremonies. I have made changes in the rituals. The people mistrust this greatly,
but only this growth keeps the ceremonies strong" (126). Tayo is forced to
modify his understanding of a tradition that is dynamic rather than static,
and his growth is predicated upon his ability to recognize the fluidity and
wholeness of the world and its people.

Tayo learns to do more than merely oppose white people; he begins to
resist the witchery. Readers also learn that the problem – and the solution –
is larger than racial categories and conflicts. Betonie tells Tayo:

> That is the trickery of the witchcraft. They want us to believe all evil
> resides with white people. Then we will look no further to see what is

really happening. They want us to separate ourselves from white people, to be ignorant and helpless as we watch our own destruction. But white people are only tools that the witchery manipulates; and I tell you, we can deal with white people, with their machines and their beliefs. We can because we invented white people; it was Indian witchery that made white people in the first place.

(132)

Targeting white people merely creates more division, not balance; it focuses on the effect instead of the cause.[7] Silko is like Betonie; both of them change the ceremonies to balance evil in the world, Betonie in his healing rituals and Silko in her novel use of clan stories.

Some critics argue that characterizing whites as a byproduct of witchery is counter-productive. Lori Burlingame writes: "Betonie's story is somewhat racist and ultimately no more explicative than the Puritans' racist notion that the Indians were in league with the devil" ("Empowerment" 6). In my opinion, however, the larger danger of *Ceremony*'s characterization of white people is that it might appear to excuse white crimes against Native Americans. By redefining Western imperialism within a tribal cosmology, *Ceremony* risks letting Euro-Americans off the hook for the massacres, land-grabs, religious intolerance, cultural dispossession, and political disempowerment. The novel seems to blame Indian witches, rather than white greed, ignorance, and violence. In a constructive response to such concerns, Owens writes: "Betonie's words and the story of witchery underscore an element central to Native American oral tradition and world-view: responsibility. To shirk that responsibility and blame whites, or any external phenomenon, is to buy into the role of helpless victim. We make our worlds, Silko is suggesting, and we thus have enormous responsibility" (*Other Destinies* 184). In a similar response within another tribal tradition, Christopher B. Teuton argues that the Cherokee origin story – in which Dayunisi (the water beetle) dives under water and returns with the raw materials for land – emphasizes "social responsibility" ("Indian Literature" 198), and it includes everyone: "Knowledge is sought and valued in relation to the collective harmony and survival of the community as a whole" (197).

Ceremony invites everyone – not just Natives – to think anew about their social responsibilities and relationships. All people are asked to revise conventional (often simplistic) notions of history and race. Gloria Bird notes the result of such rethinking and praises Silko's rejection of a Western view of colonial history: "to speak of colonization only in those terms is to stay within the realm of creating boundaries between us and them, to stay locked into a static system with no resolution" ("Toward" 103). *Ceremony*'s worldview breaks down the binaries dividing individuals and groups. No longer "us" and "them," readers are united in the need for responsible action. The novel's ceremonial power brings readers together in a solution that is simultaneously communal and individual. Rather than feel insulted, Euro-American readers should also bear the responsibility to help remake the world into a fair and just community.

Part of a responsible solution – according to *Ceremony* – entails recognition of injustice and racism. Attentive readers would be hard-pressed to conclude that white America is blameless or that Silko's goal of unity absolves them from responsibility. Silko never permits readers to forget the racism underlying treatment of Natives throughout U.S. culture and history. Tayo, for example, is justifiably angry regarding the way that Indian soldiers were used as cannon fodder in the Second World War and then cast aside after the war. He describes how white store clerks ignore him or avoid touching his hand while returning change. Likewise, the character Helen Jean is encouraged to adopt "white ways" but then funneled into menial jobs, despite her other qualifications.

Among the many examples of individual prejudice, readers are also reminded of historical atrocities that shaped the modern world. Silko writes how an Army captain gave smallpox-infected blankets to the Apaches in the 1860s, and she informs readers of how the National Forest Service took more tribal land in Arizona when politically connected ranchers came from Texas. Silko targets complacent readers with the facts, forcing them to confront the individual and institutionalized racism and its ongoing effect in the lives of Natives and others. She writes: "the lies devoured white hearts, and for more than two hundred years white people had worked to fill their emptiness; they tried to glut the hollowness with patriotic wars and with great technology and the wealth it brought. And always they had been fooling themselves, and they knew it" (191). Such sentiments reappear in other works by Silko, in which white people are trapped by ignorance and evil. In "Storyteller," for example, white men (or "Gussucks") are depicted as bestial – rapists of women as well as cultures: "They thought they could take it [something of value], suck it out of the earth or cut it from the mountains; but they were fools" (29). More recently, *Gardens in the Dunes* – like the Norton-anthologized story "Lullaby" before it – exposes the outrageous practice of institutionalized kidnapping by government employees. *Almanac of the Dead*, for its part, is a veritable tome of angry incrimination of white criminality. Silko does not shrink from explicit socio-political commentary, yet her success in *Ceremony* results from her ability to identify racist hegemony while also finding a solution that transcends such divisiveness. She rejects the wrong-headed pattern set by Euro-Americans, instead embracing a philosophy of openness and inclusion.

Fighting fragmentation and hatred

Silko's goal of unification is daunting, however. Readers are told that in the fifth world – i.e., in the modern world – everything became entangled: "all of creation suddenly had two names: an Indian name and a white name" (68). Words and language also have the power to separate, and the division contributes to Tayo's sickness. He cannot sort out which name, or which world, is correct. Tayo's war experiences demonstrate the extent to which ethnic division and individual isolation is unnatural. He joined the army to show solidarity with his cousin Rocky and with the United States. Despite military orders, he recognized his personal and human connection to the Japanese: "Tayo had realized that the man's skin was not much different from his own ... There was no difference when they were swollen and covered with flies. That had been the worst thing for Tayo; they looked too familiar even when they were alive" (7). He realizes that – despite fractious cultural teachings – all individuals are united in life and by death. In *Almanac of the Dead*, Silko includes a more spiritual vision of cross-cultural connection. Explaining early contact between black Americans escaping slave-holders and the tribes with whom they sometimes found shelter, she writes, "[G]reat American and great African tribal cultures had come together to create a powerful consciousness within all people. All were welcome – everyone had been included. That had been and still was the great strength of Damballah, the Gentle. Damballah excluded no one and nothing" (416). Spiritual unity here trumps material and cultural categories. In *Ceremony*, Tayo's intuitions of human solidarity are intensified when he envisions his uncle Josiah among the executed Japanese soldiers. Rocky tries to soothe Tayo with a conventional ideology of patriotic duty and nationalistic destiny, urging him to act according to an individualistic credo, but Tayo works to overcome the fabricated differences that separate people from others and themselves.

Silko uses several flashbacks to illustrate and emphasize a healthier sense of connection and unity. Before the war Tayo saw the limitless potential of himself and the world: "[H]e could remember times when he and Rocky had climbed Bone Mesa, high above the valley southwest of Mesita, and he had felt that the sky was near and that he could have touched it … Distances and days existed in themselves then; they all had a story. They were not barriers" (19). From his view on the mesa, Tayo sees coherence and wholeness, a perspective that contrasts sharply with his post-war world-view. His experiences at war and his encounters with bigots changed his outlook from one of inclusion to one of exclusion. Seeing only parti-alities and hierarchies, he becomes angry and violent, and he accepts a fragmented world.

Silko dramatizes what happens when Tayo initially follows the divisive example of white culture. His anger at Emo's willful ignorance and cruelty drives him to stab Emo with a broken bottle. His act, in effect, mimics Emo's own sadism, which, in turn, mirrors white violence and warfare. Violence is the simplistic reaction, and Tayo is temporarily seduced by it: "[Tayo] got stronger with every jerk that Emo made, and he felt that he would get well if he killed him" (63). Although his rage finds an outlet, it does little to make him better and offers no positive resolution. Rather, his response is as counterproductive as Emo's role during the war: "Emo grew from each killing. Emo fed off each man he killed, and the higher the rank of the dead man, the higher it made Emo" (61). Although Tayo initially follows Emo's destructive ways, his own doubts save him: "he wasn't sure any more what to believe or whom he could trust. He wasn't sure" (63). Rather than continue to grow from violence and hatred like Emo, Tayo is compelled to locate a philosophy in contradistinction to the divisive mes-sages that fragment his identity, shatter his world-view, and intensify his isolation.

Making his task more difficult is the fact that the Indian community – like the world at large – has almost splintered. Tayo was taught to feel shame for his Indian heritage, as was his mother. In a tragic irony, Tayo's mother (identified as Little Sister to Auntie in this section) was separated from her family by misguided white people: "holy missionary white people who wanted only good for the Indians, white people who dedicated their lives to helping the Indians, these people urged her to break away from her home" (68). The missions teach her to be embarrassed of her heritage, a mis-education that ultimately leads her to drink rather than take care of her son, which, in turn, disrupts the community further: "For the people, it was that simple, and when they failed, the humiliation fell on all of them; what happened to the girl did not happen to her alone, it happened to all of them" (69). Silko reemphasizes again the inter-relationship of all people: no one acts within a vacuum; everyone's choices ripple throughout the population. Tayo's Auntie illustrates a compounding divisiveness. Epitomizing the common prejudices of many people, Auntie badmouths Mexicans, blacks, whites, and mixed-blood Indians. Her willingness to categorize and divide separates Rocky from Tayo, as it earlier separated Tayo from his mother.

Yet Silko also uses Auntie's example to express an idea at the core of her performative novel: the concept of a single clan. Auntie is a Christian, and in *Ceremony* Silko distinguishes between Christianity and Pueblo spiritual beliefs: "Christianity separated the people from themselves; it tried to crush the single clan name, encouraging each person to stand alone, because Jesus Christ would save only the individual soul; Jesus Christ was not like the Mother who loved and cared for them as her children, as her family" (68). Again advocating community over individualism, Silko provides an important vision of spiritual union. She recalls "when the people shared a single clan name and ... the people shared the same consciousness" (68). The idea of the "single clan" explains Silko's choice to include the clan stories in *Ceremony*. Their power is normally reserved for members of the clan, so *Ceremony* revitalizes the idea of the original clan to maximize the effect of the stories. Every new reader expands the performative power of the stories.

Silko's treatment of the original clan tallies with Pueblo origin myths collected by anthropologist Alfonso Ortiz (like Silko, a Pueblo Indian censored by tribal members for publicizing private information). Ortiz writes: "The origin and migration myth ends with an informant's observation: 'In the very beginning we were one people'" ("Empowerment" 16).[8] At one level, references to "the people" may seem exclusive to Pueblo people. Even Betonie answers questions about why he lives near Gallup – a "filthy town" (118) – by stating: "I tell them I want to keep track of the people ... 'Because this is where Gallup keeps Indians until Ceremonial time'" (117). His statements here equate "the people" with Indian people, even a specific tribe (the Laguna), rather than all people.

Re-uniting the people

Silko's references to "the people" – at another level – include everyone, not merely one tribe of people.[9] In "Interior and Exterior Landscapes," she writes, "Each Pueblo group recounts stories connected with Creation,

Emergence, and Migration, although it is believed that all human beings, with all the animals and plants, emerged at the same place and at the same time" (*Yellow* 36). Silko defines the first people as the originators of all people, and her novel is an effort to repair divisions and to reunite humans once again. In a 1978 interview, she states, "Tayo's healing is connected to the faith which this old medicine man [Ku-oosh] had, a faith which went back to things far in the past, the belief that it's human beings, not particular tribes, not particular races or cultures, which will determine whether the human race survives" (*Conversations* 35). Silko builds upon this basic belief throughout *Ceremony*, emphasizing the unity and connectedness of all people regardless of race or tribe. Even Betonie qualifies his earlier statement about "the people," stating: "Nothing is that simple … you don't write off all the white people, just like you don't trust all the Indians" (128).

One way that Silko demonstrates human connectedness – and revitalizes the original clan – is via a shared danger and the mutual goal that results. When Tayo hides from Emo and the others, he enters a region surrounded by reminders of the atom bomb: Trinity Site, where tests were conducted, and Los Alamos, where the bomb was created. Whereas the traditional stories are a more positive indicator of mutual goals, the threat of atomic annihilation serves as a bleak reminder of our status as members of a single clan. Silko writes, "[H]e had arrived at the point of convergence where the fate of all living things, and even the earth, had been laid … [H]*uman beings were one clan again*, united by the fate the destroyers planned for all of them, for all living things; united by a circle of death that devoured people in cities twelve thousand miles away" (emphasis added, 246). With this recognition, Tayo moves further away from a world-view that encodes separation and isolation. Like his earlier vision from the mesa, he sees wholeness. Karen Piper writes, "[T]he narrative uses the ultimate signifier of violence – nuclear holocaust – to invoke a new global community" ("Police Zones" 485). Silko uses both the modern and the traditional to reunite all people within a single clan.[10] In the face of practically unutterable horror, she offers equally overwhelming hope.

Gloria Bird defines "the major trope of Native American literature" as "the interconnectedness of all things – of people to land, of stories to people, of people to people," adding: "The interdependence of parts to the whole is one of the pivotal characteristics of the plot upon which Tayo's ultimate dilemma hinges" ("Toward" 98). Despite this oft-noted theme, a common approach to *Ceremony* – and, in fact, much Native writing – emphasizes the qualities of "resistance" and "subversion." Although these elements certainly exist, they are subordinate to the effort in *Ceremony* to unify readers within a new type of ceremonial project to redefine the world. Josiah provides advice to this effect, directing Tayo (and readers) away from resistance as the primary response and toward shared challenges: "Josiah said that only humans had to endure anything, because only humans resisted what they saw outside themselves. Animals did not resist. But they persisted, because they became part of the wind. 'Inside, Tayo, inside the belly of the wind'" (27). Rather than maintain their separateness, animals move with the wind and use it to progress toward their goal. Tayo, likewise, sees a single clan under the shadow of atomic threat; he persists rather than resists, joining with others in a communal bid for survival.

Tayo, in fact, embodies the ideal of the single clan. Physically (genetically) he is both "white" and "Indian," a fact that results in bias against him. Nonetheless, the combination of racial backgrounds ultimately symbolizes his recognition and adoption of an interconnected worldview.[11] Tayo is not "half" of anything; he is whole. Josiah's cattle provide a gloss for Tayo's achievement. Mixed-bloods like Tayo, the cattle are a blend of muscular Herefords and resourceful Mexican cows. As Josiah says, "[T]hey would grow up heavy and covered with meat like Herefords, but tough too, like Mexican cows, able to withstand hard winters and many dry years" (80). Combining positive attributes of both strains, Josiah's cattle persist and triumph. Not coincidentally, Night Swan and Betonie – perhaps the two most important advisors to Tayo – are also of mixed blood, and they both condemn factionalism and articulate ideologies of fellowship and wholeness, steering Tayo toward a less individualistic, less disruptive belief system. Without fully understanding at first, Tayo progresses toward solidarity with a single clan again.

Betonie encourages Tayo to recognize the world beyond himself, to consider others, and to think holistically. Although Tayo initially rejects these prescriptions, he privately accepts his connection to others in a critical moment of realization:

> He wanted to yell at the medicine man, to yell the things the white doctors had yelled at him – that he had to think only of himself, and not about the others, that he would never get well as long as he used words like "we" and "us." But he had known the answer all along, even while the white doctors were telling him he could get well and he was trying to believe them: medicine men didn't work that way, because the world

didn't work that way. His sickness was only *part of something larger*, and his cure would be found only in something *great and inclusive of everything*.

(emphasis added, 125–26)

Tayo realizes that neither his sickness, nor the cure, is specific to him alone. His health depends upon the complex inter-relationships of all people and things, much like the strength of a spider-web depends upon the linked strands. Gradually Tayo begins to recognize patterns in seeming chaos. At Betonie's urging, Tayo re-thinks his own connection to others and accepts tribal traditions that foster inclusion and change rather than seclusion and stasis.

Night Swan actively encourages a philosophy of connectedness and change to Tayo. When he tells her about the prejudice he faces because he is part white, she tells him: "They are afraid, Tayo ... Indians or Mexicans or whites – most people are afraid of change. They think that if their children have the same color of skin, the same color of eyes, that nothing is changing ... They are fools. They blame us, the ones who look different. That way they don't have to think about what has happened inside themselves" (100). Night Swan facilitates Tayo's growth toward a more comprehensive view of the world. She advocates change as a necessary component of life. Providing a model for Tayo, Night Swan shows him how to grow beyond restrictive definitions and one-dimensional identities.[12] Her advice underlines the human dilemma – the shared problem and responsibility – at the heart of Silko's novel. Natives alone – or, for that matter, whites alone (or, anyone alone) – cannot fix a broken world.

Individual success and human promise

Near the end of *Ceremony*, Tayo faces a choice: either kill Emo (and fulfill others' low expectations) or reject the violent stereotype. He chooses change, revising the destructive story of supposed Indian savagery and reclaiming his own story to embrace hope and life. Tayo rejects the violent confrontation – unlike Abel in *House Made of Dawn* – and his choice ultimately is more admirable, because it is more unconventional and involved. By refusing to enact the stereotype, he changes the Destroyers' ceremony and instead joins a revitalized clan to perform a renewed tradition of peace and love.

His decision to change the story reflects Silko's choice to re-frame Laguna stories to promote connection and healing for everyone. In both cases, change is a positive and natural development of tradition, rather than a departure from tradition. Silko writes, "[T]he story-telling always includes the audience, the listeners. In fact, a great deal of the story is believed to be inside the listener; the storyteller's role is to draw the story out of the listeners" ("Language" 50). Silko's organic sense of story and audience necessitates reader inclusion. By sharing clan stories with outsiders, Ceremony simultaneously demonstrates and enacts change, recruiting readers into a performative act of hope and unity that aspires to balance the world. Readers are offered a tremendous opportunity and a great responsibility. They are invited to participate in a civic ceremony that not only rejects reductive stereotypes but also advocates respect, understanding, and connection. The success of Silko's novel – and the dialogue it has created – suggests that her goal is succeeding.

Ceremony's power results from its inclusion and connectedness, which Womack describes as an essential element of all literature: "[I]t has to have some element of universalism, a point of recognition that can speak across cultures to the human condition" ("A Single" 15). Silko has stated in an interview that allegiance belongs first to all people and only then to a specific group: "[F]irst of all, you're a human being; secondly, you originate from somewhere, and from a family, and a culture. But first of all, human beings" (Coltelli "Leslie Marmon Silko" 254). Placing primacy on the human connection before ethnic, religious, or national divisions, Silko disputes the category "American Indian literature" itself, stating: "I think that it is divisive. I always make very clear that I have Mexican and white ancestors, and I am very close to the old ancestor spirits in Germany and the Celts. I love that I have connections with Mexico, and I love Spanish, and I identify with the Chicanos" (Cohen "An Interview" 26). Her reaction against the limitations of labels and categories corresponds to the goals of Ceremony: to unite everyone and to dismantle the divisions that cause hatred and violence.

Like Silko, Gerald Vizenor in Bearheart challenges labels and categories, and he advocates connectedness over separation. Also like Silko, he requires and creates a participant audience. Yet few readers would conflate Silko and Vizenor. With withering satire, an often obfuscating humor, and an inherently challenging style, Vizenor's Bearheart establishes a community of individuals intrinsically linked by personal acts of the intellect and imagination, rather than through the communal performance of a novel civic ceremony.

4

INDIVIDUALISM VS. SEPARATION
IMAGINING THE SELF TO FOSTER UNITY VIA GERALD VIZENOR'S *BEARHEART*

Much has been said – and rightfully so – about Gerald Vizenor's attack on terminal creeds. They are, essentially, an intellectual stopping point, the false and arrogant moment when an individual or institution claims that he/she/it fully understands something or someone. Louis Owens describes terminal creeds as "beliefs that seek to fix, to impose static definitions upon the world," adding: "Such attempts are destructive, suicidal, even when the definitions appear to arise out of revered tradition" ("Ecstatic" 144). Terminal creeds damage adherents because they presume nothing more can be learned. Terminal believers limit their own imaginations. According to Vizenor, they exist within the defunct vacuum of their own minds, forever separated from other people, ideas, and the world around them.

Vizenor writes against one-dimensional notions of culture and identity not only because such ideological absolutism is simplistic and destructive, but also, and more importantly, because terminal beliefs divide people from each other and from themselves. In an interview, Vizenor said: "I think [anthropology] *separates* people. The methodologies of the social sciences *separate* people from the human spirit. They *separate* people through word icons, methods that become icons because they're powerful, because they're rewarded by institutions – *separate them from a kind of intellectual humanism, an integrity of humanism and the human spirit*" (my emphasis, Coltelli *Winged Words* 170). One of Vizenor's goals in *Bearheart: The Heirship Chronicles* is the opposite: he wants to foster a genuine intellectual connection among individuals – a shared intellectuality centered upon the imagination.

Bearheart poses many challenges, and readers risk falling into the easy trap of terminal belief if they fail to recognize not only what Vizenor criticizes in *Bearheart*, but also what he celebrates, namely, the ability of the imagination to link people together beyond restrictive definitions. *Bearheart* is an effort to foster freedom (intellectual, spiritual, physical, etc.) and to heal wounds (historical, social, personal, etc.). Vizenor's trickster-like presentation – with its paradoxical blend of tragedy, satire, comedy, and pathos – compels readers to use their imaginations to interpret, challenge, and redefine conventional ways of thinking.[1] Readers must struggle through an intentionally difficult novel that allows them to re-imagine the world and themselves. The process necessarily cultivates "an integrity of humanism and the human spirit," to use Vizenor's phrasing. The interpretive struggle heightens personal intellectuality and spirituality, which, according to Vizenor, has the power to bring people together.

This paradox – communal connection via intellectual individuality – is at the core of Vizenor's message. The fictional world of *Bearheart* – which is to say, the modern world that we occupy – is broken, not just economically and materially, but imaginatively, a far more dangerous problem. Vizenor hopes to repair it by linking people together again, not necessarily within a "single clan," as Silko does in her performative novel *Ceremony*, but within a community of active readers and thinkers.

Text and reader

Some of Vizenor's strategies are quite straight-forward. His fictional author, Bearheart, addresses readers directly – even intimately – in the introductory *Letter to the Reader*, creating an immediate connection between narrator and audience that helps to break down the barrier separating and isolating individuals. Bearheart invites readers into his private reflections regarding a personal story that, nevertheless, has larger communal and global applications.

Nonetheless, Bearheart is elusive, to say the least. He teases readers with information, forcing them to fill in the gaps to make sense of the emerging narrative. This narrative technique serves a larger purpose. Reader response critic, Wolfgang Iser – whom Vizenor quotes in the headnotes of *Narrative Chance* – argues that modern texts, which are often fragmented and enigmatic, "make us aware of the nature of our own capacity for providing links" ("Reading Process" 55). As readers, we must complete the text; the end-result is an intellectual collaboration. Iser states that the literary text "is something like an arena in which reader and author participate in a game of the imagination" ("Reading Process" 51). Vizenor takes this "game of imagination" to its logical extreme, pushing readers to be more active and creative in the reading process. Their imaginative output necessarily designates readers as partners in the creation of meaning.[2] Not only are they constantly forced beyond terminal creeds, but their collaboration posits the imagination as a shared site of intellectual rebellion and freedom.

Readers must struggle through a demanding novel that very purposefully challenges them to re-create the world and themselves. Vizenor has stated as much about Native texts: "If it's written by a tribal person about tribal experience, it shouldn't be so easily accessible to bourgeois consciousness" (Bellineli, "Video"). Vizenor offers no easy answers or simple platitudes. Rather, he creates sometimes bizarre and often contradictory stories that defy most stereotypes.[3] Craig Womack describes "Vizenor's famously difficult style; its impenetrability, abstraction, theoretical jargon, puzzling contradictions. Parsing Vizenor's prose and coming up with a reasonable explanation is a formidable task" ("A Single Decade" 71). Vizenor forces readers to untangle complex theories and philosophies, and he complicates their efforts on purpose. In an interview, he states: "I choose words intentionally because they have established multiple symbolic meanings, and sometimes I put them in place so that they're in contradiction, so that you can read it several ways. You can read it just for its surface trace and definition – lexical definition – or you can change the definition in this one and leave that one the same and there's contention or agreement" (Coltelli *Winged Words* 175). Vizenor intensifies the interpretative process by forcing flexibility from the reader.[4] Individual readers will likely arrive at different conclusions (and probably should), and their responses will probably also shift from reading to reading.

As a result, the process of interpretation necessitates a heightened thoughtfulness and creativity. In *Narrative Chance*, Vizenor writes, "There can never be 'correct' or 'objective' readings of the text or the tropes in tribal literatures, only more energetic, interesting and 'pleasurable misreadings'" (5). Reading Vizenor's writings is necessarily self-reflective, since, as Elizabeth Blair notes, "In Vizenor's view, one looks for neither meaning nor truth in the postmodern novel" ("Trickster" 76). Likewise, Blaeser writes, "Vizenor refrains from exercising ultimate control over the readers' responses. Apparently *what* they imagine is of less significance to him than *that* they imagine. If they imagine, then his words have brought them liberation from the text" (*Gerald Vizenor* 179). Readers create their own meaning as they sort through the sometimes competing and sometimes complementary options. The process reflects Lawrence Gross's discussion of "bimaadiziwin," an Anishinaabe concept for the way to live well: "Bimaadiziwin, however, does not exist as a definitive body of law. Instead, it is left up to the individual to develop an understanding of bimaadiziwin through careful attention to the teaching wherever it can be found. This makes the term quite complex" (442). This concept of learning situates the source of meaning within the audience as well as the text. The symbiotic relationship of readers and text coincides with Iser's theories: "The production of the meaning of literary texts … entails the possibility that we may formulate ourselves and so discover what had previously seemed to elude our consciousness" ("Reading Process" 68). Difficult texts compel readers to grow – to transcend their own limitations and those imposed by society. Stanley Fish concurs: "It is a method which processes its own user, who is also its only instrument. It is self-sharpening and what it sharpens is *you*. In short, it does not organize materials, but transforms minds" ("Literature" 98). By sifting through evidence, considering interpretive possibilities, and developing flexible theories, readers are encouraged to avoid terminal creeds and expand beyond their former selves.[5]

The dangers of language

A major challenge for readers – and for the characters of *Bearheart* (beyond physical survival) – is to reject misleadingly simple explanations and formulations, even when they seem encouraging. Vizenor's methodology involves disrupting audience complacency, as laudatory philosophies and traditions can result in not only self-congratulation but also imaginative stagnation. He dramatizes this error in the *Letter* using the AIM activist, who admonishes Bearheart for speaking playfully as a bear, believing that Bearheart is disrespecting the bear clan religion. Her stern demeanor and quick criticism suggests an automatic response. She unthinkingly equates traditional spirituality with seriousness, whereas Bearheart views humor as an essential part of a healthy spiritual life. He belittles her stereotypical response: "You would be a word bear, your religion a word pile" (x). Her beliefs are unexamined, and her stale, somber piety exposes her complacency. She does not think or imagine beyond clichéd notions. While making general pronouncements about the goals of AIM, "[s]he smiles, proud to hold freedom in terminal creeds" (xi). Her unquestioning acceptance of static philosophies reveals her intellectual and imaginative limits – Vizenor's primary target. She has trapped herself within someone else's explanation of her beliefs. Unlike Bearheart, whose creed is fluid and imaginative, she accepts dogmatic religious formulations that prevent personal growth and obstruct meaningful connection.

One of the reasons Vizenor is so playful with language – and so challenging – is because he distrusts it. Even radical statements can become empty poses if unexamined and unimagined. As a writer, Vizenor must avoid the traps that he notes in others, and the danger is, arguably, more pronounced within a standard written text since it is – by its very nature – unchanging, static.[6] The shifting, paradoxical qualities of his narrative are an effort to avert absolutist statements.[7] His view of language also recognizes the insufficiency of words when used without imagination, a danger that he exposes repeatedly in the novel. Bearheart writes: "The aimless children paint hard words on the federal windows in their material wars, and the words are dead, tribal imagination and our trickeries to heal are in ruins" (ix). Even statements of social resistance can fall into predictable patterns that suggest a lack of creative response to a critical situation. Bearheart mocks the cheap imitation of traditional customs, such as "plastic bear claws," chicken feathers, and imitative beads. He declaims upon the insidious weakening of Native traditions while he roars his independence. Vizenor repeatedly expresses suspicion regarding the tools which he himself uses – the tools typically associated with imaginative literature. Words and language can exacerbate the problem by deepening the fissures that divide people. Vizenor reveres very little beyond the inviolate human heart and mind.

Despite his caution regarding language and words, Vizenor believes that stories contain great power because they allow listeners to grow: "[S]tories are not static; there are no scriptural versions of oral traditional stories. There are great variations. A storyteller was an artist, an imaginative person. He brought himself into being *and listeners into being with his imagination*" (Coltelli, *Winged Words* 164, my emphasis). For Vizenor, the reading process works much the same way as the listening process.[8] A well-told story compels others to think anew about old notions. Vizenor said:

> If a culture lives, it changes, it always changes. If a people live, they imagine themselves always and in a new sense. And here we are in the city,

and people are still trying to figure out what was the past. Well, there isn't any past, we're it, and I am, and I'm on the intersection; and I'm finding my way through traffic and I'm going to tell some stories about it. Just as people who found their way through the imaginative traffic a thousand years ago figured out their stories as comic acts of survival.

(Coltelli, *Winged Words* 164)

Vizenor challenges readers to refresh their critical thinking strategies, their concept of tribal story-telling traditions, and their philosophies not only about their own identities but also about America's history, its past, and especially its future. He wants his stories to help bring readers "into being" with their imagination.

The power of imagination

Vizenor provides examples of how this might work in *Bearheart*. In his *Letter*, Bearheart recounts how government agents in federal schools locked him in a closet to restrict him physically as well as imaginatively. Bearheart, how-ever, insists upon his and others' ability to self-define: "We survived as crows and bears because we were never known as humans. Those cruel teachers never heard our avian voices, they never roamed with us at the treelines. We dreamed free from our chains" (viii). Using an act of the imagination as well as drawing upon elements of Native spiritualism, Bearheart explains how he escaped a cultural system that circumscribes individual autonomy. Dreaming free of his chains, he imagined himself as more than what his teachers tried to allow. His act of creativity liberated him from a society and its institutions that offer only terminal responses to expansive questions. Daniel Heath Justice writes, "Stories expand or narrow our imaginative possibilities – physical freedom won't matter if we can't imagine ourselves free as well" ("Water" 150). Rejecting all external limitations, Bearheart imagines himself free and so becomes free.

Later in *Bearheart*, Vizenor provides a similar example of how imaginative self-definition enables survival. As the pilgrims travel toward the southwest seeking an opening into the fourth world, they struggle – like Bearheart – against reductive cultural codes. The pilgrims are constantly in danger from others' small-mindedness and from their own limited view of themselves and others. At various points in their journey, they encounter people who serve as examples (both positively and negatively) from which to learn. When they come across a large group of physically deformed people, some of whom lost their faces and/or legs because of industrial toxins, the pilgrims (and the readers) receive a lesson in the use of the imagination to combat debilitating situations. Some of the "cripples" dress as moths; some wear special masks; all envision their lives as whole, so each is whole in his or her own way. They cope creatively with their handicaps: "Their incomplete bodies lived whole through phantoms and tchibai dreams" (145). Their imaginations save and complete. They live from inside out – defining themselves intellectually and imaginatively – rather than from outside in.

However, their success only translates to others as a general philosophy, not as a literal example to be followed. Little Big Mouse's imitation – and its abject failure – demonstrates the dangers of following others too closely. Little Big Mouse does not fully understand or appreciate the debilitating obstacles that they have worked so hard to overcome, and she tries to wear one of the moth's wings. In effect, she romanticizes – even fetishizes – them, and they attack her physically for this presumption (148). A moth says, "You are perfect and now you want our imagination and visions for your own … We are moths to survive and escape our lives" (149). Relying upon their own creativity to live with dignity, they resent the efforts of a non-disabled person to appropriate their successes unnecessarily. Her attempt – and its easy familiarity – diminishes their hard-won efforts.[9] Vizenor likely wishes readers to note the parallels between Little Big Mouse's presumption and the vain desire among some non-Natives to appropriate tribal beliefs and customs. The episode serves both as a warning to readers against adopting others' identities simplistically and as encouragement to exercise one's imagination fully to create oneself. Appropriation, obviously, is not a genuine link between people.

Vizenor instead wishes to highlight a connectedness based upon intellectual orientation, not imitation. He helps to shape and link readers through the inherent challenges and examples within the text. The reading process has profound implications for Vizenor that include – but go beyond – the personal transformation identified by Iser and Fish. He writes against the institutions and ideas that separate people from themselves and from others. His goal is to teach an ongoing method of interpretation (and re-interpretation) that prompts greater human connectedness.[10] Vizenor, it is worth noting, is a teacher as well as a writer, and he considers writing a form of teaching. Both are communal. In an interview, he states that his goal as a writer is to "teach" tribal history, and then he characterizes teaching as "a human activity" that is "fundamentally an ethical experience" (Bellinelli, "Video"). To Vizenor, learning and reading are similarly collaborative. By working through the complex scenarios and philosophies of Vizenor's novel, readers are linked together in an act of shared discovery that is quintessentially human.

Interpreting the novel becomes tantamount to interpreting oneself in relation to the world. *Bearheart* asks readers to exercise their imaginations and to re-think their connection to modern society. With genuine self-exploration and new self-knowledge, individuals may acquire the "intellectual humanism" that Vizenor values. Alan Velie and Zubeda Jalalzai both identify the community spirit of *Bearheart*'s trickster narrator. Velie writes, "To Vizenor the tribal world view is comic and communal; the comic spirit is centered in trickster, a figure created by the tribe as a whole, not an individual author" ("Historical Novel" 131). Further, Jalalzai notes how this positioning extends to readers: "the postmodern trickster is comic, forges communal links, and challenges isolation in a way similar to the storyteller in oral tribal cultures" ("Tricksters" 27). Neither listeners nor readers can remain separate from the narratives that they encounter. Instead, they become connected to the teller/author as well as to other listeners/readers. By engaging the narratives, they are invited to challenge the status quo and imagine themselves outside of terminal creeds, thus connecting themselves through a shared intellectual orientation. The paradox – communal connection via intellectual individuality – underlines the complexity of Vizenor's message and the ambitious goal behind it.[11]

Collaboration and individual interpretation

Throughout *Bearheart*, readers are reminded of their communal role. The terms of the relationship often shift, but the emphasis on the collaborative nature of listening/reading recurs. For example, as the pilgrims approach the word wards, Bearheart narrates: "Oral traditions were honored ... The listeners traveled with the tellers through the same frames of time and place. *The telling was in the listening*" (162, my emphasis). Listeners shape the story by understanding it in their own terms. Without listeners who question and mold a story, it assumes an authoritative, even imperious, air. In essence, it becomes terminal. We can see this most clearly when Belladonna lectures to the people of Orion, who, in turn, listen closely, ask questions, and explicitly shape her narrative. They show how the telling is in the listening; they hear her words but create their own opinions. Her fate is sealed because she is inflexible and unimaginative.

Belladonna falls prey to dangers that threaten us all, including Vizenor himself. In an interview, he faults readers/critics who were offended at the scene in which Lilith Mae has sex with several dogs. In his opinion, the scene depicts a mythic truth that is actualized, rather than a physical act that is degrading to women (Coltelli, *Winged Words* 175–76). Like Belladonna, he is frustrated by others' interpretations that run counter to his own.[12] While he clearly appreciates the multiplicity of meanings that language and word-play allow – the Bakhtinian polyglossia that so often emerges in discussions of his work – he is discomfited by how others might interpret his words in a manner disadvantageous to him. He is caught in the bind of language that he himself recognizes and manipulates. His desire for readers to establish their own patterns of meaning results in shared power between the teller/writer and the listener/reader. Paradoxically (and so fittingly), it is Sir Cecil Staples, the evil gambler, who expresses caution regarding one's audience. He tells Inawa: "There are good reasons to be dishonest in the world when people seldom believe the truth … Being honest, as you must know, little stranger, is not always being honest. Much depends upon the listener" (125). Such statements serve as a caution to writers/story-tellers, while also placing a burden on their audience. Readers and listeners are not passive receptacles; rather, their role as interpreters requires them to engage the text actively and exercise their intellect upon it. A novel as difficult as *Bearheart* requires particular energies.

Inawa is perhaps the best example of a listener. Although he is – literally – the stranger, he is – more importantly – the ideal audience. Bigfoot, Lilith Mae, Sir Cecil Staples, and Belladonna all tell him their stories, and he inevitably understands them in his own way, which is often contrarian. For example, when Bigfoot tells him that his statue could help Inawa "live without loneliness," Inawa replies, "Loneliness is not evil" (88). Likewise, while he quietly watches Lilith Mae's dogs lick her feet, she tells him, "You are strange," to which he replies, "Silence is not strange" (90). After hearing Belladonna's story of her conception at Wounded Knee and her eagle whistle, he tells a story that complements hers by explaining the origin of the eagle whistle (186–87). In Inawa, readers are given an example of how to participate in the story. He learns from others, yet he thinks for himself. At the end, Inawa enters the fourth world precisely because he listens himself "into being." He is a case study for readers, who can also find connection and transcendence via their roles as participant members of an audience.

For Vizenor, it seems, human connection cannot exist when people listen passively. Rather, individuals find community through intellectual, creative, and spiritual affinity. At the core of each of these is imagination. Vizenor states, "I do my best to imagine myself, and my acts of imagination, I believe, leave open the possibility for human and spiritual experience" (Coltelli, *Winged Words* 162). Imagining oneself free of cultural codes and social definitions makes one, according to Vizenor, more human and hence more connected to others of like mind. Without imagination, individuals become mere victims, a problem that threatens all people, for everyone is threatened with terminal creeds and their enticing simplicity. In *Bearheart*, Proude explains: "We become the terminal creeds we speak. Our words limit the animals we would become ... soaring through words from memories and visions. We are all incomplete ... imperfect" (147). According to Proude, people are too often linked, not by their openness to exploring new ideas, but instead by a failure to define themselves individually, by mere conformity, or by a negative relation (an idea that recalls Silko's unification of all people within an atomic circle of destruction). Clearly, Vizenor (like Silko) seeks a more positive unity in *Bearheart*.

Connection, non-conformity, and transcendence

Bearheart abounds with examples of people coming together philosophically, and sometimes spiritually, even while it outlines the risks and complications involved. When, for instance, First Proude defies the officials who attempt to destroy the cedar forest, one of the surveyors abandons the government project and joins First Proude because "he wanted to share his courage and defend his sovereign cedar nation" (9). He was captured and killed for his efforts, yet his intellectual adventurism demonstrates not only the genuine connections that potentially exist between like-minded people but also the dangers of thinking independently. Since physical threats abound regardless, compliant groupthink is the greatest danger in *Bearheart*. Fourth Proude explains to two agents that when they "speak as an institution" (26), they separate themselves from other people and their own goals: "When you speak as individuals in the language of your dreams I will listen, but I will not listen to the foolish green paper talking to me" (26). Their failure of imagination separates them from him. Because they cannot explain themselves using their own words, they have lost their human identity and become mere machines. Proude, on the other hand, embodies a healthy autonomy and self-determination.

  Bearheart challenges its readers to achieve their own unique humanity through thoughtful non-conformity. Readers are required to struggle through the competing interpretive possibilities, creating and explaining their own interpretations. The first stop on the pilgrimage, for example, at the scapehouse for weirds and sensitives, is clearly open to varied reader responses. Its mixture of satire and empathy, of cannibalism and orgiastic sex, of playful discourse and weighty assertions defies a single, authoritative explanation. While individual readers will likely arrive at different conclusions, the interpretive process itself provides a level of unity, as it compels readers to undergo similar intellectual exercises. *Bearheart*, like most worthwhile texts, requires that readers ask questions, challenge assertions, and imagine various possibilities in an effort to understand actions and ideas in relation to their own level of understanding. In this way, *Bearheart* is a profoundly unifying novel.

Vizenor demonstrates how this decidedly individual process prompts a new interconnectedness among quite diverse characters. During the scapehouse dinner a disagreement arises among the guests and hosts regarding the propriety of eating kittens – particularly "unpraised" kittens – but Sister Sophronia locates a connection among them, despite their differences: "We appreciate the same things. We cannot understand the secrets of living so we demand some explanation ... some praise for death and our witness" (45). From confusion and dissension comes connection. Sophronia recognizes that they are undergoing a similar thought process that ultimately manifests itself in a spiritual form. When they are most troubled, they offer "praise," a word that connotes the spiritual. She sees that they all gravitate to the sacred when they cannot find simple answers. Her understanding of their shared process – even if their notions of the sacred differ – mirrors the interpretative process that Vizenor also envisions, a process that links readers together in "a kind of intellectual humanism, an integrity of humanism and the human spirit" (Coltelli, *Winged Words* 170). The connection results from the process, not the conclusions.

Bearheart provides many examples of characters who connect philosophically and creatively, thus transcending the limiting definitions allowed by cultural stereotypes. In the scapehouse, Rosina listens to Sister Willabelle tell about her horrifying experience crash-landing in a jungle, in which she is surrounded by dismembered passengers (including her decapitated mother) and in which she is disfigured by flesh-eating insects and piranha. The experience taught Willabelle all too clearly the physicality of life and the limitations of our material existence. As her sole audience member, Rosina becomes philosophically aligned with her. When asked about

herself, "she did not have abstract answers. Her life was visual and personal. She did not see herself in the abstract as a series of changing ideologies" (39). Both women are survivors with concrete self-definitions,
realized from individual experience and developed into firm philosophies.
As a result, they connect in substantial ways – intellectually and physically – and
the chapter ends with a sensual evocation: "The women touched hands and
then together slipped in silence beneath the warm fragrant water of the
scapehouse pool" (41). By defining themselves individually according to
their own experiences – or, in other words, by imagining themselves
regardless of society's expectations – they become linked together intellectually,
spiritually, and physically.[13]

Bigfoot also uses his imagination and personal spirituality to transcend
social limitations. He falls in love with a bronze statue of a woman with big
feet: "I am a fool, but not so foolish that I must live in loneliness and
unhappiness … I am in love with a vision … She is a personal vision and
caring gives me a good time" (82). In his unorthodox manner, he finds a
connection to the statue, to himself (the statue's big feet and loneliness
suggest self-love), to Inawa (to whom he tells the story), and even to a
white anthropologist who assisted him with his vision. According to Bigfoot, the "mashed vision vine stuff changed my life" (84). His vision
expands the limits of Bigfoot's imagination that separate him from others:
"The most amazing thing was hearing the thoughts of strangers, sharing
common thoughts and feelings without words" (84). His enhanced attune-
ment to other people translates into, among other things, a lighter sentence
for the murder he committed, as the "judicial folks were downright pleased
to meet an old fashioned passion killer, a killer who made sense" (83). Bigfoot's love and vision connect him to other people (beyond his love-object)
that appreciate his devotion as well as to the larger world that embodies his
greater realization of unity.

The statue symbolizes the power of imagination to save the individual by
prompting a new awareness of the whole. Bigfoot says: "In the real life of
my dreams and visions she [the statue] is a soothsayer, a pioneer representing the sources of rivers and thunders and the snow and sunshine. She
is the curve and color of the earth and the breath of our lives" (83).
Bigfoot's vision is both a desire for love and connection as well as an
employment of his imagination to recognize the fluid inter-relationships of
the world and its inhabitants. His love for the bronze statue and the vision
that allows it – although comic at one level (almost everything about Bigfoot is comic at some level) – moves him toward a greater appreciation of

the natural world in its entirety. His imagination and independence provide connection. As Blaeser writes, "Again and again, Vizenor upholds the same basic keys to survival: balance, humor, imaginative liberation, connection, continuance – and story" (71).

At the end of the novel, the pilgrims that succeed in reaching the fourth world illustrate Vizenor's idea of connection further. When the deceptively named "freedom train" pauses on its journey, Bearheart and Inawa walk into the mountains and soon thereafter "the sound of roaring bears echoed from the mountains" (221). They emerge together after the roaring stops. Proude seems to be initiating Inawa into his beliefs. During the inquisition, Inawa is tortured – having his ears sliced off and his eyes gouged – but he does not betray the others. Instead, he defies the inquisitors in a manner that indicates his spiritual connectedness to Proude: "the stranger rose up from his chair and roared in the voice of a small bear" (232). Only Proude and Inawa gain immediate entry into the fourth world, which is the objective of their long pilgrimage. Tellingly, they are asked to use their spiritual and imaginative faculties to envision their path: "a giant bear came to them and told them to follow their vision of him to the ancient ruins of the pueblos. Dreaming together the two pilgrims traveled in magical flight over the mountains and across rivers and the divide. At pueblo Bonito, the vision bear told the two pilgrims to enter the fourth world as bears" (242). Inawa is "the stranger" no longer. He completes the pilgrimage and enters the fourth world by achieving a transcendent spirituality together with Proude as a bear.[14] His vision and his imagination – both of which connect him philosophically to Proude – help him leave the chaos and dangers of a broken world.[15] Rosina senses their success when she hears bears roar: "The bears were over time in the four directions" (244). Proude and Inawa transcend the limitations of the world and its words, and Rosina follows their lead, becoming Changing Woman – the Navajo holy woman, the creator of humans, and the teacher of balance and harmony. Rosina blends herself into the ever-changing stories, suggesting again that imaginative connection is the panacea offered by Vizenor's novel.

Dependence and self-destruction

The other pilgrims, however, fare worse because they resist meaningful human connections and instead sow division among themselves. While still imprisoned, they blame each other for their predicament, despite Proude's advice: "Mistrusting each other gives them [the self-appointed governors] evil power over us" (229). Perhaps taking his cue and temporarily heeding Proude's warning, Bigfoot (now Double Saint) mixes the remainder of his vision vines and states: "With this vision vine we share our consciousness and speak together with the animals and birds through their voices and singing" (232). Soon the drug has its positive effect, bringing the pilgrims together: "Then the pilgrims soared through the patio and over the walls with the seven clown crows. ... Time passed as shared visions" (233). They transcend not only the walls, but time itself – like Proude and Inawa – and (further emphasizing the theme of connectedness) they recognize the similarities between their imprisonment and the establishment of the United States government in New Mexico in the nineteenth century: "The twelve clown crows watched the flag of the United States unfurl for the first time in Sante Fe right now from the plaza benches on August 18, 1846. ... Space turns under and disappears" (234). Although some of them escape their prison, Double Saint forces Rosina to perform fellatio, and Pio chokes him to death for the transgression. Then Pio sneaks into Rosina's sacred bundle and is blinded as a result. Their selfishness and deceit separate them from the two successful pilgrims, and they fail to enter the fourth world.

Their failure underlines the difficulty of the pilgrimage as well as the primary challenge – as suggested by Vizenor – facing people in the modern world. Most people victimize themselves with self-indulgent complacency and self-focused philosophies. Rather than thinking independently – and so linking themselves to other individualists ideologically and spiritually – many people simply follow the majority down an easier path, never genuinely pursuing knowledge on its own terms as it relates to them personally. As a result, they merely attain a false and temporary connection to others who happen to be doing the same thing at the same time. They accept terminal creeds, described by Jalalzai as "coherent explanatory systems" ("Tricksters" 28).

Vizenor warns readers of buying into simplistic unifying systems. For example, he uses Bearheart to criticize those who seek quick comfort within trite spirituality. The narrator Bearheart tells of many non-traditional people who seek deeper purpose in the cedar forest: "The crazed and alienated were desperate for terminal creeds to give their vacuous lives meaning. Hundreds of urban tribal people came to the cedar nation for spiritual guidance. ... Pantribal people were less drawn to visions than to ceremonial entertainment" (16). Rather than searching for genuine spiritual meaning through honest personal exploration, they try to borrow someone else's beliefs for a quick fix. As a result, they become further estranged from others and themselves, instead of becoming connected to humanity through a healthy individualism. While Vizenor shows respect for Native religions, he rebels against the notion that anyone can adopt another's religion as a convenience. He suggests that true spirituality results from a profound investigation into the relationship of the self and the world, both material and immaterial. In this regard, Proude castigates his fellow pilgrims who mistake a respect for religious objects with genuine spirituality. After he trades a medicine bundle for train tickets, and the other pilgrims shun him (not realizing that the bundle contains no real power), Proude says: "The power of the human spirit is carried in the heart not in histories and material. The living hold the foolishness of the past. Good spirits soar with the birds and the sun not in secret bundles" (218). Proude's imagery echoes Bigfoot's sentiments regarding his vision of the bronze statue. Both of them relate spirituality and imagination – not simply with material objects – but with the thoughts and emotions that occur when contemplating those objects. As a result, traditionalism attached to specific items falls short of providing meaningful transcendence.

In *Bearheart*, a strong philosophy and its attendant morality comes from within. It cannot be imposed from outside. Serving as a negative example, the evil governors of the new nation in Sante Fe offer a distorted version of Proude's shared spirituality. They force their prisoners to adopt their beliefs, rather than allowing them to make individual decisions: "Now that we have founded our new nation, the new governors agreed, we must enforce high moral and ethical standards" (224). By attempting to impose a common morality, the governors separate the people from themselves. They try to define others' beliefs, rather than let individuals imagine themselves, and the result is inevitably divisive. Here the central paradox of the novel is inverted: the evil leaders fragment a community of people in a selfish attempt to unite them. Vizenor suggests again that true unity results from absolute freedom of choice.

Bearheart stops well short of advocating moral anarchy, however.[16] The fact that the majority of pilgrims fail in their quest underlines the difficulty of living according to Vizenor's individualistic tenets, rather than intimating their laxity. Moreover, *Bearheart* clearly condemns those characters who sow division and tread upon others' rights. One of the most notorious cases of separatism is Sir Cecil Staples, the evil gambler. Proude, acting as spokesperson, is explicit: "[W]e are not equals. We are not bound in common experience. ... We do not share a common vision. Your values and language come from evil. Your power is adverse to living. Your culture is death" (132). Evil and good should be balanced, but Sir Cecil's extremism creates imbalance.[17] He recognizes and desires no shared qualities with the pilgrims. Instead, Sir Cecil wants to destroy good, distinguishing it from all else and classifying it as unnecessary. If people have no connection or shared visions, their lives are fragmented and isolated – at odds with the intellectual and spiritual humanism championed by Vizenor. Sir Cecil has disconnected himself philosophically from everyone, and he loses at his own game, ultimately choking to death in one of his own torture mechanisms within arm's length of the key to freedom, a set of images both literal and figurative.

Another group in Bearheart who most obviously represent divisive thinking is white people. Vizenor repeatedly castigates Euro-Americans for their crimes against Natives. For example, he denounces the government teachers and agents of the boarding schools (viii). He describes in brutal detail the torture and rape of First Proude's wife by "whitemen" (9). The Indian Re-Organization Act of 1934 is roundly criticized, as are the "white anthropologists" that designed it (12). The founder of the Walker Art Center (in Minneapolis, Minnesota) is criticized as a "capitalist treekiller who in good conscience raped the cedar and red pine on virgin woodland reservations" (53). A movie theater shows "a film about ceremonial violence and death, starring a cast of evil whitefamilies convicted for the ritualistic murder of tribal people" (53). Vizenor describes their treatment of Native people in grisly detail, in addition to how they were released from jail early because so many others enjoyed watching their violent acts.

Tribalism versus individualism

Vizenor's criticism does not fall along rigid ethnic or racial lines, however. No individual or group seems able to escape completely the pitfalls of a modern society that uses words and images to define and limit.[18] In Bearheart he criticizes many Native beliefs and organizations, attacking especially an unthinking tribalism. Early in the novel, First Proude declares his independence not just from the U.S. government, but also from Native governing systems, declaring: "We are sovereign from all tribal and religious and national governments, he told the leaders, and we will listen to nothing more about the future. ... He and other families exposed the evil of tribal governments and taught people to control themselves" (10). From the opening pages of Bearheart, Vizenor promotes a philosophy of individualism, which, nonetheless, results in an expanded form of community. One of his characters even blames (with no shortage of situational irony) tribal societies for their inability to resist white imperialism. The hunter in the walled city of Orion says: "The histories of tribal cultures have been terminal creeds and narcissistic revisionism ... If the tribes had more humor and less false pride then the families would not have collapsed under so little pressure from the whiteman ... Show me a solid culture that disintegrates under the plow and the saw" (198). The hunter seems to forget about the gun and white "law."

Vizenor attacks all cultural classifications that separate people, including racial and ethnic divisions. In his novel *The Heirs of Columbus* (1991), Vizenor is quite explicit. At a legal deposition, Chaine Riel (the fictional descendent of the nineteenth-century métis resistance leader) explains his findings on Stone Columbus, a cross-blood trickster leader and the primary character of the novel: "Stone resists the notion of blood quantums, racial identification, and tribal enrollment. ... He would accept anyone who wanted to be tribal, 'no blood attached or scratched,' he once said on talk radio. ... His point is to make the world tribal, a universal identity, and return to other values as measures of human worth, such as the dedication to heal rather than steal tribal cultures" (162). Stone's radical idea equalizes all people, removing the arbitrary measures that divide one group from another. Individuals would be judged by their beliefs and actions, not by exterior affiliations. While Vizenor again satirizes non-Natives who appropriate Native traditions,[19] he reiterates his opposition to arbitrary separatism: "Chaine reported to the tribal president that he should be concerned, but the notion of a universal tribe would cause no harm, 'because there was nothing to lose but racial distance'" (162). Whereas in *The Heirs of Columbus* Vizenor uses science – i.e., genetic modification – to advance the unity of the human race, in *Bearheart* he focuses on an idea more available to every person – the ability to imagine.

Vizenor wants readers to understand themselves honestly – a sometimes painful process – and to reject the reductive definitions provided to them by society. He argues that most people accept their status as victims: "People have been so beaten that they have no energy left to know how to imagine themselves. And they only know how to be victims – not just mixed-bloods or Indians but loads of other people. ... It's very sad and it's extremely tragic so I'm moved by that obviously. Quite a bit of my writing is revealed therein – people don't like to read that" (Coltelli, *Winged Words* 166). He uses his fiction to encourage others to imagine themselves anew – "to listen themselves into being." He destroys the old and thus allows the new to be created.[20]

In short, Vizenor writes to change readers and society. Rather than promoting a return to cultural traditions, he encourages the development – and continual redevelopment – of new and personal philosophies via introspection and interpretation. Louis Owens describes change *per se* as "the center of traditional tribal identity" ("Afterword" 250). Vizenor himself said: "Cultures are not static, human behavior is not static. We are not what anthropologists say we are and we must not live up to a definition" (Coltelli, *Winged Words* 172).

In *Bearheart*, Vizenor offers examples of characters who are open to change and characters who reject change. Belladonna represents an example of someone who resists change. Not only does she make vague generalizations about an idealized past, but she literally turns backward away from new ways of thinking about herself and the world. Vizenor emphasizes her mistake: "[h]er vision turned backwards," "[h]er facial expressions wavered backwards," "she was breathing backwards," (203) and she even walked backwards. In essence, she reverts to the past, precisely what the people of Orion warn against: "Surviving in the present means giving up on the burdens of the past and the cultures of tribal narcissism" (198). Healthy people do not obsess over the past, he suggests; rather they constantly experiment to understand the present. The denizens of the word hospital understand this: "[W]e are still working out the models and paradigms and experiments on our language to learn where we are and where we will be, all at the same time that we consider the moment at which we meet and speak" (165). They explore an evolving language to better understand themselves. With knowledge comes personal growth.

Proude's and Rosina's act of leaving the circus is perhaps the most positive act of individual adaptation. Although they are forced from their land by politics and violence, they have long been ready to change their lives. When Proude asks Rosina about a bundle, she replies: "I made that more than ten years ago. I am prepared to leave this cedar circus and the distance between our memories" (31). Both resist the threats to their chosen way of life, yet they simultaneously prepare for a new life. Neither bemoan the lost past (although the injustice is certainly remembered); instead, they progress into their new future. During the pilgrimage, they encounter a diverse array of people, and they accept each individually. Some of them – such as Pio Wissakodewinini and the Bishop Parasimo – choose to change their identities regularly, and entire groups – like the moth-cripples – redefine themselves to fit their new circumstances.

Humor also serves as a signal of intellectual flexibility and personal change. It balances the individual and the world against disruptive forces. For instance, when the federal agent tells Proude about his father, Proude asks, "Was his hate in good humor?" (27). Without humor to balance him, he would descend into evil. Humor is the balm that soothes an agitated mind. Bigfoot asserts: "When in doubt panic with good humor" (55). Bigfoot himself uses a comedic self-defense strategy when he is threatened by rock-throwers gathered on a bridge as he and the other pilgrims pass underneath. He dances maniacally in his red leggings and umbrella: "Some of the hostiles and whitestudents began to laugh at the short clown with the huge feet. ... The punt dipped and took on water but the pilgrims passed beneath the hostiles in humor and without harm" (72). He uses humor to defuse high tensions – both within himself and in the hostiles.[21] Furthermore, Bigfoot had unknowingly resurrected a traditional tactic that his ancestors had used years before, so his use of humor demonstrates again a positive connection to others, not through rote imitation, but through interactive self-creation. The final pages of the novel are peppered with the laughter of the successful pilgrims, suggesting the necessary role and result of humor to survival.

In *Bearheart*, Vizenor hopes to inspire humor, imagination, and continued change among his readers. Traversing *Bearheart*, they set out (perhaps unknowingly) on their own pilgrimage toward a fourth world that is theirs to imagine in good humor. In the process, readers share the opportunity to transform themselves, a creative act that will ally them with others equally independent and thoughtful.

James Welch has clearly engaged upon a similar pilgrimage, and he shares his imagination and intelligence in *Fools Crow* and *The Heartsong of Charging Elk*. These historical reconstructions offers readers a range of characters, facts, and ideas that are both culturally specific and universally applicable. Not unlike Vizenor, Welch draws readers into an initially unfamiliar context in order to re-familiarize them with their own world – a potentially transformative collection of diverse cultures and shared ideas, of radical differences and mutual respect, of tribal survival, individual growth, and human connection.

5

WRITING FOR CONNECTION

CROSS-CULTURAL UNDERSTANDING IN JAMES WELCH'S HISTORICAL FICTION[1]

In *Fools Crow* and *The Heartsong of Charging Elk*, James Welch examines the social and cultural connections between Natives and non-Natives, and he demonstrates how different peoples and cultures intersect in both positive and negative ways. Without losing sight of the historical outrages committed upon Native peoples, Welch's historical fiction lessens differences between cultural groups and in the process helps to foster mutual respect. His earlier novel, *Fools Crow* (1986), recreates the period of first contact between Blackfeet tribes and Euro-Americans to illuminate the alliances and conflicts, the treaties and wars, the cultural exchanges and political inequities that nearly destroyed a way of life over 130 years ago. The latter novel, *The Heartsong of Charging Elk* (2000), begins after the historical epoch documented within *Fools Crow*, focusing on the shift to reservation life among the Oglala Sioux after white America stole most of their lands. In both novels, Welch compels readers to re-evaluate common versions of United States history. He initially places most readers in the role of outsider, but he ultimately invites them into distinct tribal cultures to deepen their understanding and expand their awareness of similarities between ostensibly different peoples.

Although Welch's fiction appeals to all types of readers – Native, non-Native, academic, general, etc. – this chapter considers the ways in which Welch targets a popular audience interested but not fluent in Native studies or specific tribal cultures. In a 1995 interview, Welch said, "I feel the need to present Indians in a way that would be educational to readers, and I hope it would be entertaining, and really to bring some sort of understanding to the outside community of what life is like for Indians on reservations and Indians in historical times" (Bellinelli, "Video"). A sizable portion of his intended audience seems to be readers in the "outside community," and he addresses this audience in a manner that highlights the links between people of different cultural backgrounds. His presentation of tribal words and near-translations, his descriptions of specific cultural practices, his retelling of traditional stories, his broad use of humor, and his emphasis upon the importance of community all offer insight into the shared qualities of a common humanity.[2]

By demonstrating similarities as well as showcasing differences, Welch's historical novels serve to empower and liberate Native people and communities, a stated goal of indigenous scholar-activists Devon Abbott Mihesuah and Angela Cavender Wilson, among others.[3] Fools Crow and Heartsong treat racial issues and relationships in a manner that defines the present as much as the past, effectively dismantling many misconceptions and stereotypes that sustain discrimination today. Although clearly intent upon correcting the historical record, Welch also offers hope for the future, and he targets a general readership to influence popular attitudes. He uses fiction to break down barriers, showing readers that intersections of belief and practice between people make assaults on one group essentially an attack on the self. James Clifford argues, "'Cultural' difference is no longer a stable, exotic otherness; self-other relations are matters of power and rhetoric rather than of essence" (Predicament 14). Harnessing the power of literature, Welch challenges rigid racial and cultural categories – while still honoring differences – and he reveals shared motivations, doubts, and ideas in order to break down constructed divisions in our past, present, and future.

Writing history as resistance

The focus on connections between people does not prevent Fools Crow and Heartsong from acting also as resistance literature.[4] Both novels explicitly subvert prevailing stereotypes about Natives. While writing Fools Crow, Welch himself said: "I'm trying to write from the inside-out, because most historical novels are written from the outside looking in. ... [From the perspective of Fools Crow] the white people are the real strangers. They're the threatening presence out there all the time" (McFarland, James Welch, 4–5).

Welch's Native-centered approach in Fools Crow decenters many readers, compelling them to rethink conventional attitudes regarding the expansion of the United States and the social and military policies that allowed it.[5] In other words, Welch's historical fiction initially "others" non-Native readers by placing white Americans at the margins of the main story.

In Fools Crow, Welch uses the historical narrative to situate readers in a cultural framework specific to the Blackfeet. The events at the novel's core are historically documented occurrences that Welch outlines in Killing Custer (1994). Owl Child, a Blackfeet warrior shunned by his own community for a murder, killed the white trader Malcolm Clark in August 1869. Although the act was revenge for a personal insult, it became an excuse for U.S. troops to attack all Blackfeet, a course of action that culminated in the Marias River Massacre (sometimes called the Baker Massacre). Welch himself has a very personal connection to this history. He has identified Malcolm Clark and possibly Heavy Runner as relations, and he ascribes much of the inspiration for Fools Crow to his great-grandmother, Red Paint Woman, who was part of Heavy Runner's band on the Marias River, and whose stories he heard from his father.

Among other things, Fools Crow informs readers that 173 men, women, and children were killed despite a signed agreement between Chief Heavy Runner and General Alfred Sully. Welch focuses on this catastrophe to publicize a fundamental event within Blackfeet and U.S. history as well as provide a context more generally to re-think popularized historical episodes such as "Custer's last stand." To Welch, the unprovoked massacre and the Battle of Little Bighorn are central both to Blackfeet history and to United States history. To separate them is to distort. Whereas Custer's death has been mythologized as part of a larger story about American providence, the massacre on the Marias River has been largely ignored. Welch hopes to change that in Fools Crow by re-constructing events from a Native perspective, compelling readers to understand them outside of the promotional narrative about "winning the West" and "manifest destiny." In this version, Malcolm Clark is not a victim, but a hapless hypocrite; Joe Kipp is not an intrepid scout, but a self-serving turncoat; General Alfred Sully is not a noble ambassador of white America, but a small-minded negotiator of meaningless contracts. Fools Crow deconstructs a white-washed view of United States' history, recreating a particular cultural moment to demonstrate how different peoples and cultures both clashed and merged.

The Heartsong of Charging Elk also seeks to alter the way that many readers think about Native history and its relation to European/American society, but it performs this task in a slightly different manner. Welch identifies his historical precedent as Black Elk, who had traveled with Buffalo Bill's show, missed the return ship home to America, and lived in Europe for two years (56–58). In Welch's novel, Charging Elk is also left in France by Buffalo Bill's "Wild West Show," and he survives in a new world that is both fascinated and frightened by him. In turn, he is simultaneously intrigued and repulsed by French culture. Inverting the imperialist pattern, Charging Elk and the other young Natives travel to Europe in search of adventure, fun, and wealth. They are the explorers who enter and occasionally disrupt the others' world, taking pride in their difference and pleasure in shocking the Europeans: "the young Indians enjoyed the spectacle of themselves reflected in the astonished eyes of the French people" (27). Not going quite so far as claiming to have discovered France, they nonetheless traverse its streets with confidence and bravado.

On the other hand, they face much bias, and Charging Elk's experiences (in some respects) parallel the hurdles faced by Native people generally during the late nineteenth and early twentieth century. For example, Charging Elk is declared officially "dead" by inept government operatives, whereas in the United States Natives were often treated as a "vanishing" people by many white officials. Both Charging Elk and early twentieth-century Natives were compelled to survive in a hostile cultural environment that refused to recognize them in any meaningful way and ignored them as inconsequential. Charging Elk's dream of Native Ghost Dancers suggests his hope for recognition and independence (114), yet his recurring dream of mass death probably refers to the massacre at Wounded Knee on the Pine Ridge Reservation in 1890. Many historians consider Wounded Knee as the end of armed resistance to white attack and the beginning of a particularly bleak period of forced assimilation. Charging Elk himself is compelled to abandon many of his traditional ways as he struggles to adapt to life in Marseille. Moreover, fetishized by a French man, who drugs and molests him, Charging Elk kills him. The experience is emblematic of how Native cultures were exoticized by outsiders (despite steady opposition), while the subsequent trial exposes the overt prejudice at the heart of such simplifications. During the proceedings, "specialists" declaim on the size of "savages' brains" and "mental capacity," all part of a process that relegates Charging Elk to a "living death" (291). Welch's narrative recalls the manner in which Natives were judged and condemned according to the prevailing culture's prejudices. In the end, though, Charging Elk gains a renewed sense of self that combines his connection to the past with a strong understanding of his place in the present. He finally gets a real choice, and his decision to stay in France with his wife and their expectant child points not only to the impossibility of ever returning fully to his previous life but also to his successful adaptation and contribution to a changed world.

Translating the unfamiliar

Welch's historical fiction does more than present Native history from an indigenous perspective, however. Both Fools Crow and Heartsong involve readers within a narrative that compels them to re-situate themselves.[6] Particularly for readers not fluent in Blackfeet and Lakota cultures, a period of readjustment must take place. Welch's use of language forces readers into the role of outsider.[7] Immediately in the initial paragraphs of Fools Crow, readers are confronted with an unfamiliar world in which "Cold Maker" and the "Backbone of the World" hold dominance. Welch describes people, places, and things using near-translations and Native words that distance many readers from their familiar world. In Fools Crow frogs are "green singers," grizzly bears are "real-bears," and fish are "the swift silver people who live in the water" (56). White people are "Napikwans," and the federal troops – appropriately enough – are "seizers." Thus, Welch defamiliarizes conventional perspectives for many readers, in effect taking control of the language to redefine popular perceptions of American history.[8]

Nevertheless, Welch's choice risks exoticizing a culture that is too often treated as a curiosity; his language could be perceived as contrived or wooden. Critics have discussed the efficacy of writing subversively in English, or "reinventing the enemy's language" (Harjo and Bird, Reinventing). Robert Gish notes briefly that Welch risks "silliness" but that ultimately his "scheme of naming … has the intended effect of establishing an older (but for the reader newer) way of knowing" (71). Welch asks readers to do more than suspend their disbelief; he asks them to transform their beliefs by re-visioning the world using new terms and a new context. Blanca Schorcht praises Welch's use of hyphenated coinages: "This kind of translation simultaneously prevents the exoticization of Native American history while it emphasizes differences in experience" (96). However, while his use of language may initially highlight differences, it ultimately allows similarities to come to the forefront.

To this end, Welch's terminology recalls Ernest Hemingway's language in For Whom the Bell Tolls. Set in Spain, Hemingway "translates" Spanish language and culture into English in a manner that retains the flavor of the original. Hemingway's protagonist, Robert Jordan, who hails from Missoula, Montana (which was, incidentally, also home to Welch), uses diction that reflects both the formality of Spanish ("thou hast," "thee") and the literalness, even the stiffness, of translation ("not even in joke" [30], "we are various" [151]). Welch, an avowed admirer of Hemingway, uses language in a similar manner. Both writers initially compel readers to navigate an unfamiliar world, but ultimately provide enough information for readers to achieve a greater level of understanding. Welch, in particular, invites readers into a unique but often misunderstood culture, allowing them first to become comfortable with differences between languages and cultures – and then to recognize the similarities between people.

Likewise, The Heartsong of Charging Elk asks readers to understand western European society via a Native perspective and language. This time, however, Welch defamiliarizes the "white" world, rather than, as in Fools Crow, rendering a Native cultural and physical environment in new terms. Early in the narrative, Charging Elk wakes up in a "white man's healing house" after an injury and illness, and he must explain to himself – and to readers – where he is and what he sees. His descriptions interpret French society from the perspective of an Oglala Sioux, while also commenting humorously on non-Native customs (and on Charging Elk's own personal attitudes). Dollar bills are "frogskins," coffee is "pejuta sapa, black medicine" (17), and alcohol is "mni wakan, the white man's holy water" (21). Whites themselves are "wasicuns." Welch also details Charging Elk's response to a Christmas nativity scene and the "naked iron tree" (i.e., Eiffel Tower) (42). Interestingly, he describes national anthems as "power songs" (66), a phrase that redefines a typically conservative point of pride into an indigenous intellectual framework. This reference takes a nationalistic icon (i.e., the anthem) – something that distinguishes one group of people from others – and transforms it into something that crosses cultural borders. In Welch's treatment, it serves as a connection between people, not a separator.

In this way, Welch does more than disorient readers within his historical fiction; he also re-orients them. While his terminology might initially decenter readers, it ultimately invites readers into a rich and vibrant Native world. Welch uses Fools Crow especially to teach readers a new way of seeing and understanding. A good example of how this works occurs during a conversation between Fools Crow and Red Paint on the night before he leaves to revenge Yellow Kidney's mutilation. As he and Red Paint lie in their lodge, they hear "the barking and howling of Kis-see-noh-o" (135). While the description of the sounds may signal the specific animal to some readers, others might not immediately make sense of the reference, and, in fact, several different animals bark and howl. In the next line, Welch aids readers by identifying Kis-see-noh-o as the "little-wolves," thus using a calque to rule out wolves proper and to give a strong hint as to the animals he is referencing. Not until two pages later, however, does Welch identify with certainty the animals as coyotes (137).

This relatively minor detail demonstrates how Welch instructs and includes readers. He first destabilizes or de-centers them with a non-English word or a near-translation; then he provides textual clues that allow readers to figure out his reference; and finally he gives them (sometimes) the opportunity to double-check their conclusions. As a result, Welch allows readers to overcome their lack of knowledge and the resulting discomfort. At first, they are outsiders, and his language excludes them from full participation within the narrative. However, he does not sustain this exclusion. They gain a small piece of knowledge that involves them more fully in the novel and perhaps promotes their understanding – and hopefully their respect for – Native American experiences.

Teaching readers with cultural connections

Readers are asked to perform a daunting task in Fools Crow – learn about a complex culture probably unfamiliar to many of them – and so Welch makes efforts to alleviate anxieties that readers might have about being placed in the role of student. Even prominent characters must learn the ways of their own culture. For example, when Mik-api teases Fools Crow about his crush on Red Paint, Fools Crow asks him to speak on his behalf, and Mik-api responds: "Slow down, you foolish young one. … First, you must go to your father and mother and tell them of your intentions. If they agree, I will talk to Yellow Kidney" (105). Like readers, Fools Crow must be taught the proper courtship procedures of the Pikunis. As Fools Crow grows and learns, Welch undoubtedly hopes that readers will also mature in their knowledge. Fools Crow contains strong elements of the bildungsroman, a component of the novel that undoubtedly rings familiar to many readers. Yet Fools Crow also attempts to cultivate public opinion about unfamiliar or underappreciated components of Native cultures. To create a comfort zone suitable for learning, Welch shows how all people must learn their own cultures. By doing this, he not only encourages readers to understand and respect Blackfeet culture, but he also motivates them to learn (or relearn) their own culture and history.[9]

An important way that Welch teaches readers is with Blackfeet stories, a traditional tribal manner of imparting information and wisdom to successive generations. He provides fairly detailed accounts of Seco-mo-muckon, of Akaiyan and Nopatsis, and of So-at-sa-ki (Feather Woman) and Poia (Scar Face). At one level, these Blackfeet stories provide commentary upon the novel's events. Seco-mo-muckon's pride and deceit echo that of Fast Horse, as does Akaiyan's treacherous betrayal of his brother. Nopatsis' patience, learning, and success parallel the experiences of Fools Crow. On another level, however, these stories draw readers more deeply into Pikuni culture, inviting them to understand and appreciate the worth of the culture that created the stories. Readers receive information that should lessen the differences between cultures, rather than make one seem more exotic or foreign than the other. Some critics even locate a "merging of two cultures" in Welch's depiction of Blackfeet stories. Velie states that Welch's bildungsroman draws upon both the Native tradition of Scar Face and the Euro-American tradition of Horatio Alger ("Indian"199–200). Whether Welch consciously thought of Alger as he wrote is perhaps less important than that Velie makes the connection himself. The stories allow bridges between cultures by sharing messages that transcend a specific culture. These stories undoubtedly have specific cultural meanings for the Blackfeet, but when shared with a national and international audience, they will also be understood (as Welch was well aware) in terms already familiar to readers.

Because of this, Welch again risks himself. Some might argue that publishing Native stories allows them to be distorted by removing them from their traditional cultural context and place them within a historically exploitative belief system.[10] However, Native writer and teacher Sidner Larsen argues that making connections across cultures is a specifically indigenous methodology. He asks his students to read Native texts "with strong emphasis on students relating their own lives to the materials" (*Captured* 14). Likewise, Blanca Schorcht notes how traditional tribal stories should be incorporated into readers' ways of thinking: "Their different worlds engage in dialogues with each other as they converge with the real world of the contemporary reader" (*Storied Voices* 88). Welch himself values just such connections. In *Killing Custer*, he recalls a moment of revelation in his ambition to become a writer. In his adolescence, he believed that real writers had to live in New York City and, presumably, write about it too. As he tells it, his mother showed him some documents that demonstrated how Sitting Bull lived in and journeyed through northern Montana. He writes: "Suddenly, the area did not seem so remote. Suddenly, my part of the country had history, a *connection* with the rest of the country – at least the west" (232, emphasis added). Welch appreciates this connection because it links Native American history to Euro-American history. He did not see the overlapping histories in conflict with each other; rather, they inform and complement each other. Welch's insight apparently encouraged him to write about the Blackfeet experience as part of U.S. history. Whereas Fast Horse in *Fools Crow* foolishly resists any meaningful dialogue about his past (200), Welch uses his historical fiction to open up a dialogue with readers that promises further understanding rather than more violence.

One of Welch's primary goals is to dispel misconceptions about tribal cultures by inviting readers into it. His most successful strategy is his direct description of specific customs within their traditional cultural framework. For example, the Sun Dance ceremony, according to *Fools Crow*, is an annual unifying celebration during which individuals make sacrifices for themselves and their people. Readers learn of the important role of the Sacred Vow Woman, about the process by which the center pole of the Medicine Lodge is chosen and prepared, and about how individuals dance around the pole for a greater good. Welch's rendering of the ceremony demonstrates its purposes and, as a result, its normalcy, thus demystifying an important tradition that was criminalized by the U.S. government and is still sometimes treated as an exotic curiosity by non-Natives.[11] Welch's willingness to share details of the Sun Dance with readers is a gage of his desire to combat the distorted images that revolve around the celebration.

In addition, his personal involvement in the ceremony as a child helped Welch become fully aware of his Blackfeet identity. In a foreword to William Farr's photographic history, *The Reservation Blackfeet, 1882–1945*, Welch recalls attending the ceremony with his father and watching the procession of holy people: "A voice, high and distant, sang to the sun and it entered my bones and I was Blackfeet and changed forever. I remember. Thirty-four years later the image of that Sun Dance procession is still with me, and *in my novels and poems I have tried to maintain the spirit of that moment*" (Farr, vii, emphasis added). *Fools Crow* captures the spirit of that moment by inviting readers into a literary rendering of the experience. By sharing such an essentially Native ritual with readers, he trusts them with knowledge of the ceremony. In doing so, he offers some level of connection or even belonging – comparable in a small way to his own experience of new self-awareness.

Welch reinforces this philosophy of connectedness in *Heartsong*. During a flashback to the Sun Dance, Charging Elk "heard the beat of the drum and he knew it was the heartbeat of the *can gleska*, where all becomes one" (64). His vision of unity suggests again the inclusiveness that Welch associates with the ceremony. Even if readers are not "changed forever," as Welch was, their experience reading about the Sun Dance – and the culture generally – has the power to alter perceptions and foster respect for tribal beliefs and customs. In an interview, when asked whether "the word" is sacred, Welch doubted whether "sacred" was the correct term, but he emphasized the ability of language to educate, entertain, and foster intimacy, adding: "Words are probably the strongest link between people. I think in any form of communication people can develop a more emotional relationship over a book. From the writer to the reader it's a very intimate relationship" (Bellinelli, "Video"). Welch fosters this relationship by detailing Native customs in print, at a time, moreover, when many prefer to keep spiritual and cultural practices out of the hands of those who might mishandle them (and, in fact, have in the past). In this way, Welch constructs a bridge between cultures – showing a trust and honesty that perhaps points to how all might become one.

The trans-cultural bridge, of course, goes both ways.[12] In *The Heartsong of Charging Elk*, Welch demonstrates a similar connection between different spiritual systems, but he reverses the cultural direction. While Charging Elk is traveling with the "Wild West" show, he meets a French woman, named Sandrine, who gives him a picture of a man with "a woven chain of thorns" around his heart. He refers to it afterward as "the picture of the man with the bloody heart" (72). His factual description reveals that Charging Elk does not initially understand the spiritual message likely intended by Sandrine. He interprets the image literally. Charging Elk eventually understands and accepts the image in terms of his own spiritual beliefs: "it had become part of her *nagi* that he must carry always, just as he always wore his badger claw necklace" (72). The gift, to Charging Elk, signifies a cross-cultural relationship – even if not necessarily intended in that way. Rather than becoming interested in Christianity, he incorporates it into his own belief system, demonstrating a respect for others' beliefs as well as asserting equality between them: the image of Jesus is parallel to his badger claw necklace. Welch's depiction also suggests a satiric intent. With its oblique reference to the many depredations done to Natives in the name of Christianity, Welch implies that Jesus does, after all, have a bloody heart. The irony fades, however, in light of Charging Elk's genuinely sympathetic response. His redefinition of the Christ-image emphasizes an intersection of beliefs rather than a conflict between them.

Welch fosters cross-cultural relationships further in *Heartsong* by providing information about Oglala beliefs and by exhibiting those beliefs in action. For example, as Charging Elk thinks about Armond Bretueil, the man who drugged and molested him, Welch defines quite explicitly the roles of *heyokas* and *siyokos*. He does not suggest or infer, and he does not expect readers to know already how they differ, as more challenging authors might do. Rather he patiently explains that heyokas "act crazy but deep within them, they possess much power. They are to be respected but feared" (180). On the other hand, siyokos are "evil spirits" (181), and, as a result, more dangerous than the heyokas. These small gestures of explanation suggest that Welch is attempting to meet readers at their level of knowledge and promote further understanding. Moreover, Charging Elk himself is not quite sure whether Bretueil is heyoka or siyoko, and as a result readers are led to believe that the distinction is difficult even for those immersed in Lakota culture.[13]

Ambiguity and interpretation

Welch, in fact, seems to delight in his ability to foster ambiguities about culturally specific knowledge. He rarely misses an opportunity to undermine cultural absolutes. For example, in *Fools Crow*, readers are told that a married man should not look directly at his mother-in-law; then later, Fools Crow and Heavy Shield Woman stare at each other: "now this taboo seemed far less important than the bad spirit in the boy they loved" (264). In effect, Welch demonstrates how every culture has rules, and every rule most likely has exceptions. This both prevents us from fully understanding the Blackfeet world and makes us more dependent upon the text itself to determine Welch's goals. And yet if Welch sometimes provides readers with the necessary information, he other times forces us to confront the inevitable ambiguity. For example, Fools Crow tells Boss Ribs about Fast Horse's dream (199), even though he knows that "to tell another's dream could make one's own medicine go bad" (48). His change of plan takes place without explanation, demonstrating the grey area surrounding some cultural beliefs and their implementation. Likewise, when Charging Elk visits a new restaurant and finds himself surrounded by hostile American sailors, he sings his death song to escape. On the one hand, readers are shown an Oglala man utilizing an important part of his belief system to avoid danger. On the other hand, even Charging Elk realizes that the song did not help him in the standard way: "He knew that the purpose of the song had become distorted into a kind of defense mechanism but he didn't know why – only that it worked this time" (177). Both Charging Elk and Welch seem relatively comfortable with how traditional aspects of tribal cultures transform themselves into something new. This both complicates our ability to comprehend the Native worlds in Welch's fiction and – in a way – relieves us from assuming that we require an encyclopedic knowledge of distinct tribal cultures to understand (and enjoy) his novels. Welch teaches us what we need to know (in the same way that Momaday and Silko also assert the self-containment of their texts).

Furthermore, in both Fools Crow and Heartsong, Welch focuses on questions, doubts, and other negative reactions that individuals have regarding traditional elements of their belief systems. Even clearly admirable characters do not subscribe to a monolithic view of Blackfeet culture. For instance, despite the fact male Blackfeet society was organized around raiding and war honors (as much as hunting and trading), Fools Crow vomits from his horse after a raid against Bull Shield. The danger and violence of his killing were apparently too much for him. Although he is initiated into manhood as a result, Welch does not glamorize the moment or the man, and in fact Red Paint questions the necessity of the war party, even though it seeks revenge for her father's mutilation. Welch portrays the misgivings that would have inevitably arisen, and that also clash potentially with his positive presentation of a warrior culture. In the end, however, the complications and paradoxes of Pikuni life and thought make the people and their culture more admirable, because more complex.

Perhaps the most sensitive issue that Welch confronts is the doubt that individuals likely experienced regarding their spiritual beliefs. Facing a potentially overwhelming cultural onslaught, some characters question their Blackfeet faith. Rides-at-the-door says despairingly: "Sun Chief favors the Napikwans. Perhaps it's because they come from the east where he rises each day to begin his journey. Perhaps they are old friends. Perhaps the Pikunis do not honor him enough, do not sacrifice enough. He no longer takes pity on us" (177). Welch risks much by voicing such doubts so openly. Historically, much of white America would have likely agreed that tribal religions were false, and undoubtedly a portion of U.S. citizens would still consider Blackfeet spirituality as quaint mythology. Welch's portrayal confronts an understandable part of the Indian experience – the potential for religious misgiving[14] – while ultimately demonstrating how such questioning can lead to a stronger belief. Fools Crow's journey to Feather Woman at the end of the novel is a good case in point. Along the way, he doubts both his dream and his dream helper; he blames Skunk Bear – his animal helper – for betraying him; and he repeatedly questions his ability to help his people. Yet in the end, the tribal beliefs and stories more than adequately inform and support his own experiences.

Similar situations occur throughout Fools Crow. Heavy Shield Woman, for example, is naturally apprehensive about her decision to be Sacred Vow Woman, and she re-evaluates her own worth and motivation. Her self-examination is an effort to understand herself better and conduct herself more appropriately. Welch is not alone in his examination of religious doubt among tribal people. In The Surrounded, D'Arcy McKnickle expresses similar misgivings via the elder Modeste, who tells Archilde:

> Many went off alone on praying-fasts. It was clear that something had gone wrong, the people had lost their power.
> [...]
> So our wise ones began to say that we must find something new. Our voices, they said, no longer reach Amotkan ['The old word for God']. Maybe he has gone too far away or maybe our voices have become weak, but when we speak in the old ways we are not heard.
>
> (73)

Like McKnickle, Welch is not inviting disbelief regarding tribal religions. Rather, he demonstrates the full range of his characters, presenting them as intellectually honest and spiritually brave rather than shrouded in mysticism and mystery.[15] To his credit, Welch resists the urge to create idealized characters. While sometimes heroic, they are always human.

Charging Elk faces similar doubts – and reassurances – about himself and his spiritual beliefs. He remembers how his friend Sees Twice had told him that the white "God Almighty" was "even stronger than Wakan Tanka." Years later, Charging Elk thinks: "Although he hadn't believed Sees Twice then, now he wasn't so sure. After all, the wasicuns ruled the world" (183). His isolation in France challenges his beliefs, causing him to question his conception of God. In the end, he retains his belief in Wakan Tanka, thanking the Great Spirit for sending people like Yellow Breast to help him. Despite marrying a Christian, and even attending services with her, Charging Elk does not become Christian; instead he simply demonstrates his open-mindedness to others' beliefs. As James Clifford writes, "It is easier to register the loss of traditional orders of difference than to perceive the emergence of new ones" (*Predicament* 15). Welch resists developing an undue focus on loss alone, and he veers away from a purely syncretic model. Instead, he describes cultural co-existence and individual persever-ance. Welch shows the normalcy of self-questioning and how doubt is (or should be) part of all faiths.

His European characters share similar moments of uncertainty, demon-strating again the connectedness of all peoples. The ultra-pious René prays regularly to the Christian figure, Mary, but he acknowledges that "he had no sign that she had heard him" (266). His wife, Madeleine, admits to herself: "Sometimes his piety was a burden" (100). Likewise, the farmer Vincent Gazier responds to his wife's illness with religious despair. After Charging Elk tells him that he will pray to Wakan Tanka for her, Gazier gains hope, saying, "'Thank you, Charging Elk. That is all I ask. Perhaps your Great Spirit ... ' The gaunt man suddenly stopped. He had almost committed a sacrilege" (317). Apparently he had almost acknowledged the equality of their differing definitions of God — just as Charging Elk had done (and Fools Crow). By showing how individuals respond to life's challenges in similar ways, Welch equalizes the people and their belief systems. Neither is exotic; both are normal.

The normal and the negative

One of Welch's great accomplishments in Fools Crow is that he normalizes Native people and cultures in a historical work that might invite romantic nostalgia. An especially noteworthy example is on the morning that Fast Horse again leaves the Pikuni camp. A blizzard had just blanketed the region, and Welch takes the time to outline the typical activities "on almost any other day" (191) and, in the process, again invites readers into a Blackfeet community before white intrusion: "Some of the men would go off hunting, or just exploring, always with their weapons. The women would prepare hides or continue with bead- or quillwork and gossip. The children would throw stones into the river or play with dolls or sleds" (191). In the extended description, Welch shows domesticity and contentment without descending into romanticism. Focusing on mundane daily activ-ities, he avoids sentimentalizing a past lifestyle and instead informs readers of its normalcy. The historical perception created by Welch extends to the present, and it represents a viewpoint voiced by other Native writers as well. Paul Chaat Smith writes: "One decade we're invisible, another dangerous. Obsolete and quaint, a rather boring people suitable for schoolkids and family vacations, then suddenly we're cool and mysterious. Some now regard us as keepers of planetary secrets and the only salvation for a world bent on destroying itself. Heck, we're just plain folk, but no one wants to hear that" (in Shanley, "Metacritical" 223).

Refusing to romanticize tribal cultures or people, Welch instead creates a range of characters that includes the negative. For instance, the egotistical Fast Horse rejects Blackfeet culture because he fails to gain instant honor within it. The usually honorable Yellow Kidney rapes a dying Crow girl during a raid. The vindictive Owl Child endangers all Natives by obsessively seeking revenge against all white people. The jealous Running Fisher rapes his father's wife, Kills-Close-to-the-Lake, and then engages in an adulterous affair with her. Writing an historical novel about white America's usurpation of Native land, Welch could have focused simply on the obvious villain, but he took the more difficult path. He was willing to explore ambiguities and allow for exceptions, and he opened himself to charges that he is perpetuating negative images of Native Americans. By showing his characters' mixed motives and bad decisions, however, Welch eludes the either/or mentality that has traditionally presented Natives as simply good or bad.[16]

Of course, in his effort to equalize – and to be historically accurate – Welch also shows white characters in *Fools Crow* as criminally small-minded (such as Captain Snelling and General Alfred Sully) and as dangerous turncoats (such as Joe Kipp). Nevertheless, he also presents some whites as fair-minded, mostly the early traders but also the "long robe" painter Long Teeth and the doctor Sturgis. In *Heartsong*, Welch described the French as "genuinely sympathetic" to Natives (51), despite their fear and prejudice. In its small way, this opens Welch's fiction to more readers, some of whom might become defensive if they sense that the "good" and "bad" guys are entirely good or bad. Kimberly Blaeser asks the question: "What if white society were envisioned as the demonic 'other'?" ("The New 'Frontier'" 164). Welch's historical novels suggest that such a presentation would amount to extremism or absolutism (and tantamount to the distorted treatment of Natives by some white writers).

In *Heartsong*, his European and Euro-American characters have decidedly mixed motives. The fishmonger and philanthropist René fosters romantic conceptions of Indians that tend to be reductive, while also having positive liberal leanings that encourage him to help people in need. Whereas he is openly racist regarding African immigrants (165), René recognizes his complicity in Charging Elk's murder of Armand Bretueil. Franklin Bell, an American diplomat who tries to aid Charging Elk, is motivated both by professional self-interest – "It was just business, this whole thing" (142) – and by what seems like a sincere desire to help Charging Elk return home. His contact with Charging Elk also prompts him to express private doubts about Euro-American society. As Bell watches him eat, he thinks: "They must have picked up the niceties of civilization. But what did they think of the white man's civilization? Did they consider it an improvement over their own primitive ways?" (107). His questions simultaneously show an unexamined prejudice as well as a curiosity about other ways of thinking. His interest in Charging Elk's response to "the white man's civilization" perhaps suggests uneasiness about it himself. Like Bell, the reporter St-Cyr is both self-focused and curious, "wish[ing] desperately that he could understand what was going on inside that Indien's head" (259). His desire to understand is admirable (if largely impossible), and he generalizes unfavorably about Natives even while he shows respect for Charging Elk.

Rather than separating Natives from whites, Welch reveals their similar thought processes, including those involving ambivalence, hatred, and pride. Among other things, individuals from both groups make identical mistakes. For instance, in Fools Crow, Owl Child's anger over Joe Clark's insult prompts him to think: "All the Napikwans would pay for those words" (209). He does not distinguish between individual white persons; rather, he discriminates against them all, holding each accountable for Clark's insult. Likewise, an unnamed white man traveling in winter with his son thinks fearfully of recent killings, and, as he approaches the war lodge containing Yellow Kidney, he admits: "I want to kill an Indian" (244). As with Owl Child, he blames an entire population for one person's transgression; any Native will serve his purpose, not just those actually responsible for the killings. Such characterizations help equalize people, even as it exposes the lowest common denominator. Stated more positively, Welch transcends narrow definitions of either race as either wholly innocent or guilty, and thus he rejects categorical absolutes.

Despite the weight of historical evidence against white people, Welch seems ultimately to focus on the cynical motivations of humankind in general. In Killing Custer, he writes: "Custer's last stand has gone down in history [unfairly] as an example of what savagery the Indians were capable of; the Massacre on the Marias [one of the closing incidents in Fools Crow] is a better example of what man is capable of doing to man" (47). Welch would be quite justified in condemning Euro-American behavior here, particularly since massacres and other atrocities were conducted by white Americans throughout United States' history, but he focuses instead upon the capacity for evil by people in general. Avoiding racial generalities, Welch sees the problem as a human one. Perhaps this attitude is what prompts Alan Velie to write, "The politics of Fools Crow might best be described as accommodational. Welch presents a number of viewpoints in the novel, but the most responsible and sympathetic leaders advocate compromising with the whites, chiefly on pragmatic grounds" ("Historical Novel" 201). This response, however, seems unfair. Rather than "accommodational" and "compromising" – with its undertone of obliging weakness – Welch instead creates characters (both Native and non-Native) linked by their mixed motives and conflicted desires. Rather than exposing Native concessions, he shows human complexity and universality.

Humor as connection

Fools Crow, however, avoids outright cynicism and does more than demonstrate the shared ambivalence of individuals or the inevitable confrontation between groups. He also provides a positive counterbalance to the impending threat by honoring the people and culture endangered. One of the ways Welch does this is with humor. Much has been written of Indian humor, and many commentators have demonstrated how humor deconstructs the pervasive stereotype of the stoic Indian – severe, joyless, wooden.[17] Welch taps into this tradition to display the joy of Native life. His characters are often laughing and teasing. In this way, he demonstrates to readers that – despite the looming danger – Natives lived healthy lives replete with a sense of fun. For example, after a council meeting focusing upon such overwhelming issues as possible extermination, religious failure, and their children's future, the men are still capable of ending the meeting with laughter. Not consumed by the white presence in their land, they relish life and its pleasures (178). Welch prevents readers from reducing them into unfortunate historical victims deserving of nothing but pity.

Throughout Fools Crow there is much bawdy humor among the young warriors who tease each other about sexual experiences (or the lack of them). Blackfeet culture appears quite masculine in Fools Crow, and the young men engage in playfully competitive banter about lovers, desire, masturbation, and bestiality. Their willingness to accept such kidding points to its good-natured quality. In fact, teasing seems to be a preferred method of communication within the community. When Fools Crow asks permission to marry Red Paint, his mother states: "People will make jokes. People will say, There goes Rides-at-the-door's son, he marries whole families" (106). Welch paints a portrait of a people who find humor in almost all things. Even Feather Woman laughs at Fools Crow when he fears that he died and went to the Sand Hills (332–33). (However, it should probably be noted that Welch is more likely to describe *how* Pikunis enjoy a joke rather than concoct a joke for readers to relish, a departure from the more explicit, if ironic, humor in *Winter in the Blood*.)

Welch's authorial instinct often seems to be levity in the face of tragedy, even when it involves typically sacrosanct topics such as respecting elders. In an exchange between Fools Crow and Raven, Welch deflates the exaggerated reverence for elders that is simultaneously genuine and clichéd, a trope of sorts that Robert Dale Parker describes as "worn generalizations" (*Invention* 1). Discussing human death, Fools Crow solemnly intones the benefits of continual death (as opposed to temporary death), and Raven asks: "'Did your grandfather tell you that?' [Fools Crow gravely responds:] 'He was a wise man.' [Raven rejoins:] 'Not always.' Raven laughs" (163). Whereas Fools Crow displays the proper veneration for his grandfather, Raven's comment humanizes the man, and he goes on to describe the grandfather as once comically poor and luckless. Fools Crow shows a profound respect for the "long-ago people," but Welch – in trickster-fashion (here, in fact, using Trickster) – takes the opportunity to deflate a truism that might become as hackneyed as the verity, "Natives-respect-nature."[18] In *Heartsong*, Welch weighs in briefly on the same issue. During a Christian holiday dinner, Charging Elk and René's widowed mother seem to share a secret joke amid much laughter, a joke that Charging Elk admits he does not quite understand. On his way out, the grandmother "laughed and made a gesture that looked disturbingly like the Lakota sign for fucking" (209). Again eschewing stale images of august elders, Welch humorously breaks stereotypes and simultaneously lessens differences between cultures.

Community versus individual

Ultimately, Welch seems more interested in displaying similarities between people than in exposing disagreements or publicizing concessions. Toward this goal, he stresses the importance of community repeatedly in both *Fools Crow* and *Heartsong*. Individual action is valued, but primarily insofar as it contributes to the larger good. In *Fools Crow*, Fast Horse enriches only himself with raids that jeopardize the lives of other tribal members, but Fools

Crow risks his own life to gain a vision important to the tribe. Likewise, the Sacred Vow Woman at the Sun Dance ceremony represents the entire community: "If you are successful, the Pikunis will prosper and enjoy favor with the spirit world. If you fail, if you are not strong or virtuous enough, great harm will come to us" (102). Moreover, Welch ends the novel, not with the massacre, but with the spring rains beginning to fall on a cere-monial dance conducted by Mik-api with the rest of the community. Like Fools Crow's infant Butterfly, these images promise renewal and connec-tion: the rain indicates their link to the quickening world (including the blackhorns in the novel's final sentence) after the severe winter; and the ceremony promises rejuvenation to the Native community, an expan-sive focus that increasingly overshadows Mik-api and Fools Crow in the closing paragraphs. The people, not the individuals, will survive, and Welch completes the novel by pointing to the future rather than the past and thus offering hope to all readers who value community and connection.

Heartsong highlights a sense of community in ways that are both subtler than *Fools Crow* and yet more obviously cross-cultural. Charging Elk increas-ingly finds acceptance in French society. Employed loading ships, he joins the union: "And they accepted Charging Elk as one of them, a member of the union, in a way that he hadn't been used to ... And he felt, for the first time since he had left the Stronghold, that he was a part of a group that looked out for each other. And he liked it" (349). Charging Elk's will-ingness to join French society springs from his understanding of cultural connection that he learned in the Stronghold. He had, after all, promised René's son, Mathias, that they will travel together to America: "Charging Elk had assured him that one day he could go to the land of the Oglalas and become a brother by ceremony" (171). To Charging Elk, inclusion in dif-ferent communities is fluid. He accepts the idea that such connections are inevitable and even desired. His love for and marriage to the French-woman, Nathalie, suggests the depth of his connection to his new world, and their expectant child symbolizes a merging of cultures and a promise for the future. As Charging Elk states, "My wife is one of them and my heart is her heart. She is my life now and soon we will have another life and the same heart will sing in all of us" (367).

Both Fools Crow and Charging Elk come across as compassionate and flexible thinkers. They show self-respect and strength in the face of adver-sity, and their characters provide examples of men who build upon a solid cultural foundation to grow within a changing world. Despite its dangers and restrictions, they live freely, bridging gaps between cultures and exerting influence upon those around them. To this end, their stories are liberating and empowering for readers as well, and they attest to the role of literature to make the world a more inclusive and humane place. By shaping their stories in this manner, Welch upholds literature as a cultural force for good. He uses fiction to educate readers about U.S. history as well as the human relationships and connections that contributed to past failures and that might lead to future successes – for Native Americans and for all people.

6

THE APPROXIMATE SIZE OF HIS FAVORITE HUMOR

SHERMAN ALEXIE'S COMIC CONNECTIONS AND DISCONNECTIONS IN *THE LONE RANGER AND TONTO FISTFIGHT IN HEAVEN*[1]

In Sherman Alexie's directorial debut, *The Business of Fancydancing*, the primary character, Seymour, is a Spokane Indian who moves to Seattle to attend college and pursue fame as a poet. Many of his Indian friends who remain on the reservation accuse him of selling out to white society. To a degree, the film echoes Alexie's own choices and their repercussions. Although he often earns praise as a clever manipulator of language, Alexie, like Seymour, is also criticized for his depictions of Indians and Indian culture. His detractors characterize his writing as harmful pandering to white expectations, arguing that Alexie not only avoids the moral and social obligation to educate white readers and re-instill cultural pride in Indian readers, but he also works actively against such goals with his humor. To some critics, his playfulness may demonstrate skill as a writer, but it betrays Indian people by presenting them as clichés who deserve to be laughed at.

From another perspective, Alexie's humor is central to a constructive social and moral purpose evident throughout his fiction, but particularly in his collection of short stories, *The Lone Ranger and Tonto Fistfight in Heaven*. He uses humor – or his characters use humor – to reveal injustice, protect self-esteem, heal wounds, and foster bonds. The function of humor changes from scene to scene, shifting to serve these varied goals. In *Indi'n Humor*

Kenneth Lincoln explains the many different roles of humor within Indian communities. He describes "the contrary powers of Indian humor" as "[t]he powers to heal and to hurt, to bond and to exorcize, to renew and to purge" (5). Like the Trickster figure, humor in Indian communities embodies shifting meanings and serves conflicting ends. Rather than a sign of his "hip" irreverence, Alexie's sophisticated use of humor unsettles conventional ways of thinking and compels re-evaluation and growth, ultimately allowing Indian characters to connect to their heritage in novel ways and forcing non-Native readers to reconsider simplistic generalizations.

In *The Lone Ranger and Tonto Fistfight in Heaven*, humor allows characters to display strengths and hide weaknesses, to expose prejudices and avoid realities, to create bonds and construct barricades. These "contrary powers" often co-exist simultaneously, requiring characters and readers to position and then re-position themselves within shifting personal and cultural contexts. Alexie's cross-cultural humor alternately engages readers – creating positive connections between individuals of diverse backgrounds – and disrupts communities (both Indian and white), erecting barriers that make constructive communication difficult. Here lies its principal challenge for readers. Alexie's shifting treatment of humor serves as a means of connection as well as an instrument of separation. However, it is precisely this plasticity that allows him to negotiate successfully the differences between Indian communities and non-Native American society, while simultaneously instigating crucial dialogue about social and moral issues important to Native communities (and all people).

Theorizing the frontier of humor

Humor is defined by its fluidity, paradoxes, and incongruities. In a discussion of American Indian creativity in *Mixedblood Messages*, Louis Owens conceptualizes a literary post-modern "frontier" as "always unstable, multidirectional, hybridized, characterized by heteroglossia, and indeterminate" (26). More importantly, within this "frontier" exists "the dangerous presence of that trickster at the heart of the Native American imagination" (*Mixedblood* 26). Owens argues that contemporary Indian writers create an inclusive frontier comprised of diverse perspectives resistant to one-dimensional definitions. This frontier is not easy or absolute; it changes and challenges. Whereas Frederick Jackson Turner had defined the frontier as "the meeting point between savagery and civilization," thus creating a simplistic binary that presupposes conflict, Owen's "frontier" is a polyglot intellectual borderland that resists limiting stereotypes and definitions.

Alexie's particular brand of humor is "that trickster at the heart of the Native American imagination" (Mixedblood 26). It embodies the potential for facilitating mutual understanding and respect between diverse peoples. By exploding expectations and compelling dialogue, humor teaches self-knowledge and social awareness, much like the trickster figure. Alexie's use of humor encourages readers to think anew by creating a space of shared inquiry and reciprocal empathy. According to Mikhail Bakhtin, the power of laughter generates "a crude zone of contact" that "demolishes fear and piety," allowing the "absolutely free investigation" of its subject (Dialogic 23). Alexie's humor creates that zone – or offers that space – to his readers. He provides an emotional and intellectual meeting ground for his readers to reconsider reductive stereotypes and expectations. While Owens defines the frontier as "a multidimensional zone of resistance" for Indians (Mixedblood 41), Alexie uses humor to add a new element to it, one that extends beyond resistance (although that is certainly part of it). Alexie challenges readers of diverse backgrounds to join together to re-evaluate past and present ideologies. Humor generates a freely occupied space in which readers can begin sorting through the myriad connections and disconnections that define us today.

Stephen Evans, in an evaluation of Alexie's re-fashioning of stereotypes (particularly that of the "drunken Indian"), notes how satire compels "the collaborative making of meaning between Alexie and his readers" ("Open Containers" 54). Readers are not passive receptacles; they engage, question, resist, learn, and grow during the reading process. They join Alexie on Owen's "frontier" and in Bakhtin's "zone" to hash out interpretations to the past, responses to the present, and prospects for the future. This delicate alliance between author and audience – facilitated by humor – is more effective at promoting understanding than purely logical or historical efforts. With its shifting layers and elaborate surprises, Alexie's humor (in an adaptation of Vizenor's tactics discussed in Chapter 4) disrupts readers' complacency and necessitates analysis, clarification, and, ultimately, identification.

Aware of his demands on readers (and seemingly anticipating critics), Alexie demonstrates the ambiguity and difficulty of responding con-structively to humor. In "A Drug Called Tradition," the second story in The Lone Ranger and Tonto Fistfight in Heaven, readers are thrust into the middle of a wild party thrown by Thomas, who received some money from a power company that ran its line across his land. Despite the good times, the revelry feels tainted, as Victor senses: "When Indians make lots of money from corporations that way, we can all hear our ancestors laughing in the trees. But we never can tell whether they're laughing at the Indians or the whites. I think they're laughing at pretty much everybody" (13). Victor admits his own ambivalence about the situation (and its humor), expressing uncertainty about whether he benefits from the money or whether he is harmed by it. Significantly, he focuses on his ancestors' reaction, a response that suggests the importance of generational connections to him. He wants to feel some alliance with past Indians, to share with them a small triumph over white aggression. Yet Victor senses that perhaps he is the target of their laughter. His misgiving illustrates the problem many critics have with Alexie. They cannot be confident who or what represents his satiric target. Reviewing *Reservation Blues*, Gloria Bird writes, "To derive *meaning* from the novel for the native audience is to become lost in its ambiguity of purpose" ("Exaggeration" 52). Readers prefer assurance and certainty, but instead they hear laughter, and its target is indefinite and shifting. Alexie rarely offers an easy moral-to-the-story; the questions he raises – and the world he depicts – have few simple answers.

Like many readers, Victor is initially confused by his options. At one level, he appears eager to laugh at the white companies who cough up cash to his friends. On another level, he is unsettled by the idea that power lines dissect Indian land. The double meaning of the "power lines" underscores how white society exerts its power to divide Indian land and, in effect, disconnect Indians from their heritage. Alexie's caustic humor shows how the situation cuts both ways. His unflinching portrayal of Victor's discomforting new knowledge serves a vital function: readers have ventured onto Alexie's rendering of Owen's "frontier," and they are forced to recognize its ambiguity and to evaluate their resulting uneasiness. By creating situations that resist formulaic responses, Alexie fits into a long-standing tradition of Indian storytelling.[2] In *Native American Renaissance*, Kenneth Lincoln describes "Old Man," or Trickster, as one who "makes up reality as people unfortunately know it, full of surprises and twists, contrary, problematical" (123). Evaluating a Blackfeet story, Lincoln writes, "A 'married' dialectic of absurd initial impressions distorts the world comically, then must be corrected by a firmer sense of why-things-are-what-they-are" (*Native* 151). Likewise, the painful and wrenching realization of possible complicity – accentuated by ancestral laughter – provokes Alexie's readers to re-think the circumstances that allow the sad and sardonic humor. In short, our reality is distorted and needs to be "corrected."

However, Alexie does not abandon readers to the task. Instead, Victor himself demonstrates how this "correction" might work. Recognizing his separation from his ancestors, he ultimately accepts (albeit uneasily) the importance of their traditions, particularly that of story-telling. He acknowledges the value of Thomas' vision of sobriety and traditionalism, and he acquires a stronger connection to tribal elder and spiritual leader, Big Mom. If he had not been discomfited by the duplicitous nature of laughter, Victor would have remained closed to the wisdom within Indian stories. In "A Drug Called Tradition," the protean nature of humor itself compels new knowledge about Victor's relation to the cultures that compete for his loyalty. He has "corrected" – to a degree – his own complacency and resistance to his Indian heritage.

Story-telling and its equivocal potential

Interestingly, Alexie finds himself – as a story-teller – in much the same place as Thomas, a connection that James H. Cox has noted.[3] Both offer stories that challenge and disrupt the status quo. Rather than creating a cultural void, however, both Alexie and Thomas force readers/listeners to re-evaluate accepted ways of thinking. Perhaps as a result of their unconventional and confrontational roles, neither gain widespread acceptance within their own communities. Thomas Builds-The-Fire is shunned or abused by many fellow Indians; few want to bother with his stories. Erik Himmelsbach writes, "While Alexie has enlightened the world at large about the contemporary American Indian experience, his tribe has essentially shunned him. Back at the Spokane Reservation in Wellpinit, Washington, people have strong, often unfavorable opinions about the author who, as a child, often whiled away his days alone in his room playing Dungeons & Dragons or Nerf basketball. 'I was a divisive presence on the reservation when I was 7,' he recalls. 'I was a weird, eccentric, very arrogant little boy. The writing doesn't change anybody's opinion of me. If anything, it's intensified it.'" This type of reaction re-appears within his art. For example, in the film, *The Business of Fancydancing*, Seymour is rejected by his boyhood friends on the reservation, and in *Reservation Blues*, the band Coyote Springs is reviled in the Spokane press for supposedly being "representative" of the entire tribe (175). More recently in *The Absolutely True Diary of a Part-Time Indian* (2007), Arnold is rejected by his best friend

Rowdy as well as other members of the community when he transfers to a "white" school off the reservation.

Nevertheless, story-telling, like humor, offers the potential for increased understanding. In the film Seymour defends his choices by describing himself as a public relations specialist who attracts attention to issues vital to Indians. Seymour, Alexie, Thomas Builds-The-Fire, Arnold, and Coyote Springs obligate others to think about problems too often ignored. As Lincoln writes, "Storytelling personally brings people together; it engages them collectively in giving and receiving the events of their lives. In such storytelling times, people occupy space with focused attention; they enter their common world more fully" (Native 223). Alexie's use of humor, in particular, adds a complex new dynamic to the communal space allowed by stories.

In "The Approximate Size of My Favorite Tumor" in The Lone Ranger and Tonto Fistfight in Heaven, Alexie focuses explicitly on the equivocal place of humor in daily life. In this story more than any other, he demonstrates the power of humor both to bring people together and to tear people apart. The title itself toys with the varying degrees – the approximate size – to which the first-person narrator, Jimmy, makes use of his favorite thing – humor – to deal with his cancer. Both the humor and the tumor are potentially dangerous aspects of Jimmy's life. While cancer slowly kills him, his jokes about it – particularly his "favorite" tumor that he insists is shaped liked a baseball – drive a wedge between him and his wife, Norma. Jimmy's preoccupation with the baseball-sized tumor ("even had stitch marks" he says) emphasizes the game-playing that he prefers to hide behind. Jimmy's humor appears to be an attempt to transform a very real threat to his life into a benign token of a national past-time. The comic treatment is a coping mechanism that borders on denial. He makes light of a serious danger to his life by connecting it to – and reducing it to – a mere game. His humor seems like an effort to hide from the reality of cancer.

From this vantage, Jimmy's joking might reflect the concerns of those critics who feel that Alexie wants to ignore real threats to indigenous cultures and identities. Alexie's humor is sometimes viewed as a screen that belies the anger and frustration felt by many Natives in the face of the United States' criminal history. Writing specifically about Alexie, Owens writes:

> I would argue that self-destructive, self-deprecatory humor provides an essential matrix for this fiction because such humor deflects any "lesson in morality" from the non-Native reader and allows authors to

> maintain an aggressive posture regarding an essential "authentic" Indianness while simultaneously giving the commercial market and reader exactly what they want and expect in the form of stereotype and cliche: what Vizenor terms the "absolute fake".
>
> (*Mixedblood Messages* 76)

Jimmy does indeed seem to be faking, but his masquerade fails to fool Norma or, I suspect, many readers (Indian or otherwise). Rather his humor suggests the extent to which Jimmy will go to try to protect himself from real pain: he does not want to face the horror of his cancer. Who can blame him? Coming to terms with the pain and loneliness of a terminal disease is no easy matter. Nevertheless, watching him undergo various stages of denial does not blind readers to his suffering. Rather, it emphasizes the personal pain that Jimmy is experiencing. His humor may appear self-destructive on one level, but its effect upon readers is the opposite. It begs the question: what has prompted Jimmy to pretend the pain does not exist?

Humor as protection

Perhaps one answer is offered by the first story in the collection. "Every Little Hurricane" highlights the larger cultural context that causes characters to drink too much and fight with each other. These personal "storms" result from "a specific, painful memory" of racism for each individual Indian: "Victor's father remembered the time his own father was spit on as they waited for a bus in Spokane. Victor's mother remembered how the Indian Health Service doctor sterilized her moments after Victor was born" (8). Providing such background flashbacks, Alexie demands that readers recognize the wider cultural and historical context. He is not simply re-playing the hackneyed stereotype of "vanishing Americans" who destroy themselves and thus fulfill generic white expectations; his characters are not self-destructive losers. They are sympathetic, complex individuals trying to cope within a racist society. Likewise, understanding Jimmy's use of humor as a screen for his multi-layered pain in "The Approximate Size of My Favorite Tumor" requires attention to his formative experiences, which, in turn, prompt a more constructive response to his cancer.

In this regard, we might argue that his use of humor in the face of adversity shows real personal strength. In *Custer Died For Your Sins*, Vine Deloria, Jr., writes, "When a people can laugh at themselves and laugh at others and hold all aspects of life together without letting anybody drive them to extremes, then it seems to me that that people can survive" (167). In this light, laughter replaces Jimmy's fear and demonstrates his ability to survive and even triumph over debilitating circumstances. His jokes make him feel larger than life, allowing him to transcend his daily fight against cancer by magnifying himself into someone famous and beloved. For instance, Jimmy confides to his friend, Simon, what he had already said to Norma: "I told her to call me Babe Ruth. Or Roger Maris. Maybe even Hank Aaron. ... I told her I was going to Cooperstown and sit right down in the lobby of the Hall of Fame. Make myself a new exhibit, you know? Pin my X-rays to my chest and point out the tumors. What a dedicated baseball fan! What a sacrifice for the national pastime!" (157). Attempting to rise above his tragic personal situation, he imagines (and projects) himself as a world famous sports star, acting as if such popularity will allow him to surmount the day-to-day fear and frustration of living with cancer. As Deloria states, "The more desperate the problem, the more humor is directed to describe it. Satirical remarks often circumscribe problems" (147). To allay his desperation, Jimmy imagines himself in a position of honor at the baseball Hall of Fame – earning gratitude from fans for his apparent selflessness and fanatic commitment to the game – in an effort to limit the extent of his problem and to control it. His humor aims for self-definition and autonomy.

From yet another perspective, however, this comic attempt at self-aggrandizement works against Jimmy by putting him on display for tourists to gawk at. Readers might regard him as simply fulfilling reductive stereotypes of Indians as cultural curiosities and historical souvenirs for the entertainment of white America. To borrow Owens' phrase, he has become an unwitting victim of "inner-colonization" (Mixedblood 82). However, Alexie enlists these images to recall to readers the social injustices perpetrated upon Indian peoples. In fact, the connection to the national pastime renders Alexie's provocative humor all the more poignant, as images of Indians have long been used – from the Boston "tea party" to the Atlanta Braves – by white Americans to symbolize what they imagine is quintessentially American (something Phillip Deloria outlines in Playing Indian). Within the context of his joke (and Alexie's story), Jimmy becomes, in part, a living symbol of a wounded people, and his cancer exemplifies and highlights the physical and psychological assault upon Indian cultures by Euro-American society. Moreover, his ability to joke about self-involvement in his own humiliation – and thus about the supposed complicity of Indian people in their exploitation – shows cultural awareness, self-knowledge, and personal strength, even while it reveals an irreverence (shared by Alexie) toward normally sacrosanct topics. The humor of Jimmy's assertion depends upon our recognition of its absurdity in relation to historical facts – and, more importantly, its sad relevance in the face of cultural misconceptions. As Lincoln writes, "The potshots make both sides think, if disagreeably, then finally dialogically" (Indi'n 25). Alexie's humor has this effect; it shocks readers into regenerate perspectives via their own discomfort.

Humor as self-destructive avoidance

Alexie recognizes the potential danger of his "potshots" and takes pains to illustrate when and how humor can obstruct personal growth and productive relationships. After all, not everyone appreciates Jimmy's sense of humor. One problem is that he so constantly depends upon games and jokes about his disease that he comes across to others as selfish and myopic. His humor fails to consider the feelings of friends and family. Rather than appreciate his strength and patience, much less his humor, the other characters often react instinctively against him. Even his friend Simon, after listening to his Hall-of-Fame joke, says, "You're an asshole" (157), and Jimmy can only agree. But he does not do anything to change. Instead, he appears determined to drive away even his closest friends with his unrelenting humor. For example, in the first section of the story, Jimmy and his wife Norma had just finished a verbal fight, and neither seem willing to make up. When Jimmy finally seeks out Norma to resolve their differences, she makes it clear why she's annoyed, asking: "Are you going to make any more jokes about [your cancer]?" (159), then adding: "If you say anything funny ever again, I'm going to leave you." Obviously this is a critical moment, a time for carefully chosen words and feelings. Instead, Jimmy describes to readers what he did: "I lost my smile briefly, reached across the table to hold her hand, and said something incredibly funny. It was maybe the best one-liner I had ever uttered. Maybe the moment that would have made me a star anywhere else. But in the Powwow Tavern, which was just a front for reality, Norma heard what I had to say, stood up, and left me" (159). Jimmy lost his wife – whom he loved – because his joke de-personalized a very personal situation. A joke – even from the funniest Indian in the world (and Jimmy's pretty funny) – was guaranteed to destroy his relationship because it denied real intimacy. Humor in this situation erected a barricade between him and his wife. The parallel to Alexie's position is fairly obvious: he has lost the favor of some critics with a brand of humor that "made him a star" rather than garnering respect within the Indian community.

By Jimmy's own accounting, his joke would have won him fame some place else, a description that reinforces the distance between him and Norma. He imagines himself in an entirely different situation than his reality – fantasizing a popularity that helps negate personal pain. Jimmy's wish to be a star mirrors his self-image of celebrity super-fan at the baseball Hall of Fame. Professional athletes and entertainment industry stars look good and smile at the camera; they have become national symbols of health and success. Jimmy's desire to be famous – couched in the guise of humor and placed between him and his wife – seems like an attempt to avoid the honesty required within one-to-one personal relationships. His self-indulgent, almost obsessive, use of humor destroys or prevents any real closeness to anyone. Like the Pow-Wow Tavern where he finds Norma, his joking seems like a front for reality, a sad effort to laugh off and ignore what will not go away. Instead, his effort to be funny drives away what he probably needs most: support and friendship. Here, Alexie implicitly acknowledges the danger within Owen's "frontier," Bakhtin's "zone," and his own humor: the possibility of misunderstanding, backlash, and failure is real.

More explicitly, the short story "Amusements" not only illustrates the fact that humor can separate characters from their friends – and from themselves – but it also demonstrates how Alexie's comic style can prompt readers' disgust and anger. In the story, Victor and Sadie play a cruel prank on Dirty Joe (possibly an echo of Mark Twain's similarly stereotyped character, Injun Joe, in The Adventures of Tom Sawyer). They put the inebriated man on a roller coaster at a crowded amusement park, and white onlookers respond with horror and delight. Critical response has been largely negative. Owens writes, "[T]he two young people are enacting in miniature precisely what Alexie has done with his work thus far" (Mixedblood 80). To Owens, "Amusements" is the best example of how Alexie "simply reinforces all of the stereotypes desired by white readers: his bleakly absurd and aimless Indians are imploding in a passion of self-destructiveness and self-loathing" (Mixedblood 79).[4] However, Owens focuses upon the act alone, and he overlooks – within the story and the collection – both the causes of their actions and the results. Alexie demonstrates how their ill-conceived joke stemmed from years (even centuries) of racism. Remembering the "white ... faces twisted with hate and disgust," Victor confesses, "I was afraid of all of them, wanted to hide behind my Indian teeth, the quick joke" (55). His thoughtless prank does not occur in a cultural vacuum. Rather, it results from a lifetime of fear and frustration living in a society that too often reduces Indians to one-dimensional stereotypes.

Throughout *The Lone Ranger and Tonto Fistfight in Heaven*, Alexie repeatedly emphasizes the personal and historical contexts that help explain the difficult problems facing many Indians today. For example, in "The Only Traffic Signal on the Reservation Doesn't Flash Red Anymore," the narrator states: "[I]t's almost like Indians can easily survive the big stuff. Mass murder, loss of language and land rights. It's the small things that hurt the most. The white waitress who wouldn't take an order, Tonto, the Washington Redskins" (49). Likewise, in *Reservation Blues*, which seldom reaches the virtuosity of *Lone Ranger and Tonto*, Alexie provides the cultural context that affects individual choices. He describes "a woman who grew up without electricity and running water, who grew up in such poverty that other poor Indians called her family poor" (67). In contrast to this, "White people owned everything: food, houses, clothes, children. Television constantly reminded Thomas of all he never owned. For hours, Thomas searched the television for evidence of Indians" (70). Alexie expects readers to interpret his characters' actions in light of the societal realities that he details. While stories like "Amusements" may present lamentable situations, few readers, I suspect, and this includes my primarily white middle-class students, interpret Alexie's fiction as other than a harsh indictment of white complicity.

Moreover, Victor himself recognizes the problem with his joke within the story. He understands exactly whom he has become, and obviously he does not like it. Hiding in the fun house, he stares at his reflection in the crazy mirrors: "The kind that distort your features, make you fatter, thinner, taller, shorter. The kind that make a white man remember he's the master of ceremonies barking about the Fat Lady, the Dog-Faced Boy, the Indian who offered up another Indian like some treaty" (58). Victor admits that he has become a circus monstrosity, an aberration without identity or self-respect. The story ends immediately after his realization. Part of what makes Alexie's fiction difficult and fascinating is its elusive, even poetic, prose style. The narrative rarely expostulates at length, instead forcing readers to puzzle out the meaning for themselves. Whereas Owens suggests that Alexie "does not perhaps understand what he is doing" (*Mixedblood* 80) – I think Alexie effectively identifies the problem of culturally taught self-hate to readers. Without sermonizing or simplifying, he exposes the years (and centuries) of neglect and prejudice that can result in obviously regrettable decisions. In this way, Alexie invites readers onto the dialogic "frontier": Victor's revelation at the end of "Amusements" is the beginning of his self-examination and possible growth. Victor senses the need for change, and so should readers. Alexie's story forces us to re-think our own level of culpability in a culture that fosters racism, self-hatred, and despair.

Throughout his fiction, Alexie emphasizes the need for a revaluation of personal morality and social ethics. In addition to his provocative use of humor, Alexie creates characters who showcase individual strength and ability as well as an expansive pan-Indian belief system. Whereas Owens complains that "there is no family or community toward which his characters ... might turn for coherence" (79), *The Lone Ranger and Tonto Fistfight in Heaven* contains many positive examples of personal strength and development, even while exploring the disruptions that plague Indian communities. In "The Fun House," for example, the narrator's aunt becomes angry with her ungrateful family. After a day spent by herself, she returns to the house, dons an exceedingly heavy bead dress, and dances: "She stood, weakly. But she had the strength to take the first step, then another quick one. She heard drums, she heard singing, she danced. Dancing that way, she knew things were beginning to change" (82). The story ends on a distinctly positive note. While the woman draws upon her inner strength to rise above the skewed ethics of her husband and son, the dance and the bead dress connect her to a traditional Indian culture as well as signal the beginning of a new tradition.

Tradition, change, and context

Her actions show how longstanding traditions can be successfully transformed – sometimes even merged with those of other cultures – to operate effectively within a changing world. As she says of the dress: "It's just like the sword in the stone" (76). Like King Arthur, who gains the crown by removing the sword, she proves herself a leader by wearing the dress. One of Alexie's concerns is the blending of cultures and the transmutations that result.[5] In this regard, he is not far removed from Leslie Marmon Silko, a writer that critics usually contrast to Alexie.[6] In *Ceremony*, Night Swan and Betonie tell Tayo that rituals must evolve to maintain their strength. Alexie's fiction falls squarely within an American Indian literary tradition advocating growth and change. Always writing with a keen historical awareness, Alexie transforms past traditions – whether dancing, drumming, or story-telling – to fit a changing world reality. He states that his fiction does not seek to resurrect a past heritage, but instead to depict its truth within the present.[7] In an interview with Juliette Torrez, Alexie said:

> I'm not talking about four directions corn pollen mother earth father sky shit. I'm not talking about that stereotypical crap about being Indian. There's always a huge distance between public persona and private person. In my art I try to keep that as narrow as possible. I try to write about the kind of Indian I am, the kind of person I am and not the kind of person or Indian I wish I was.
>
> (Alexie, "Interview")

In this vein, his short stories delineate not only the harsh cultural realities facing Indians (both on and off the reservation) but also the pride and strength that sustain them.

Alexie no more advocates the unexamined adoption of mainstream culture than he would suggest the irrelevance of past cultural traditions, despite his often positive depictions of change and renewal. In "The Fun House," for example, he exposes the sometimes grotesque distortions that can result from blended cultures. The female protagonist – the unnamed wife and mother – is angered by misogynist jokes. In an interview, Alexie describes what frustrates him most about white culture: "Pretty much everything patriarchal. We've resisted assimilation in many ways, but I know we've assimilated into sexism and misogyny" (McFarland, "Polemical" 27). "The Fun House" exposes the flaws within white culture and how they harm Indians and their local cultures.[8] Likewise, in the copiously titled "Because My Father Always Said He Was the Only Indian Who Saw Jimi Hendrix Play 'The Star-Spangled Banner' At Woodstock," Alexie not only satirizes the hippies "trying to be Indian" but also explains a negative change within Indian cultures, writing: "On a reservation, Indian men who abandon their children are treated worse than white fathers who do the same thing. It's because white men have been doing that forever and Indian men have just learned how. That's how assimilation can work" (34). Whereas Alexie often uses humor to reveal social injustice and immorality, he does not simply blame Indians. White America is the root cause of Indian problems.

Nonetheless, some critics excoriate Alexie for suggesting that Indians themselves have failed. As Owens writes, "[N]o one is really to blame but the Indians, no matter how loudly the author shouts his anger" (*Mixedblood* 80). However, Alexie blames white culture over and over again in no uncertain terms. In "The Fun House," for example, part of the woman's bitterness results from a sterilization program enacted by the United States government: "[T]he doctor tied her tubes, with the permission slip my aunt signed because the hospital administrator lied and said it proved her Indian status for the BIA" (81). Here, Alexie points an accusing finger at a society that systematically trampled upon the rights of Indian people for over five hundred years. While white America often shakes its head over the sins of the distant past, few want to acknowledge the illegal and immoral machinations of the present. Likewise, "The Trial of Thomas Builds-The-Fire" also highlights atrocities perpetrated upon Indians. A courtroom situation allows Thomas the opportunity to recount a series of stories regarding white crimes upon Indians, including lynchings, massacres, and thefts. It ends with Thomas being carted off to jail with "four African men, one Chicano, and a white man from the smallest town in the state" (103). Alexie shows the sad reality of modern-day justice in America: the poor – particularly poor people of color – face systemic oppression and inequity. Thomas' stories in "The Trial" offer the most compelling context to explain how Indians have been kept poor for so long.

Humor as intra-community connection

However, Alexie seems more focused upon showing the importance of community than exposing a culture of neglect, and he provides examples of positive familial connection throughout *The Lone Ranger and Tonto Fistfight in Heaven*. For example, in "This Is What It Means to Say Phoenix, Arizona" – the prototype for the movie *Smoke Signals* – Victor and Thomas take a pilgrimage to Arizona, and their friendship re-emerges as a result of their shared respect for Victor's father. Thomas says, "Your dad was my vision. *Take care of each other* is what my dreams were saying. *Take care of each other*" (69). Alexie's message seems obvious: friendship and support are essential to a fulfilling life and a healthy community. In the first three stories in another collection, *The Toughest Indian in the World*, Alexie also explores various efforts by urban Indians to re-connect to more tribally grounded Indians. Likewise, toward the end of *The Absolutely True Diary*, Arnold and Rowdy move toward a reconciliation. Rather than insult Natives and their diverse cultures, Alexie shows in his fiction how personal pain and honesty can bring renewal, change, and solidarity.

Alexie's use of humor is his most important strategy for demonstrating Indian friendship and connection. Humor offers a bond to individuals otherwise alienated within a hostile culture. In "The Approximate Size of His Favorite Tumor," Alexie flashes back to Jimmy and Norma's first meeting, showing how humor brought them together by creating an intimate space separate not only from other Indians, but also from antagonistic white people. Jimmy tells readers how he first met Norma at a reservation bar; both were drinking Diet Pepsi. Because he was laughing so loud, Norma approached his table to join the fun and cracked her own joke. Jimmy explains their response: "And we laughed. Then we laughed harder when [my cousin] Raymond leaned in closer to the table and said, 'I don't get it'" (160). Although they laugh harder, in part, because of Raymond's inability to understand, they also recognize the bond that occurs over a shared joke, especially a private joke. They are the insiders who understand and appreciate the humor, and, naturally, it brings them closer. Their response, however, shows more than two people simply having a good time together, although that is certainly part of it. They are reacting to the ability of humor to create a private space. A new-found intimacy is allowed by a joke that only they comprehend. Raymond does not "get it," and so he is left outside of their "zone of contact," to reiterate Bakhtin's phrase. In their case, humor functions positively to unite two like-minded people within an environment that otherwise might exclude them. Neither of them drink – except for Diet Pepsi – and they are in a bar. Whereas bar patrons more typically rely upon alcohol to create a sense of community, Jimmy and Norma use their shared sense of humor to create a community of two.[9]

A similar situation occurs after they are married, only this time humor constructs a protected space for them in a hostile white world. Their joking allows an intellectual and emotional safe zone that shelters them from a destructive society. Alexie records an event in which Jimmy and Norma have a run-in with an institutionalized representative of white America. While driving down a highway, a state patrolman pulls them over and threatens them with a variety of fabricated charges (a situation that Alexie also explores in "Traveling" from the collection The Business of Fancydancing). Soon enough, the cop offers "some kind of arrangement so none of this has to go on your record" (165), an arrangement that turns out to be precisely the amount of money Jimmy and Norma have in their pockets. Rather than responding to this racist and illegal shakedown with open anger or frustration, they use humor as a defense. When the officer tells them about a "new law against riding as a passenger in an Indian car," Jimmy says, "[w]e've known about that one for a couple hundred years" (165). After giving up all his money, he adds: "Your service has been excellent" (166), a sarcastic jibe that forces a laugh from Norma. No longer able to resist, she also "jumped into the fun," as Jimmy puts it. When the officer threatens them with more serious charges, she facetiously tells him: "I'll just tell everyone how respectful you were of our Native traditions, how much you understood about the social conditions that lead to the criminal acts of so many Indians. I'll say you were sympathetic, concerned, and intelligent" (166). Their humor helps to diffuse their anger and fear. It shows strength and intelligence in the face of adversity, while it also shields Jimmy and Norma from a common threat. Not allowing themselves to be bullied – as the driver does in "Traveling" – they use humor to take control of the situation. Jimmy explains to readers: "[Y]ou have to realize that laughter saved Norma and me from pain, too. Humor was an antiseptic that cleaned the deepest of personal wounds" (164). Their joking provides a relatively secure psychological space for them to share together – a space that defies a world filled with hatred and prejudice.

For both of them, as for many of Alexie's Indian characters, the "deepest of personal wounds" is the lack of recognition – on the part of white society – of their basic human rights and dignity. Whereas ethnic bias can tear people apart, humor allows them to identify with each other more firmly by creating a common space – a zone of contact – that rejects the outside threat. Despite his often light-hearted tone, Alexie writes with a firm social and moral purpose: he wants all readers – Indian and non-Indian – to recognize the possibility of this common space, to understand and appreciate their shared humanity. In an interview, Alexie defines how he arrived at this conviction: "I think there are three stages of Indian-ness: The first stage is where you feel inferior because you're Indian, and most people never leave it. The next stage is feeling superior because you're Indian and a small percentage of people get into that and most never leave it. At the end, they get on realizing that Indians are just as fucked up as everybody else. No better no worse. I try to be in that stage" (Alexie, "Interview"). Most of Alexie's characters deal with a variety of problems; they are typically complex and multidimensional. As he puts it, they are "as fucked up as everybody else." In other words, they are the same as his readers, the same as anyone. Their particular challenges, however, often result from racial prejudice and social disadvantage. In his stories, Alexie reveals a nation that many Americans might not want to acknowledge or deal with. He writes about the lack of options open to Indians – both on the reservation and off. He exposes the extreme poverty, the alcohol and drug abuse, the broken families, the isolation. This is not cheerful stuff; in fact, it is a national disgrace – the inevitable result of centuries of abuse and neglect. Alexie shrewdly presents this socio-political reality with humor to soften its initial impact. Ron McFarland states that humor "makes the pain and anger bearable for the reader" (*James Welch* 31). Alexie himself said in an interview: "You make people laugh and you disarm them. You sort of sneak up on them. You can say controversial or rowdy things and they'll listen or laugh" (Alexi, "Interview"). He uses humor to draw readers in and entertain them; once he has them, he communicates his world view, one that does not necessarily reflect the comforting, traditional American ideals of equal opportunity and democratic justice for all.

Humor as cross-cultural outreach

More important than Alexie's use of humor to advance possibly controversial ideas, however, is his understanding of the potential for humor to link different sorts of people together despite ethnic, racial, and cultural boundaries. Vine Deloria, Jr. writes: "People have little sympathy with stolid groups. Dick George did much more than is believed when he introduced humor into the Civil Rights struggle. He enabled non-blacks to enter into the thought world of the black community and experience the hurt it suffered" (*Custer Died* 146). Alexie understands this fully. Since his Indian characters find a sense of community in humor, humor also allows bonds between Indians and whites. In "The Approximate Size of My Favorite Tumor," for example, Jimmy is back in his doctor's office for more radiation treatment three months after Norma left him. He and Dr. Adams seem to inhabit entirely different worlds, but their joking lessens the distance between them. Jimmy again plays with visions of fame and power, saying: "A few more zaps and I'll be Superman." And she replies: "Really? I never realized Clark Kent was a Spokane Indian" (162). Jimmy then writes, "And we laughed, you know, because sometimes that's all two people have in common" (162). Although their laughter has a sad, hollow element, it nevertheless offers some sense of comfort and connection. It lessens the distance between them and humanizes a clinical, potentially sterile, situation. After another joke, Jimmy writes, "And we laughed, you know, because sometimes you'd rather cry" (162). Again, the laughter provides relief from the realities of cancer treatment by allowing them to share something uniquely human and life-affirming. Humor forces their differences to the sidelines and permits them to connect in a positive manner. Jimmy clearly appreciates his alliance (however temporary) to the doctor. As she prepares to leave, he "wanted to call her back and make an urgent confession, to ask forgiveness, to offer truth in return for salvation" (163). When he calls out her name, and she asks him what he wants, he only says, "Nothing. Just wanted to hear your name. It sounds like drums to these heavily medicated Indian ears of mine" (163). His response expresses a cross-cultural compliment that includes Dr. Adams in the Indian world. Her name is like drums, a traditional part of tribal life. Whereas humor offers solidarity and protection to Jimmy and Norma in the face of white police aggression, humor allows Jimmy to bond with his doctor and gain temporary respite from his sorrow and fear. Their connection fosters a sense of community that can be shared by all people regardless of background.

Although Indian/white relations in The Lone Ranger and Tonto Fistfight in Heaven are usually fraught with racial tension, Alexie offers occasional glimpses of sympathy, friendship, and love. These instances tend to re-emphasize the hope for mutual understanding and attachment. In the title story, "The Lone Ranger and Tonto Fistfight in Heaven," for example, the bored narrator amuses himself by silently provoking a convenience store clerk working the graveyard shift. In spite of his antagonistic attitude toward the clerk, the narrator admits his sympathy for and identification with him, saying: "There was something about him I liked, even if it was three in the morning and he was white" (184). Whereas their racial differences prompt separation, they eventually connect using humor. The narrator launches a couple Brady Bunch jokes to break the ice, jokes that are slightly insulting to the white guy, but serve to highlight a shared sense of humor: both appreciate ironic self-deprecation in the face of a perceived threat (a tactic that Alexie uses throughout the collection). As Lincoln writes, "In addition to survival and renewal, a comic vision can be amicably competitive, even pleasurably engaging. … [It] targets issues with an attention that roughs its audience affectionately, Indian-to-white" (Indi'n 25–26). Both young men are poor, disenfranchised outsiders who take dangerous jobs that few others want. They recognize their status (or lack of status) and resort to humor as a chance to transcend their meager positions. Their jokes offer them a brief connection that rejects the unfair world of moneyed hierarchies. Momentarily, they are not a white guy and an Indian guy. Instead, they are both underpaid workers in low-level jobs. Their shared laughter repudiates the culture that hands them peanuts. Before the narrator leaves, the clerk gives him a free Creamsicle because "those little demonstrations of power tickled him" (184). Not quite friends, but extending friendly gestures, both characters take pains to show that they live on their own terms and not those dictated by society. Their moderately rebellious stances – and their use of humor – bring them together in an ethical stance at odds with mainstream society.

Likewise, in the final story of the collection, "Witnesses, Secret and Not," the young Indian narrator, his father, and a white detective discover that they can join together in laughter. They are discussing, again, the father's friend who disappeared several years earlier and is presumed murdered. The rehashed interview involves an implied hostility, tempered only by the apparent routine of the situation, until the narrator begins to laugh about the childish way that the detective writes (with his tongue poking out of his mouth). He tells readers: "I shook my head and laughed harder. Soon all three of us were laughing, at mostly nothing. Maybe we were all nervous or bored. Or both." (221). Their laughter not only breaks the tension, it offers them a chance to bond together in some vague way. For a moment, they can forget the grim detective business at hand. Perhaps they can even forget about the implicit harassment of white detectives repeatedly interviewing an Indian man about a murder. Their shared laughter suggests a desire to unite over something untainted by racial bias. Humor allows them to transcend the situation temporarily, to forget their roles as detective/white and suspect/Indian, and instead to connect in a more humane manner over something as innocent and playful as a child's private joke.

Many of Alexie's short stories serve the same end. In fact, Alexie himself has stated that many of his jokes are private: "I load my books with stuff, just load 'em up. I call them 'Indian trapdoors.' You know, Indians fall in, white people just walk right over them. ... I really want the subtext for Indians" (Purdy, "Crossroads" 15). If Alexie creates a subtext of humor that brings Indians together, he offers enough clever jokes, ironic witticisms, and absurdist rejoinders to engage and include white readers as well. (Of course, I cannot comment upon the jokes for Indians only ... because I can't find them.) Alexie repeatedly employs humor to forge a bond between Indians and whites, between himself and his diverse readers. Humor acts as a transcendent force. When we laugh, we join together in a largely affirmative, entirely human response to an often unfair world. It creates a shared, protected space that invites everyone's participation. Alexie's joking asks readers to recognize our similarities rather than notice our differences. Laughter is the great unifier, and it has the power to lift us – if only temporarily – beyond many racial tensions and cultural conflicts. In *Reservation Blues*, Father Arnold understands this connection: "He was impressed by the Spokanes' ability to laugh. He'd never thought of Indians as being funny. ... Father Arnold learned to laugh at everything, which strangely made him feel closer to God" (36). Humor is a part of Indian cultures – and Alexie's fiction – not as a sign of his supposedly hip irreverence, but instead because it offers varied solutions to real worldly pain. Humor permits escape to an enlightened zone in which people can appreciate their similarities rather than focus only on their differences. Perhaps for this reason Alexie's title has the Lone Ranger and Tonto fistfighting in *heaven*. The comic divination of two fictional creations boxing competitively not only recalls Lincoln's description of humor as "pleasurably engaging. ... target[ing] issues with an attention that roughs its audience affectionately, Indian-to-white" (*Indi'n* 25–26), but it also elicits laughter that might, like Father Arnold, make readers "feel closer to God." Both the fight and the humor constitute "heavenly" activities that aspire to equalize readers in a transcendent humanism.

Likewise, the final line of *The Lone Ranger and Tonto Fistfight in Heaven* – "All of us" (223) – emphasizes human unity over ethnic division. At the end of "Witnesses, Secret or Not," as the narrator's father cries over his disappeared friend, Alexie identifies everyone as witnesses to his tears: "All of us" includes not only the characters and perhaps the dead friend himself, but also the readers who have observed the suffering, heartache, love, and joy of Indian life as presented by Alexie throughout the collection. As readers, we have witnessed varied glimpses of Native lives and worldviews, and, as a result, we are culpable for continued injustices and stereotypes. Alexie uses his collection of short stories to change the way people think. As Craig Womack writes, "Native artistry is not pure aesthetics, or art for art's sake: as often as not Indian writers are trying to invoke as much as evoke" (*Red* 16–17).

Anger and joy

Alexie takes pains to educate readers. He repeatedly reveals the causes and effects – both historic and contemporary – of Indian anger and frustration with white America. Over and over again, he warns of the potentially violent reactions to cultural indifference.[10] One example, in "Jesus Christ's Half-Brother is Alive and Well on the Spokane Indian Reservation," has the

narrator imagining the rebellion of his adopted son: "He's going to dyna-
mite Mount Rushmore or hijack a plane and make it land on the reservation
highway" (120). Such images disallow readers from feigning ignorance.
Pretending to believe in a supposedly innocent America (a strangely
recurring trend over the past two-plus centuries) is impossible. Alexie
makes clear that America was never innocent, something any person familiar
with white/Indian relations (not to mention black slavery) has long
known. His novels, *Indian Killer* (1996) and *Flight* (2007), stand as testa-
ments to the rage and aggression seething within individuals torn between
multiple sets of incompatible cultural expectations. In some respects,
Alexie's fiction is a call to arms – or, more accurately, an arming of the
intellect. Reviewing James Welch's *Killing Custer*, Alexie wrote that "the war
between Indians and whites has never ended" (Richardson "Magic" 46).
Likewise, in "Imagining the Reservation" he begins with a series of requests:
"Imagine Crazy Horse invented the atom bomb in 1876 and detonated it
over Washington, D.C. ... Imagine Columbus landed in 1492 and some
tribe or another drowned him in the ocean" (149). Alexie understands
that wars also are fought within the imaginations of the populace. Those
who win the battle of popular opinion are one step closer to success. *The
Lone Ranger and Tonto Fistfight in Heaven* is part of Alexie's ongoing fight against
complacency and ignorance. Ultimately, it forces readers into a position
comparable to Victor in "A Drug Called Tradition." Laughter might discomfort
and confuse us, but it also prompts rethinking, growth, and change.

As a result, an essential part of Alexie's battle is his boisterous affirmation
of Indian life, a facet of his fiction too often ignored. He repeatedly enu-
merates the hopefulness, creativity, humor, pleasure, and strength of
Indians. His characters are neither consumed by rage nor obsessed with
revenge. Rather, they are often delighted with each other and pleased
with the details of their lives. In "The First Annual All-Indian Horseshoe
Pitch and Barbecue," Alexie uses a recurring refrain – "there is something
beautiful about" – to introduce positive elements of reservation life: the
"beautiful dissonance and implied survival" of Victor's piano playing;
the braided boy who wins the wrestling match; the man who prevailed in
the story-telling contest as well as the basketball tournament; and particularly the dreams "crackling like a campfire ... [and] laughing in the saw-
dust" (148). These positive images provide a necessary balance to the
sometimes harsh images of Indian life. They are spare, poetic, elusive, even
cinematic. Alexie is at his best when writing in this vein (a style he returns to
it superbly in *Flight*). Moreover, the life-affirming images are as realistic as

the negative representations. Like anywhere, good and bad – success and failure – exist together. Alexie makes clear that Indian communities are really not much different than others, and any attempts to distinguish too finely are ultimately counterproductive.[11] The final image of "The First Annual All-Indian Horseshoe Pitch and Barbecue" reinforces the idea that Indians and whites are linked equally: "she held the child born of white mother and red father and said, 'Both sides of this baby are beautiful'" (148).

In "The Approximate Size of My Favorite Tumor," Alexie also ends on a relatively positive note by reuniting Jimmy with Norma via humor and love. When Norma returns to Jimmy, she enters the (childless) house with the classic joke of the unconventional pretending she fits the Ozzie-and-Harriet, Leave-It-to-Beaver convention: "Honey, I'm home. ... Where are the kids?" After momentary surprise, Jimmy extends the joke, saying: "They're asleep. Poor little guys tried to stay awake, you know?" (169). The humor breaks the ice – letting them reconnect and then proceed to more serious matters. In fact, Norma admits that humor is one of the reasons why she left another man to come back to Jimmy, saying: "he was so fucking serious about everything" (170). The second reason for her return is more grave, but just as significant as her need for laughter; she says: "someone needs to help you die the right way" (170). Thus, it seems, the two things that bring them together are humor and death. Both equalize and unify; both prompt common fears and frustrations. Of course, both also threaten separation. Lincoln writes, "Like the redness of blood, or jokes about failure, dying remains a universal for all humans (the last joke?)" (Indi'n 27). Jimmy and Norma use humor as an antiseptic for their wounds, for their pain, for their anxiety about dying. The inevitability of death – and its universality – compels them to forget their differences and brings them back together.

It also reminds them of the importance of humor, which offers relief from the pain and loneliness of life. Such shared human dilemmas cause Indians, as Alexie put it, to be "just as fucked up as everybody else. No better no worse." Norma and Jimmy end up together because they need each other, just as every person needs others. Their humor shows that they also genuinely enjoy each other, which is what, I believe, Alexie hopes his readers (and critics) will learn to appreciate more. The emphasis on humor forces readers to appreciate our common humanity; it compels us to rethink our usual answers. Ultimately, Alexie asks: "Do you believe laughter can save us?" (152). The question is a serious one.

Despite its potential dangers, humor creates an intimate space that includes everyone willing to recognize our similarities and laugh at our anxieties. Whereas humor can provide a method of self-defense in a divisive world, it also offers the opportunity to surmount the false distinctions that separate people and to reinforce the connections that demonstrate our unity and equality.

7

STITCHING THE GAP

BELIEVING VS. KNOWING IN LINDA HOGAN'S *POWER*

In *Power*, Linda Hogan challenges readers to expand their understanding of the environmental and spiritual forces that shape the world. Such rethinking compels the recognition of both human and cultural connections. *Power* leads readers on a demanding journey that goes beyond mere belief and toward shared knowledge. According to Barbara Cook, Hogan writes "to tell the stories of Native people's experiences in the world and to encourage others to view the world – especially the natural world – from the perspective of traditional Native ways of knowing" (1). Without denying philosophical differences or avoiding acts of political resistance, Hogan advocates cross-cultural understanding to protect the environment, help threatened cultures and people, and encourage wholistic thinking and unity.

Hogan uses an introspective young narrator, Omishto, to prompt readers to reconsider the human relationship to the natural world.[1] Avoiding easy formulas, Omishto struggles to make sense of the radical choices of a respected Taiga woman, Ama, who kills an endangered panther in Florida to heal a broken world. Her choice thrusts Omishto into a demanding search for answers that facilitates her personal growth. In this regard, *Power* is a Native American female bildungsroman. Omishto grows into a woman via her relationship to a more experienced woman, Ama, who simultaneously follows and modifies sacred tribal traditions, forcing Omishto to re-examine her understanding of female power, traditional spirituality, and the environment.

Power also invites readers to experience, grow, and think outside of convenient but reductive categories. To facilitate this process, Omishto serves as a witness and an interpreter for readers. As she struggles to define herself in relation to unfolding events, Omishto voices the questions and misgivings that many readers likely share. Those familiar with Hogan's previous work – such as her novel *Mean Spirit* (1992), which chronicles the oil industry's abuse of Indian land and people in Oklahoma – probably expect and appreciate her emphasis upon environmental concerns. However, reading a novel in which the protagonists hunt and kill an endangered animal probably requires many to rethink assumptions about human/ nature relationships within the novel. The guidance that Hogan offers her audience in *Power* is uneven and somewhat sparse. Readers are forced to undergo a learning process via the fluctuating stages of Omishto's own adolescent understanding. Omishto is immensely confused by Ama's killing of the panther (and her own involvement in the act). As a result, readers are not *told* how to understand the hunt within a tribal context; instead, readers are *shown* the process by which Omishto struggles to make sense of Ama's act and its implications for all people. Readers are invited to undergo a similar process.

Moreover, Hogan's choice to create a fictional tribe and culture – rather than develop her story around an actual tribe and its beliefs – prevents readers from bringing specific cultural knowledge to the narrative. Even readers with encyclopedic knowledge of many indigenous cultures are forced to learn as they read. No one arrives with definitive information that will answer all questions. Instead, readers are compelled to understand the situation (and interpret the novel) while Omishto also attempts to define her response to events. As a result, the search for meaning is shared between Omishto and the audience, making readers more likely to identify with Omishto as she struggles to develop a coherent response to emotionally charged and culturally ambiguous circumstances. Hogan uses her narrator to demonstrate and encourage the interconnection of all people in the face of the earth's mysteries.

Narrative and interpretive processes

Omishto speaks in the present tense. She does not narrate retrospectively from the past, which would suggest completion and finality. Instead, she is embroiled within the cultural and personal conflict as it takes place, thus emphasizing process and continuity. Readers see her moments of doubt and revelation; they perceive her mistakes and advances. In short, readers are constrained by a limited perspective. As they recognize her fallibility, they also must admit their own. Reading *Power* places the audience in a vulnerable position, similar to that of Omishto, who negotiates a vaguely defined spiritual realm within a hostile material world. Lee Schweninger writes, "[T]he narrator becomes, by extension, spokesperson for the reader's own responsibilities and culpabilities, bringing to light what would otherwise have gone unremarked and thus misunderstood" (*Listening* 193). Readers are decentered and forced to reposition themselves repeatedly over the course of the novel. Hogan uses Omishto's narrative voice – which is alternately defiant, hopeless, speculative, and assured – to lead readers through a learning process that offers unity and hope in an otherwise fragmented world.

Omishto, of course, occupies a much more precarious situation than Hogan's readers, and she represents – to a degree – Native peoples and cultures under duress from mainstream society. Not only is she pressured intellectually to accept conventional ways of thinking about the world, but she is also threatened physically by rock-throwing boys and an abusive stepfather. Her immediate environment is endangered also. The animals are disappearing, and the land and water are polluted. Native plants are choked by kudzu and dwarfed by Methusaleh, both imports of European Americans. Omishto lives in a heavily contested physical and cultural space, and she strives to develop an outlook that offers some resolution. *Power* allows readers this same opportunity. James Ruppert has explored the implied reader within Native texts, and how Native authors "maneuver the readers into these different ways of knowing" (*Mediation* ix). Hogan uses Omishto's narrative perspective to lead readers through a learning process that transcends a divided world and recognizes connection and wholeness. To borrow Ruppert's term, Omishto "mediates" between conflicting cultures as well as changing reader responses.[2]

In *Power*, however, the end result is not guaranteed, and the process is anything but simple. Omishto repeatedly reveals her confusion when faced with unfamiliar situations and feelings. Often she senses that a larger force is working. When her sister Donna and she see Abraham Swallow run past in terror, neither of them is able to help. She says, "It was the worst feeling, like we didn't have any control over it. I kept saying, 'We've got to call,' but we just sat there like we couldn't move a muscle, and neither one of us could explain it, why we couldn't move" (12). Because Omishto cannot explain it, readers cannot understand it fully either. They might speculate, but they are denied certainty. Like the narrator, readers are confronted by their own lack of knowledge and power. Within the text, readers are embroiled within a search for meaning, which, it seems, requires them first to admit how much they do not know. Readers start fresh, much like Omishto, who is repeatedly portrayed using birth imagery. For example, her first appearance occurs in a boat on the water. The birth image is made explicit with her own narration: "It's as if I am curled inside an opening leaf in this boat covered with algae, as if I am just beginning to live" (1). Similar imagery recurs throughout the narrative, and the novel essentially records Omishto's re-birth to a new way of knowing the world. During this process, she rethinks old ideas and discovers new ones, struggling toward a healthier – and, potentially, a healed – world.

Tradition and renewal

Among conflicts with her mother, the community, and her own identity, Omishto must decide whether traditional Taiga beliefs are valid and sustainable. Early in her narrative, she tends to reject them, wavering between an adolescent over-confidence and a world-weary despair. She initially discounts the tribal elders as "superstitious," dismissing their manner of gaining knowledge as "just another old belief" and adding: "I don't give superstition even an ounce of weight" (22). Her skepticism extends to Ama, despite their friendship, and Omishto's attitude toward her vacillates between respect and embarrassment: "But my feelings about Ama are mixed, I admit. Sometimes I love her, and in those moments I think the gap between her teeth is beautiful. But there are times I don't even like her, and on those days I think she's ugly" (19). Her uncertainty about Ama appears again and again: "My feelings about her change. One moment I think she is a stranger and she is insane. I don't know her anymore. She is a stranger to her own self, too. The next moment I am surprised and proud, wishing I could believe like she does" (61). Her wavering opinion underscores the difficulty of her position. It also highlights the challenge for readers. They, too, struggle to decide whether Ama makes the best decision in killing the panther, and they seek to understand the spiritual beliefs that prompt her actions.

To Omishto, Ama represents a traditional way of living. When she views Ama through the lens of mainstream culture, Omishto distances herself from Ama, thus reflecting the extent of her own colonization.[3] However, even this formulation – with its easy equation of American society as bad and Native culture as good – is a simplification. Michael Hardin argues that *Power* "disrupt[s] conventional binaries" ("Standing" 50) by refusing to accept or reject any cultural narratives absolutely. Ama herself advocates a combination of diverse beliefs, as Omishto notes: "Ama said the old ways are not enough to get us through this time and she was called to something else. To living halfway between the modern world and the ancient one" (22). Ama advocates a blending of old and new, and, in doing so, she hints at the intersections between Native and Euro-American cultures. Ama accepts and modifies various elements of different cultures and times, blending their components into a new system that allows renewal and balance.

In an interview, Hogan explains that traditions and cultures necessarily merge and change:

> Traditions move around. When I was a girl, there were no sweat lodges in Oklahoma. After the American Indian Movement and the occupation at Wounded Knee, Oklahoma nations took up this Plains tradition. The different tribes started coming together to talk with each other again and people incorporated more and more into their own traditions. It didn't make those traditions less. It meant that they were more.
>
> ("Interview")

Rather than sustaining mutually exclusive categories in *Power*, Hogan reveals the inevitability – and the desirability – of interconnected ways of understanding and living within the world.

All cultures change to remain viable and survive. Such merging necessitates cross-cultural interactions that affect both (or all) cultures involved, mainstream American society included. *Power* invites readers – Native and non-Native – to respond to the novel with a show of constructive resolve. Ruppert identifies this tendency in other Native works, explaining "how their texts create a dynamic that brings differing cultural codes into confluence to reinforce and re-create the structures of human life: the self, community, spirit, and the world we perceive" (*Mediation* 3). Hogan asks readers to develop a world view that privileges connection over fragmentation. Despite Omishto's sometimes accusatory tone and teenage self-righteousness, Hogan uses her to mediate between readers of different backgrounds and belief systems. Dan Jaffe notes a similar goal in the poetry of African American poet Gwendolyn Brooks: "The purpose of art is always to communicate to the uninitiated, to make contact across seemingly insurmountable barriers" ("Gwendolyn" 94). If readers accept the novel's challenge, then they take part in a process that recognizes and creates relationships between seemingly disparate people, ideas, and cultures.

Storm as metaphor

The storm both facilitates the process and illustrates the primary idea. Serving as the central plot device to advance the action, it embodies the concept of wholeness and connection that recurs throughout the novel. Omishto states, "The wind is a living force. We Taiga call the wind Oni. It enters us all at birth and stays with us all through life. It connects us to every other creature" (28). Omishto's description of Oni emphasizes the inter-relationship of all living things, an idea that Hogan also emphasizes in her memoir *The Woman Who Watches Over the World*. After describing how she helped an oil-soaked bird, she states: "Its fate was interwoven with our own human fates in this world we humans have diminished because we have failed to understand how each thing connects with all the rest" (25). In *Power*, Hogan seeks to reconstruct the relationship not only between people and the environment (including animals, plants, rocks, etc.) but also between all people. Oni serves this function; it permeates, links, and changes all people and things.

During the storm, Omishto undergoes a radical change, although she seems only partially aware of it at first. When the winds begin, she describes the storm as "a bigger enemy" (33) and notes the "brute force of nature" (34). Only later does she begin to accept the larger implications of the storm and of Oni: "And then I say, 'God!' calling out to what has never heard me before" (37). The storm renders her completely naked, having torn off her dress. The imagery and language point (again) to her rebirth, a process that necessarily involves new ways of knowing. Reflecting upon the storm, she states: "I think again of breath, and how we Taiga people have that word – Oni – for breath and air and wind. It is a force. Oni is *like God*, it is everywhere, unseen" (41, my emphasis). Omishto makes a connection between different language systems as well as different belief systems. She uses a simile to equate Oni (a Taiga concept) and God (within the novel, largely a Christian formulation). Both are defined as creators; both promise individual rebirth; both offer world renewal.

Considering Ama's philosophy of connectedness and Omishto's struggle to understand it, readers should note moments when Hogan highlights the shared qualities of different belief systems. They demonstrate Omishto's growth by showcasing her ability to see past the divisiveness of the world she lives in. In one such example, Omishto recognizes that knowledge gained at school – portrayed as a predominantly white institution – intersects with Ama's teachings. She states: "At school I learn that storms create life, that lightning, with its nitrogen, is a beginning; bacteria and enzymes grow new life from decay out of darkness and water" (95). Her description of storms and lightning echoes her understanding of Oni: "This was how the world was created, Ama told me once, out of wind and lashing rain" (42). Rather than being in conflict with each other, physical science offers corroborative evidence for cultural beliefs. Omishto makes a connection between two seemingly disparate thought systems. In a similar example, her science lesson furthers her movement away from her mother's brand of Christianity: "at school I have learned there's no room in sky for my mother's heaven; there's no room at the center of the earth for hell, either. It is new worlds I will have to look for" (106). Again, a way of thinking that might initially appear opposed to Ama's beliefs instead facilitates her movement toward an integrated philosophical outlook. Omishto seems increasingly aware of how supposedly competing knowledge systems intersect and overlap.

Knowledge versus belief

Despite the relationships that she begins to recognize, Omishto remains quite explicit about her ongoing personal conflict. She vacillates between Taiga beliefs and Euro-American beliefs, between what she is taught by Ama and what she learns at school: "I used to believe in that preacher, but when it comes to this kind of thing I can't say what I believe anymore. I can't say even what I think or know. Believing and knowing are two lands distant from each other" (40). Her doubts are normal and healthy, part of a learning process that involves hard work more often than moments of revelation. Her misgivings link her again to readers, who must sort through a narrative both elusive and evocative. Hogan's writing style is often more lyrical than factual, and the ambiguities and inconsistencies complicate efforts to define Hogan's purpose. Omishto's shifting perspective seems intended to make readers admit how much they do not know.

A central question appears twice in the text, and it is directed from Ama to Omishto and, by extension, to readers: "What do you know and what do you just believe?" (67). The question emphasizes an important distinction central to Hogan's novel. Beliefs are culturally specific to certain groups (organized by region, race, ethnicity, religion, etc.). To a degree, people can choose their own beliefs. However, knowledge transcends cultural categories. Whereas beliefs may be seen as local or individual, knowledge is universal and independent. Knowledge can be shared; it connects everyone and everything. During an NEH Institute presentation in 2003, Hogan argued that many so-called "belief systems" should more properly be labeled "knowledge systems." She made the distinction to underscore the solidity, even factuality, of Native ways of understanding the world. Beliefs are a choice, and they are subject to doubt and distortion, whereas knowledge is less mutable, less transitory, less optional. Hogan also stated that laws of nature should take precedence over tribal laws. The distinction suggests that cultural divisions should not fragment a more expansive understanding of the world. In short, Hogan stresses philosophical connectedness and inclusion over factionalism.

This concept becomes manifest when Ama suggests that they hunt the endangered panther, and Omishto tells readers: "I say to her as I did in the dream or in another time – and I don't know why I say it. It's as if something speaks through me – I say, and don't even know what it means, 'I know what will happen'" (44). Although her certainty is made suspect by her previous fluctuations, her confidence in this situation – and the compulsory nature of her actions – are similar to the description of the episode involving Abraham Swallow. In both cases, Omishto is not in control, realizing instead that she is involved in something larger than herself. Within the context of Power, Omishto is connected to an expansive knowledge system that she is only beginning to recognize. Hogan suggests that Ama's hunt and Omishto's involvement transcend mere belief and culture. Their predetermined quality implies that they exist in a pure realm outside the arbitrary categories created by human design.

Over the course of the hunt, Hogan emphasizes the stages during which Omishto discovers new knowledge. First, Omishto begins to realize what they are doing and its significance. After following Ama on the hunt, she states: "I am surprised I didn't think of it before, when I said, 'I know what will happen' … It has been in [Ama's] face all along, what will happen, but I have only now seen it clearly" (57). Her sense of the situation is slowly dawning upon her. Despite her awareness of Taiga culture, and its connection to the panther, Sisa, she does not immediately perceive the significance of their actions. Likewise, readers only understand what is occurring as

Omishto understands. The hunt is a learning process, a search for meaning, and each stage causes new doubts and anxieties. Omishto repeatedly states her misgivings: "I know what she will do and I don't want any part of it" (58); "I want to turn back[;] … I am more afraid now of what we're doing than I am afraid of the panther" (59); "I am already sick by this act Ama has entered into, this act I don't yet comprehend except that it is both grace and doom, right and wrong" (62). Such statements do little to clarify the situation. Rather than explicitly explaining the Taiga kinship to specific animals, Hogan uses Omishto to illustrate the difficulty of understanding a very complex relationship. Since readers are necessarily approaching the Taiga culture as outsiders, they likely experience Omishto's confusion directly.

Witness

Omishto's role in the hunt seems to be quite specific. Carrying the water and assisting Ama is only tangential to her real role. She is a witness. Her name, Omishto, means "watching," and her central act in the novel is to watch Ama kill the panther, and then to bear witness in two trials – one in the U.S. justice system and the other in the tribal hearing. In addition, she witnesses for readers. To narrate is to shape and define. Her challenge is to discover the significance of the hunt and share her knowledge with others. In a sense, readers are also witnesses, experiencing vicariously what Omishto experiences immediately. Hogan invites her audience into a culturally specific situation (albeit via a fictional tribe) from which outsiders would normally be excluded. Readers are compelled to answer the same challenging questions that face Omishto. The search for meaning, again, is shared; connection is emphasized.

After the hunt, Omishto has a dream that reinforces an inclusive understanding of the world. She narrates: "I dream of people who do not yet know they are human. Maybe they are only now being born. It includes me, this cast of people" (94). Using birth imagery again, Hogan connects Omishto's new life – her new understanding of her spiritual relationship to the environment – to other people around the world. Hogan suggests that renewal is required to transcend divisions, join together, and heal a broken world. The immensity of the project necessitates everyone's involvement. As stated, during the hunt, both Omishto and Ama are compelled to continue, despite their hesitancy and doubt: "We are carried in something larger" (62). That "something larger" exists beyond tribal beliefs, and it encompasses instead a knowledge system available to all people. Omishto seems to recognize that once she accepts this new knowledge, the course of her life will be forever altered. Everything she once believed will be called into question. Hogan has her articulate this new understanding using the second-person pronoun "you," perhaps to force readers to undergo a similar thought process: "But the wind leaves you changed without knowing how, just knowing something unsayable has changed and it has changed forever and you cannot go back and you can never be the person you were only a day before" (67). When asked, Hogan describes her authorial intentions vaguely but evocatively, stating that she writes "for the future" ("NEH"). Omishto's words imply that the future which Hogan envisions is a radically changed place, a place where "you" and I and Omishto are reborn and, as a result, unified by our shared knowledge of the natural world and our relationship to it.

Hogan provides an interpretive key to readers when Omishto writes a school essay that tells the story of the Panther Woman. The story explains how "[a] sacrifice was called for and if it was done well, all the animals and the panther would come back again and they'd be whole" (111). Omishto, however, tears up the explanatory essay, evidently believing that her teacher and classmates would not accept the story with equanimity. In short, she does not trust in others' ability to understand. Her reaction is unsurprising, considering the history of Indian/white relations and Omishto's own recurring frustration with U.S. culture.

Hogan, on the other hand, seems to believe that readers will make a good-faith effort to understand unfamiliar beliefs, perhaps even integrating them into their own. While Omishto tears up her essay, Hogan includes it in her novel. Their choices are illuminating. Whereas Omishto chooses the safe but cynical route, Hogan risks misunderstanding in an effort to solve seemingly intractable problems. Her gamble testifies to a belief that diverse people can understand and even accept the underlying principles in a culture other than their own.

Hogan's emphasis upon cross-cultural connection does not suggest that she lacks respect for individual tribal cultures and their specific beliefs. On the contrary, she created a fictional tribe in *Power* because she wished to avoid publicizing private stories and sacred beliefs of a specific tribe. Her invention of the Taiga allows her to discuss general principles underlying some sacred rituals without being irreverent. Likewise, her subtle but self-conscious effort to foster cross-cultural unity does not mean that she fails to recognize the very real damage done by Euro-Americans to Natives. In fact, *Power* exposes many atrocities committed upon Indian peoples, and it often rejects the influence of mainstream society upon tribal cultures. For example, she recounts the torture of indigenous people by the Spanish (73); she describes the environmental degradation in the name of progress (114); and she repeatedly illustrates the pressures on Omishto and her family to embrace an ethics of materialism and one-dimensional beauty. Omishto herself is scarred by conflict and hatred, and she describes herself as "broken and divided" (143).

Power contains a great deal of justified rage, but its strength is that it moves beyond this anger toward a solution that includes everyone. Like Leslie Marmon Silko in Ceremony, Hogan recognizes that if everyone is not invited to participate, then harmony cannot be achieved.

Trial and error

For Omishto, the official court case – with its structured questions and answers – provides her an opportunity to rethink her beliefs. Initially, she feels hopeless and lost. As the lawyer questions her, however, she has an epiphany: "Every word I say sounds wrong. And then with surprise, I realize that I have lied, because I do believe what Ama believes. I have been lying, even to myself" (128). Omishto recognizes a deeper affinity for Ama and her beliefs, but her new position remains untenable as long as she cannot accept that others might also understand what she now understands. By excluding others, she appears divisive and out of balance. She states, "The strange world of it [the panther] is private as another language. Its gold light of eyes is a secret door. It follows people but they don't see it. It is nothing they can imagine. But Ama, too, is nothing they can imagine. And likewise, this world of theirs is none of [Ama's] affair" (129–30). Similar to when she tore up her essay, she still fails to see humans as linked in substantive ways. Omishto is in danger of seeing the world only according to its human categories, according to false divisions: "I see what they do, that they look at her, at us, and see that we are different kinds of people, that we are not like them, and I think for the first time that this is true" (132). Her acceptance of superficial differences contributes to the fractured world that Ama attempted to heal with the panther hunt.

As the court case continues, Omishto ultimately rejects this view of the world. It is Ama that compels her to rethink her position once again. Many in the courtroom want to blame Ama for killing the panther; they think she did it for selfish reasons. Omishto instinctively reacts against their limited understanding of Ama's act: "I see what they think. That she wanted something for herself, that this was all done for herself, which angers me" (132). She knows that Ama did not do this for personal reasons. Paula Gunn Allen writes, "At base, every story, every song, every ceremony tells the Indian that each creature is part of a living whole and that all parts of that whole are related to one another by virtue of their participation in the whole of being" (*Sacred* 60). Ama sacrificed herself for all people, animals, and ecosystems. Omishto says, "The word I think of is 'pure.' It was pure, her killing, her reason. A pure, clear motive" (134). Far from excluding others, Ama acted in a way that sought to benefit the entire world and all its inhabitants. When Omishto realizes this, she openly rejects the divisive categories that fragment people: "I don't like the way the lawyer says 'Their world' – as he calls it – is different than 'ours,' meaning the one he and others like him have been shaped by, have inhabited. He tries to make us different and not ever to be understood" (136). To believe that Ama acts only for herself or for her own tribe would not only reduce the significance of her decision, but it would also render the people within each culture tragically alien and incomprehensible to each other.

Hogan has a more inclusive goal in mind. Like Silko in *Ceremony*, Hogan suggests that traditional ceremonies must change in order to be effective. Carrie Bowen-Mercer states that Ama "acts against tradition to restore that tradition" (158). She does not bring the panther to the group of elders in the traditional way. Instead she secretly gives the hide to two elders, thus prompting other tribal people to believe that Ama has betrayed their ritual and culture. As Omishto points out, "they believe she wanted power" (174). That the Taiga have the same response to Ama as the white people is a realistic reminder that different people are connected in base ways as well as positive ways. Both Natives and whites expect the worst of Ama, thus revealing the worst in themselves. Ama, however, changes the tradition to expand its influence. She is faithful to the idea behind the ritual, rather than to the human directives regarding its performance: "Ama takes directions not from people, but from earth itself. She believes in earth" (142). Within the framing question of the novel, she is faithful to knowledge, not belief. She alters the ceremony in order to adhere to its goal: creating harmony in a world already fractured by myopic thinking. Ama's actions transcend cultural boundaries and embrace all things. In *Dwellings: A Spiritual History of the Living World*, Hogan writes: "We remember that all things are connected. Remembering this is the purpose of the ceremony" (40).

Future connection and community

Although Omishto still struggles to understand, she comes to recognize the unifying goal of the hunt. Ama's directions come from the earth, and her acts are for the earth and its inhabitant. Omishto says, "It has all fallen, this poisoned, cut world. … Unloved and disgraced and torn apart. Fallen, that's what this world is. And betrayed" (85). She knows that the entire world requires renewal, not simply the Taiga land, or the Florida swamps, or the panthers, or even herself. Ama's sacrifice is – necessarily – for everything and everyone, for all of the fallen. The altered ceremony has applications well beyond Omishto and the past: "there are the four women singing and they are the future, not the past, like I first thought" (94). As Omishto revises her original ideas, she understands that the hunt is about preparing for the future, not returning to the past. In her vision of the future, all people become humanized; all people are reborn.

Omishto increasingly recognizes the interconnected nature of the world and her role within it. Her Taiga beliefs link her – rather than separate her – from others. Critics have noted how Hogan rejects the binaries that suppose dualism and not unity. Bowen-Mercer writes: "She asks us to question history as Euro-Americans know it: a linear continuum that divides one time from another and one space from another" (159); adding that Hogan "conflates singular experience into plural, individual into communal, human into animal" (164). Hogan does this primarily through Omishto's growing awareness of herself and her relation to others and the world. At a climactic moment within the novel, Omishto announces to readers and to herself: "I am more, at this moment, than myself. I am them. I am the old. I am the land. I am Ama and the panther. It is all that I am. And I am not afraid anymore of the future or the past" (173). Omishto no longer accepts the cultural distinctions that separate her from others and the natural world. As Michael Hardin writes, "The world is changing, the ancient is confronting the modern; but instead of abandoning one for the other, Ama and Omishto seek the space between the two, the space that is neither, or the space that encompasses both" ("Standing Naked" 151).

Ama has shown Omishto how to see past human distinctions and recognize the transcendent truths that connect different people and belief systems. Rather than dismiss others' cultural views, Omishto finds parallels between seemingly opposite ways of viewing the world. For example, during the Taiga tribal trial, she states: "Maybe when it comes right down to it, we're looking *for the same thing and we could call it salvation*" (158, my emphasis). She makes a similar cross-cultural link after Ama has been banished: "I know this; this earth, the swamp, it's *the same thing as grace*, full of intelligent souls of cat, deer, and wind" (231, my emphasis). By specifically referencing "salvation" and "grace," she brings together Taiga and Christian beliefs, highlighting the shared knowledge that underscores spiritual systems.[4]

These brief moments of illumination not only lead Omishto to a more expansive and inclusive view of the world, but they also help clarify Ama's distinction between belief and knowledge: "I see that this is how it's supposed to be. This is a design not of human making, but of something I don't know, no one knows. It came from the invisible" (168). She becomes aware of "something alive that tells me we are in the presence of something large that is all around us" (169). Ama's act and its consequences extend beyond Taiga beliefs and beyond Christian beliefs. According to *Power*, humans have not created a single system that accounts for everyone and everything. Hogan strives to connect all people in a constructive manner – by recognizing how our inter-relationships allow for the possibility of renewal, wholeness, and benevolence. One person – merely a fraction – cannot change the world. Ama's effort works for Omishto, but unless all creatures participate then the goal will remain unfulfilled.

Effort and achievement

Her goal is ambitious, to say the least, and the question inevitably arises regarding whether Ama's act results in the intended effect within the fictional world that Hogan creates in the novel. The evidence – coming from the narrator Omishto – is often inconsistent. During the court trial, she states: "And the thing is, the worst and most sad thing is, that it didn't work, that it seems like things have gone on as before, that belief has failed her, failed all of us, and the boys are still out there chasing down the world" (156–26). Omishto's cynical view, of course, is part of her struggle to understand, and she fluctuates regularly throughout this learning process. However, she also tends to make clearly divisive (and contradictory) statements that seem to reject Ama and her philosophy of connectedness, even late in the novel. For example, during the tribal hearing, she states: "I am thinking that Ama was wrong in what she did even if she doesn't know or believe it. She has committed a terrible act; she has sinned against the earth, the animals who are our allies, the one who was our ancestor.

She has broken natural law" (169). Omishto's reasoning here echoes Hogan's environmental rationale for opposing the Makah whale hunt in 1999. Like Ama, the Makah chose to hunt an endangered animal in a ritual act central to their culture and beliefs. Unlike Ama, their right to hunt was protected by the 1855 Treaty of Neah Bay.

Perhaps Omishto's most damning rejection of Ama's goals is the reasoning behind her choice to join the elders at Kili Swamp. That she joins them is perfectly consistent with a unifying view of the world; after all, she is connecting to a culture that recognizes the primacy of the earth and the life force of Oni – both of which connect all people to each other. What is contrary to Ama's world-view is how Omishto defines her relationship to the non-Taiga world. She states: "And leaving I become their enemy. It was always this way for those who tried to escape. I will be their other side, the shadow they cast, invisible, dark, dangerous. But I am not sorry. It will come to me, that world, and tug at me. It will impose itself on me. It will be here, all around me. But I will no longer be dissolved salt" (232). Her explanation fails to uphold Ama's philosophy of unity and inclusiveness (even if her choice is admirable for its strength and resistance). In effect, Omishto betrays Ama and the knowledge of "something large" that directs her actions. By rejecting Ama, she forsakes the earth that gave Ama directions.

So the question remains: did Ama fail? In regard to Omishto, it is diffi-cult to determine. She has, at times, acted like a self-centered teenager. When her family watches television together, for instance, she interprets their choice as an act of defiance against her: "I can hear everyone in the living room watching TV. They are together, as if to show that now I am outside this family. I am the source of their problems. I have brought them closer together, joined them in their judgment of me" (95). Her stereo-typically adolescent response does not even consider other possibilities: they may watch television simply because that is how they pass their eve-ning; like so many people, they may seek to escape their own lives by living vicariously through TV drama and sitcom humor. But Omishto is self-focused, so their choice becomes a judgment of her. Likewise, she rejects her mother's kindness: "I'm nervous about going to school. Mama prepares me by fixing a bowl of oatmeal. 'This'll stick to your ribs,' she says as if I'm still a child and nothing has happened. Later, when she walks me to the door, she says, 'Hold your head up, you hear?' As if oatmeal and directions will carry me through the day" (103). Her mother's words and acts seem intended as expressions of love and support, and Omishto's response reveals an unwillingness to accept (or even recognize) kindness from a person that she categorizes as an enemy.

In Omishto's defense, however, she occasionally resumes a positive connection to friends and family. In fact, she has moments of great generosity right up until the end of the narrative. For example, some white boys repeatedly terrorize her and Ama, breaking windows and shouting vulgar names, yet she finds a way to understand them in humane terms: "They have families, good grades, friends, and for some reason I can't fathom they are able to be good and honest, evil and dangerous, all in the same person, at the same time, in the same skin" (219). Omishto acknowledges the fullness of each person, even those who appear largely hostile. Seeing their goodness increases the chances for positive connection. Likewise, Omishto also returns to a more genial relationship with her mother. In fact, she identifies a link that extends beyond the mother/daughter attachment and reinforces the recurring theme of cultural and philosophical connectedness. Responding to her mother's Christian rituals, Omishto notes: "She believes that prayer, that the goodness in the world, will rise up if only she believes hard enough and kneels down on her knees long enough saying words to her friend in the sky, 'Our father who art,' and I suppose this means, after all of it, that she *still believes in the power and owner of breath, Oni, but by another name*" (188, emphasis added). Omishto here rejects the fragmentation that threatens the world, instead seeing her mother's prayer in the light of a larger knowledge. Even though her mother does not accept Taiga ways, Omishto sees beyond false distinctions.

Omishto's new open-mindedness suggests that Ama's act does, in fact, result in positive consequences in the world. Omishto seems more willing to accept connections between people; she no longer sees only differences. Hogan orchestrates a general turning of events toward more favorable outcomes at the end of *Power*, implying that the beneficial results of Ama's act will gradually unfold. Omishto, for instance, gains a stronger sense of her own identity (211) and recognizes the importance of hope (227). Omishto's mother also develops a better understanding and connection with her daughter, who reciprocates in kind (221–22). Omishto explains her mother in a way that emphasizes, once again, the cross-cultural connections that Ama represents:

> I stand and watch her [mother] go and I think of salvation. The church is saving Mama, the old ways are saving the people at Kili. Ama is saving a world. But I am saving myself being here, and in all these savings, the

path of things is changed forever. And I can't help thinking that it's God Mama believes in, but it was the old people who saved us.

(224)

The healing power of words

Toward the end of the novel, Hogan increasingly emphasizes the power of words and thus the power of her novel.[5] She writes, "When spoken, words stand up straight as a stick before her, standing like thin gods, and if she stays by tradition, as if it, too, is a person, then *something newly born and alive will remain in air, in water, in this world*" (181, emphasis added). Hogan has – through Ama and Omishto and perhaps her readers – created something new that "will encircle the future and bring it all whole and together as one" (181). This vision of unity combines words and ritual within a newborn entity that has the power to change the world.[6] As Omishto states, "[O]nce again, it all rests on my words. Everything does" (202). Hogan offers Omishto's narrative to readers in an effort to expand the success of Ama's ceremony, which suggests that no real distinctions exist between diverse ceremonies or between words, acts, and thoughts. Readers are reminded here that "[s]ong and prayer and wind are all the same word, Oni" (182). Oni connects everything, physically, linguistically, spiritually, philosophically. The world is shaped and ordered by Oni in *Power*.

In my copy of *Power*, Linda Hogan wrote the phrase, "With care for the words." I think that she wanted both to urge me to pay close attention to her phrasing and to emphasize the power of language itself to effect change. In a world fragmented by confrontation and hatred, Hogan uses words to heal and correct. As Omishto states, "[T]here is a fracture in the world, a gap between Ama and those for which the world is silent and dead. I reach for words or thoughts that will fill this gap, stitch it together like thread sewing two unmatched pieces of cloth into one" (199). Hogan has written a novel to stitch this gap. She does not simply *believe* that the environment can return to its once flourishing state, that different cultures and peoples can live in community with each other, that understanding and respect can replace competition and greed. She *knows* it can happen: "What people believe, falsely, is that all this can no longer be so" (229).

Hogan's novel, *Power*, contains the power to change the world. It represents renewal and hope, and it asks readers to bear witness to this shared knowledge. Writing for connection, Hogan invites her audience to struggle toward healing and wholeness for the sake of all people.

NOTES

Introduction

1 Warrior writes, "Though certainly not always the case, much of what [Linda Tuhiwai] Smith describes as traditional practices and specialized knowledge are based in spirituality and require a high level of belief in what is usually understood as the supernatural and the extra-worldly" (Weaver, *American* 203).

2 Robert Warrior – building upon the ideas of his former teacher Edward Said – advocates a "secular" criticism, writing: "The Native world needs criticism that is self-consciously and aggressively radically inclusive" (Weaver, *American* 206). Craig Womack disagrees: "A compassionate literary nationalism makes religious studies a key feature of its interests" (Weaver, *American* 170).

3 Joanne R. DiNova writes, "I would argue that Native literature is (in some respects) written for a non-Native audience" (107).

4 James Ruppert also explores the implied reader within the text, and how Native authors teach him/her: "my goal has been to explore how the texts maneuver the readers into these different ways of knowing" (ix).

5 Womack writes, "[W]e are not mere victims but active agents in history, innovators of new ways, of Indian ways, of thinking and being and speaking and authoring in this world created by colonial contact" (*Red* 6).

6 Likewise, Womack states that, although he writes to Muskogee Creek people as his primary audience, "I am not naive enough to believe that only Creek people read my work, nor am I disappointed at having a larger audience. Writers want to be read" (Weaver, *American* 143).

7 Similarly, Jace Weaver writes: "NAS is more than any text or class *about* Indians or in which Indians play a part. It must seek to understand the material from the perspective of the Natives ... As important as exposing and deconstructing non-Native representations of Indians is (and I have engaged in it myself), ultimately the story being told is about white people. It has little or nothing to do with Natives" ("More" 236).

8 Regarding popular Native authors, Justice writes, "My own list includes N. Scott Momaday, Leslie Marmon Silko, Louise Erdrich, Sherman Alexie, Diane Glancy, Gerald Vizenor, Joy Harjo, the late James Welch, and Paula Gunn Allen, although others might include Joseph Bruchac, Linda Hogan, and the late Owens and Michael Dorris" ("Seeing," 120; footnote 11).

9 Dee Horne writes: "When non-Natives construct the category of American Indian literature, they are often perceived by American Indians and others as creating a false homogeneity. Their efforts are perceived by some American Indian critics as endeavors to marginalize Native writers – to position them as peripheral to the eurocentric canon – or to create a sub-canon of select American Indian writers that excludes many talented writers" (*Contemporary* xiv).

10 In an interview with Paula Gunn Allen, John Purdy states, "People look down on the New Critical approach and brand it as something outdated and insignificant, but actually it's all in how you use it. Isn't it?" Allen answers: "I'm a firm defender of the New Critical approach. I just don't think there's anything else you can do. All the rest is extra" (Purdy, *Writing* 14).

11 Womack advocates that other areas of interest for Natives catch up with the focus on literature: areas such as "sovereignty, religious freedom, treaty rights, land claims, language retention, tribal education" (*Red* 11).

12 In a 1997 interview, Paula Gunn Allen states, "I'm on the eve of retiring and I feel completely comfortable, in terms of my responsibility to the community, because my job has been to work in the literary field, and that's my contribution to our people, and I feel completely comfortable. It's not a problem. There's enough people out there doing enough variety of things, with really some solid approaches, that are useful to the Native people as well as to the literary community" (in Purdy, *Writing* 3).

Chapter 1

1 Donald Fixico estimates that there are nearly 600 Indian nations in North America (*American Indians* 39). Billy J. Stratton and Frances Washburn write that "there are now over 550 federally recognized tribes in the United States" ("The Peoplehood Matrix" 57).

2 Bernd Peyer writes about "the countless letters, sermons, petitions, and tracts penned and published by educated Indian intellectuals who sought to secure Native rights to a prosperous future in the United States through what might be characterized as a strategy of selective adaptation" ("Introduction" 3).

3 Fixico puts the number of treaties ratified during this period at 389 (*American Indians* xiv).

4 Ruoff lists several newspapers begun in "Indian Territory" – as well as other locations – after removal, all written and operated by Natives ("Native" 149).

5 Boudinot's numbers are supported by Georgia censuses; see Loewen, *Lies my Teacher Told Me* 131.

6 Another collection, *Navajo Stories of the Long Walk Period* (prepared under the supervision of Ruth Roessel, 1973), provides oral accounts of the event translated by Navajo scholars.

7 Nevertheless, approximately five thousand agreements and laws were enacted between 1871 and 1940, but no more treaties (Nabokov, *Native* 120). And, of course, many treaties were written to extend into perpetuity, or "as long as the grass grows and the waters run," to employ common treaty language.

8 In his preface to *Narrative Chance*, Gerald Vizenor writes that "what is seen or published is not a representation of what is heard or remembered in oral cultures ... Anthropologists, in particular, are not the best listeners or interpreters of tribal literatures" (x).

9 See the online guide created by the Association for the Study in American Indian Literatures at https://facultystaff.richmond.edu/~rnelson/asail/guide/guide.html (accessed August 20, 2010) maintained by Robert Nelson.

Chapter 2

1 Susan Scarberry-García's *Landmarks of Healing* examines the specifically "Navajo, Pueblo, and Kiowa oral traditions that provide the symbols, structures, and themes of the healing patterns that Momaday has embedded" (2) in *House Made of Dawn*.

2 Bernard Selinger writers, "[R]upture and disjunction, not development and continuity, are the novel's guiding principles. This is blatantly indicated by the regular fracturing of the narrative line" (*"House Made of Dawn"* 42–43).

3 Contrary to my assertions here that Momaday obstructs reader identification, Dee Horne follows Louis Owen's lead in suggesting that Momaday won the Pulitzer Prize in 1969 because his novel fit into an established tradition of Euro-American writing: "Colonizers privilege writing and experiences that conform to the rules of recognition of the dominant society" (*Indian Writers* xxiii).

4 Sean Kicummah Teuton writes, "It is startling, however, how few of the novel's critics recognize U.S. colonialism as the primary force in the erosion of the characters' urban tribal social world" (*Red Land* 71).

5 Sean Kicummah Teuton writes, "The Kiowas are not the keepers of a static collection of values and practices, indelibly adhered to a single essential geography. Much to the contrary, the Kiowa people attained their 'golden age' by evaluating and incorporating new knowledge into their views of themselves, the land, and the world" (*Red Land* 69).

6 Louis Owens mentions "Momaday's phallic description of Abel's woodcutting, worthy of D.H. Lawrence at his least subtle" (*Other Destinies* 106).

7 Kenneth Lincoln describes Angela as an "insidious threat" (*Native American Renaissance* 119); Kathleen Donovan writes, "That she will work in opposition to his healing is foreshadowed by Abel's perception of natural phenomena" (*Feminist Readings* 75).

8 Lawrence Evers argues that Angela's bear story is "as rootless as a Disney cartoon" ("Words and Place" 21). Responding positively, Scarberry-García links Angela's story to bear stories from Navajo and Jemez traditions. Owens writes that "Abel's healing has also been aided by the reappearance of Angela St. John" (*Other Destinies* 115).

9 Louis Owens writes: "It is out of the search for an identity that Momaday's writing grows" (*Other Destinies* 92).

10 See Lawrence Evers and Susan Scarberry-García.

11 Although Christopher B. Teuton focuses on culturally specific knowledge in *The Way to Rainy Mountain*, his description compares to my discussion here: "[T]he Kiowan concept of the 'good life' begins with wonder. The physical ability to see far into a limitless landscape is linked metaphorically to intellectual openness and curiosity, imagination motivated by wonder" ("Indian Literature" 212).

12 This particular description of Tai-me is from *The Way to Rainy Mountain* (6).

13 Likewise, Evers writes that "Abel appears to kill the albino then as a frustrated response to the White Man and Christianity" (13).

14 In his analysis of *The Way to Rainy Mountain*, Christopher Teuton writes, "The seven sisters, the bear, the rock tree, and the stars all play a necessary role in explaining a cosmology that reaches from earth to sky and is defined by interconnectedness" ("Indian Literature" 213). Likewise, Sean Kicummah Teuton notes that Francisco "remembers the function of ceremony to reaffirm the interrelatedness of all life" (*Red Land* 56).

15 Owens writes, "The obvious reading is that [the albino] signifies the 'white man' who has disenfranchised Indian people and Abel in particular – a simplistic reading that tells us little" (*Other Destinies* 101).

16 Regarding the appearance of "culebra," Owens writes, "Abel's lesson is that evil cannot be killed" (*Other Destinies* 113).

17 According to Scarberry-García, "Abel does not receive the full power and blessings of the song, however, until he sings it himself in the closing scene of the novel" (*Landmarks of Healing* 104).

Chapter 3

1 Louis Owens writes, "*Ceremony* is a 'cure' for all of us – inhabitants of a Western world that has, for more than a century, been increasingly acknowledging and even embracing its own fragmentation, deracination, and inauthenticity" (*Other Destinies* 172). Elaine Jahner writes: "The ebb and flow of narrative rhythm in the novel creates an event in the process of telling about event. The entire process is ceremonial" ("An Act of Attention" 43).

2 Likewise, Sean Kicummah Teuton writes, "As an ever-changing body of tribal philosophy, the oral tradition thus accepts and negotiates challenges to tradition" (*Red Land* 24).

3 Womack warns against falling into the "'the Indian world is falling apart' trap, where nothing is as good as it used to be, which is implied by the pure versus tainted framework" (*Red* 65–66), particularly regarding discussions of Native stories translated into English.

4 Gloria Bird and Kenneth Lincoln have identified *Ceremony*'s readers as "participant." Bird writes, "*Everything* depends upon something else. Our ability as readers to enter as participants of the story ultimately relies upon our ability to make those connections" ("Decolonization" 98). Lincoln writes that *Ceremony* "frames the people's lives from within, casting the participant audience in tales that have always been tribal" (*Native* 246).

5 Sean Kicummah Teuton writes that "the language of this Laguna song does not merely celebrate an object but instead acts performatively to change the physical world" (*Red Land* 129). He later adds: "As readers, we too are drawn into this universal convergence, figured in the most creative terms" (*Red Land* 136).

6 Kenneth Roemer also notes this difference between the novels ("Arroyos" 21).

7 Ellen Arnold writes, "The progression of Tayo's ceremony then is not so much an imposition of order on chaos, as some interpreters have suggested (see Owens 169; Nelson 12), but a developing awareness of the relationship between order and chaos, creation and destruction, good and evil, separation and participation" ("Rereading Ceremony" 80–81).

8 Anthropologist Elsie Clews Parsons also describes the diffusion of the original population in the "Variant" of "The Emergence" (*Tewa Tales* 172–75).

9 Also, in "Language and Literature from a Pueblo Indian Perspective," Silko writes, "Everything in this world was a part of the original Creation; the people at home understood that far away there were other human beings, also a part of this world" (*Yellow* 49).

10 Dee Horne notes that racial and tribal categories persist, despite the interconnectedness of all people: "Yet even this more inclusive vision [of the atom bomb] can never fully escape the paradox inherent in collective identity. An international Indian consciousness excludes those who are not Indian. A Laguna collective excludes those who are not Laguna" (*Unsettling Literature* 18).

11 Kenneth Lincoln has focused on the two primary critical responses to mixed bloods in fiction: either they are not accepted by either group (*Native* 236–37), or they bridge/fuse the two groups (*Native* 249).

12 Kimberly Blaeser writes that contemporary writers – including Silko and Vizenor – refute the "enshrined Indian stereotype [that] dictates a static identity that precludes growth, change, and adaptation" (*Gerald Vizenor* 41).

Chapter 4

1 On the trickster figure, Kimberly Blaeser writes: "Its employment becomes one of his most effective innovations in evolving a dialogue with his audience and in inciting the reader's dialogic relation with his or her larger experience," she adds that "the imaginative portrayal of trickster stimulates reader participation" (*Gerald Vizenor* 137). Elizabeth Blair and Elaine Jahner also have excellent discussions of Vizenor's postmodern tricksterism.

2 Kimberly Blaeser also explores "reader-response aesthetics" in Vizenor's work – his haiku as well as *Dead Voices* – arguing that Vizenor "demands [readers'] involvement in the search for truth, for meaning; he demands their involvement in experience, in life. His writing sends out a call for imaginative recreation of our reality" (*Gerald Vizenor* 12).

3 James Ruppert writes, "Vizenor's program is to disrupt the expectations of both audiences [Native and non-Native] implied in his text" (*Mediation* 93). David Murray writes, "[I]n true postmodern fashion, Vizenor is trying to find a form which is both encouraging us to form patterns, to draw conclusions and yet preventing us from building on them" ("Crossblood Strategies" 31).

4 Womack writes, "Important to all of Vizenor's writing, no matter the genre, is the idea of the reader's responsibility to facilitate that participation, to leave part of the story open for the reader's completion" ("A Single Decade" 69–70).

5 Tom Lynch also sees Vizenor's goal as transformative, exploring how Vizenor's poems "melt fixation and celebrate the transformative possibilities of impermanence" ("To Honor" 203).

6 Blaeser notes: "Most scholars agree that the oral can never be fully expressed in the written, experience cannot be duplicated in text" (*Gerald Vizenor* 15).

7 Alan Velie argues that Vizenor "is aware that you can't break out of the prisonhouse of language, but catachresis is his way of kicking at the walls" ("Historical Novel" 136).

8 Ruppert notes the link between oral stories and written fiction: "Oral tradition, which flourishes in contradiction, is essential for survival, and Vizenor wants his fiction to have the healing power of oral stories" (*Mediation* 94).

9 Meg Armstrong also notes Vizenor's focus upon the dangers of fetishizing the body, although from a different perspective: "The emblematic use of body parts suggests not simply the desire for perfection unavailable to them [the cripples] but also the elevation of the fragmented body to an art form, indicating a fetishistic valuation of aesthetic concerns at the expense of spiritual vision. The text implies that this fetishistic interest in body parts is a fatal substitute for the transformative powers of love and goodness" ("White Ash" 290).

10 Hartwig Isernhagen writes: "Gerald Vizenor's work occupies the ground between writing and teaching, and between 'the creative' and 'the critical,' in very original ways that appear to be designed to abolish the very borderline between those categories" (*Momaday, Vizenor, Armstrong* 7).

11 Owens writes: "Those who know Vizenor's work will also be familiar with the powerfully utopian impulse that drives his often harsh satires" ("Last Man" 234).

12 For more on this scene, see Ruppert's discussion of the traditional "Dog Husband" story (*Mediation* 100–102), and Blair's comparison of Lilith Mae Farrier within different Vizenor texts ("Trickster" 85–86).

13 Armstrong writes, "Sister Willabelle's pain, transferred to Rosina through the tale and the tracing of the wounds, serves here to create an erotic bond between the women just as in other contrasting instances the rape and dismemberment of women is imagined as the circulation of their parts, given value for their 'love' or 'perfection,' in the hands and bellies of hateful and imperfect beings" ("White Ash" 288).

14 James H. Cox writes, "Bearheart narrates the pilgrims across the landscape toward the tribal future he envisions in an attempt to liberate them from Eurowestern story-telling traditions and the colonial third world" (*Muting* 104).

15 Barry writes, "Vizenor moves the human connections with bears and bear metaphors from the spiritual to the secular, from past to present, from the pastoral to the technological, from oral to written, from reservation to city. Bear motifs in these texts serve most often as ways for characters and readers to bridge the inconsistencies, even chaos, of post-modern life and be renewed, just as the initiates in the midewiwin ceremonies are reborn with the help of bear guides. ... They bridge the gaps between the secular and the spiritual and connect the physical and the spiritual" (95).

16 Ruppert also argues that Vizenor does not "attempt to avoid claims to absolute truth or uncontested meanings" (*Mediation* 94). Jalalzai writes, "Bearheart still relies on good, evil, and redemption" ("Trickster" 28).

17 Later in the novel, Sun Bear Sun tells his inquisitors that Proude "takes care not to upset the balances of good and evil and the energies of demons" (233). Also, Barry writes, "Above all, the concern for balance (good and evil, physical and spiritual, humor and sadness) pervades his [Vizenor's] texts" ("Postmodern Bears" 109).

18 Murray states that Vizenor avoids "recourse to such an ideologically over-determined term as blood or race," adding later: "he has been able to make meaningful connections with his personal and tribal past, largely through reading and writing, not through any unmediated sense of Indianness" ("Crossblood Strategies" 24).

19 Vizenor writes in *The Heirs of Columbus*, "Germans, at last, could be genetic Sioux, and thousands of coastal blondes bored with being white could become shadow tribes of Hopi, or Chippewa" (162).

20 Cox writes, "Vizenor's primary focus in both *Bearheart* and *Heirs* is on liberating Native people from the narratives of emigration and discovery that capture them in plots ending in their domination" (*Muting* 139).

21 Gross notes this quality in Anishinaabe culture: "In promoting solidarity with those in the group and outside it, humor in this situation brought all parties together into an integrated whole" (453).

Chapter 5

1 A version of this chapter was published previously in *Studies in American Indian Literatures* 20:3 (Fall 2008): 1–28.

2 Some critics argue that specific elements of Blackfeet culture are central to understanding *Fools Crow*. Nora Barry outlines how Welch "retells and extends traditional Blackfeet myths, and connects his hero to these myths and to historical events" ("A Myth" 3). Kathryn Shanley argues that reading dreams "comprises an indigenous science of probability" ("Lady Luck" 94), which explains Fools Crow's growth as well as his contribution to the community. Bruce Murphree suggests that Welch uses Indian legends "to clarify the dangers of straying too far from Pikuni tribal heritage" ("*Fools Crow*" 186).

3 See *Natives and Academics: Researching and Writing about American Indians* (1998) and *Indigenizing the Academy: Transforming Scholarship and Empowering Communities* (2004).

4 Louis Owens critiques the way that many so-called post-colonial critics ignore "the existence of a resistance literature arising from indigenous, colonized inhabitants of the Americas" ("As if an Indian" 13).

5 Regarding Native writers' focus on history, Kimberly M. Blaeser writes: "By a deft twist of the popular vision of history, they submerge their readers in the 'what ifs' of historical interpretation" ("The New 'Frontier'" 163).

6 Kathryn Shanley writes: "Changing the hearts and minds of readers habituated to see 'Indians' as exotic Others requires a shift in mainstream worldview, the paradigm through which social interactions and cross-cultural perceptions fall categorically into place" ("Metacritical Frames" 225).

7 Andrea Opitz, who translated *Fools Crow* into German, writes that his language "forces the reader to recognize and adapt to his or her own marginal position in relation to the particular text" (*Fools Crow* 126).

8 Louis Owens writes that Welch's use of Blackfeet language "underscores the Indians' sense of still controlling their world, of being the privileged center within this world wherein the whites are 'other'" (*Other Destinies* 158).

9 Sidner Larson describes his position similarly: "[M]y lifework has evolved to a place of attempting to interpret to predominantly white middle-class students those American Indian worldviews that I believe may be helpful to them" (*Captured* 4).

10 Peter Whitely writes, "Dissemination of ritual knowledge, either orally to unentitled parties or *ipso facto* in published accounts, violates ritual sanctity and effectiveness and may damage the spiritual health of the community" (quoted in Krupat, *Turn to the Native* 21). See also my discussion of the negative critical response to Silko's *Ceremony* in Chapter 3.

11 William Farr describes how early twentieth-century observers wrote of the "heathenism and bloodshed" of the Sun Dance celebration (*Blackfeet* 66–68).

12 Many writers have written about two-way cultural influences. James W. Loewen outlines this "syncretism – blending elements of two different cultures to create something new" (*Lies* 103). Craig Womack explicitly rejects "the supremicist notion that assimilation can only go in one direction" (*Red* 12).

13 When I presented these ideas at the 2004 Western Literature Association Conference in Big Sky, Montana, an audience member (who self-identified as Native American) indicated that some Lakota felt that Welch himself failed to define these terms accurately in *Heartsong*.

14 James Loewen argues that many Natives abandoned their spiritual belief systems after debilitating epidemics swept through their regions (*Lies* 81).

15 Robert Gish, on the other hand, argues that Welch fosters mystery within many of his works.

16 David Murray notes: "The concern for mixedness, for impurities of all sorts, whether formal or racial can be seen not so much as a refusal or betrayal of an Indian heritage or identity as a refusal of the limiting and simplified purities and archaisms of mainstream representations of Indians" ("Representation" 90).

17 See Kenneth Lincoln and Kimberly Blaeser, among others. Chapter 6 also examines Sherman Alexie's use of humor in *The Lone Ranger and Tonto Fistfight in Heaven*.

18 Vine Deloria, Jr. writes, "[T]he relationship of Indians with the natural world has become so much of a cliché that it no longer communicates anything except the need for petting zoos for urban children" ("Preface" vviii).

Chapter 6

1 A version of this chapter was published as an article in *American Indian Quarterly* (26:1 [Winter 2002]: 94–115).

2 Stephen Evans also notes: "[W]hat may be taken as repetitiveness in a casual read-through of Alexie's work actually reveals ongoing development that is entirely consistent with oral tradition techniques" ("Open Containers" 48).

3 Cox writes: "Thomas Builds-the-Fire, like Alexie, is a story-teller who subverts the image of Tonto constructed by the dominant culture" (*Muting* 60–61).

4 Stephen Evans writes, "Victor counters his own impulses: Alexie's satiric mirror turns back on his readers a searing view of Indian self-victimization and shame, an 'inside' agent for the defeat of Indians by white civilization through alcohol and humiliation – engaging in what Owens calls 'inner-colonization'" ("Open Containers" 61).

5 In *American Indian Ethnic Renewal*, Joane Nagel outlines how local cultures often fuse with other cultures in order to better survive (188).

6 Janine Richardson offers a rare exception and considers Alexie a magical realist influenced by Gerald Vizenor and Leslie Marmon Silko ("Magic" 49).

7 In an interview with John Purdy, Alexie said: "Most of our Indian literature is written by people whose lives are nothing like the Indians they're writing about. ... Momaday – he's not a traditional man. And there's nothing wrong with that, I'm not either, but this adherence to the expected idea, the bear and all this imagery. I think it is dangerous, and detrimental" ("Crossroads" 8).

8 Alexie makes a similar statement about homophobia in "Somebody Kept Saying Powwow": "Years ago, homosexuals were given special status within the tribe. They had powerful medicine. I think it's even more true today, even though our tribe has assimilated into homophobia. I mean, a person has to have magic to assert their identity without regard to all the bullshit, right?" (203).

9 See Stephen Evans' article "'Open Containers': Sherman Alexie's Drunken Indians" for an extended discussion of alcohol and alcoholism in Alexie's writings.

10 Ron McFarland writes that Alexie's humor is laced with a hard message: "Especially for non-Indians, it can get rather uncomfortable" ("Polemical" 31).

11 For this reason, some criticism of Alexie seems to promote unhelpful generalizations. For example, Jane Hafen writes, "While gritty realities of Alexie's reservation life may serve as an outlet for white liberal guilt, they are all too familiar to me" ("Rock and Roll" 76). Countering this tendency, Janine Richardson writes, "On the surface, Alexie's novel is a tale of twentieth-century American Indians trying to find their way into adulthood, as all post-adolescents must. They hang out with friends, drink, and kill time as their equally deprived counterparts do in other dead-end, small town locales" ("Magic" 40).

Chapter 7

1 Lee Schweninger writes, "Hogan's interest seems to lie in discovering the human's place in and responsibility toward nature" (*Listening* 189).

2 Likewise, Benay Blend writes, "By navigating social, political, and identity frontiers, she mediates across cultures in her writings" ("Division" 67).

3 Roland Walter writes, "Omishto's quest for selfhood constitutes an act of cultural survival in response to the disruption of communal identity and memory through internal colonization" ("Pan-American" 73).

4 Michael Hardin's disclaimer might also suit my argument here: "I am not suggesting that Hogan is validating the Christian myth, merely that she is appropriating some of Christ's more mythic, archetypal qualities. To reject the entire myth could imply participating in the good–evil binary, whereas selective appropriation moves beyond the distinctions of self and other" ("Standing Naked" 148).

5 Benay Blend writes, "For Hogan, as for many indigenous writers, the process of writing becomes an act of resistance – a way, she discloses, of making herself visible" ("Geography" 69).

6 Roland Walter writes, "In this process, speaking/writing becomes a healing process in which all things and elements are united in a flux of shared creative power. In this sense, spoken/written words, being a materialization of consciousness, re-create this consciousness" ("Pan-American" 72).

BIBLIOGRAPHY

Alexie, Sherman. *The Absolutely True Diary of a Part-Time Indian*. New York: Little, Brown, and Company, 2007.

———. *Indian Killer*. New York: Warner Books, Inc., 1998.

———. "Interview: Juliette Torrez Goes Long Distance with Sherman Alexie." *(Sic) Vice & Verse* (31 August 1999): http://poetry.about.com/arts/poetry/library/weekly/aa083199.htm?terms=alexie (accessed on August 27, 2010).

———. *Reservation Blues*. New York: Warner Books, 1996.

———. *The Business of Fancydancing*. Brooklyn: Hanging Loose Press, 1992.

———. *The Lone Ranger and Tonto Fistfight in Heaven*. New York: Harper Perennial, 1993.

Allen, Paula Gunn. "A Stranger in My Own Life: Alienation in American Indian Prose and Poetry." *MELUS* 7 2 (Summer 1980): 3–19.

———. "'Border Studies': The Intersection of Gender and Color." *The Ethnic Canon: Histories, Institutions, and Interventions*. Ed David Palumbo-Liu. Minneapolis, MN: University of Minnesota Press, 1995. 31–47.

———. "Problems in Teaching Silko's *Ceremony*." *American Indian Quarterly* 14:4 (Fall 1990): 379–86.

———. *The Sacred Hoop: Recovering the Feminine in American Indian Traditions*. Boston, MA: Beacon Press, 1986.

Apess, William. "An Indian's Looking-Glass for the White Man." *Norton Anthology of American Literature: Shorter Seventh Edition*. Ed. Nina Baym. New York: W. W. Norton, 2008. 483–88.

Armstrong, Meg. "'Buried in Fine White Ash': Violence and the Reimagination of Ceremonial Bodies in *Winter in the Blood* and *Bearheart*." *American Indian Quarterly* 21:2 (Spring 1997): 265–98.

Arnold, Ellen. "An Ear for the Story, An Eye for the Pattern: Rereading *Ceremony*." *Modern Fiction Studies* 45:1 (Spring 1999): 69–92.

Bakhtin, Mikhail. *The Dialogic Imagination: Four Essays by M. M. Bakhtin*. Ed. Michael Holquist. Trans. Caryl Emerson and Michael Holquist. Austin, TX: University of Texas Press, 1981.

Barry, Nora. "'A Myth to Be Alive': James Welch's Fools Crow." *MELUS* 17:1 (Spring 1991): 3–18.

——. "Postmodern Bears in the Texts of Gerald Vizenor." *MELUS* (27:3) [Fall 2002], 93–112.

Bell, Robert. "Circular Design in *Ceremony*." *Leslie Marmon Silko's* Ceremony: *A Casebook*. Ed. Allan Chavkin. Oxford: Oxford University Press, 2002. 23–39.

Bellinelli, Matteo. "Video: Native American Novelists – James Welch." *Films for the Humanities & Sciences: A Production of TSI Swiss Television*. 1995.

Bird, Gloria. "The Exaggeration of Despair in Sherman Alexie's *Reservation Blues*." *Wicazo Sa Review* (Fall 1995): 47–52.

——. "Toward a Decolonization of the Mind and Text: Leslie Marmon Silko's *Ceremony*." *Reading Native American Women: Critical/Creative Representations*. Inés Hernández-Avila. Lanham, MD: Atlamira Press, 2005. 93–106.

Black Elk, Nicholas, (as told through John G. Neihardt). *Black Elk Speaks*. Lincoln, NE: University of Nebraska Press, 1932.

Blaeser, Kimberly M. *Gerald Vizenor: Writing in the Oral Tradition*. Norman, OK: University of Oklahoma Press, 1996.

——. "Native Literature: Seeking a Critical Center." *Looking at the Words of Our People: First Nations Analysis of Literature*. Ed. Jeannette Armonstrong. Penticton, BC: Theytus Books, 1993. 53–61.

——. "The New 'Frontier' of Native American Literature: Dis-Arming History with Tribal Humor." *Native-American Writers*. Ed. Harold Bloom. Philadelphia, PA: Chelsea House, 1998. 161–73.

Blair, Elizabeth. "Text as Trickster: Postmodern Language Games in Gerald Vizenor's *Bearheart*." *MELUS* 20:4 (Winter 1995): 75–90.

Blend, Benay. "Linda Hogan's 'Geography of the Spirit': Division and Transcendence in Selected Texts." In *From the Center of Tradition: Critical Perspectives on Linda Hogan*. Ed. Barbara Cook. Boulder, CO: University Press of Colorado, 2003. 67–80.

Boudinot, Elias. "An Address to the Whites." *Cherokee Editor: The Writings of Elias Boudinot*. Ed. Theda Perdue. Athens, GA: University of Georgia Press, 1996. 65–83.

Bowen-Mercer, Carrie. "Dancing the Chronotypes of Power: The Road to Survival in Linda Hogan's *Power*." In *From the Center of Tradition: Critical Perspectives on Linda Hogan*. Ed. Barbara Cook. Boulder, CO: University Press of Colorado, 2003. 157–77.

Brooks, Lisa. "Afterword: At the Gathering Place." *American Indian Literary Nationalism*. Eds. Jace Weaver, Craig S. Womack, Robert Warrior. Albuquerque, NM: University of New Mexico Press, 2006: 225–52.

——. "Digging at the Roots: Locating an Ethical, Native Criticism." *Reasoning Together: The Native Critics Collective*. Eds. Craig S. Womack, Daniel Heath Justice, Christopher B. Teuton. Norman, OK: University of Oklahoma Press, 2008. 234–64.

Brown, Michael F. *Who Owns Native Culture?* Cambridge, MA: Harvard University Press, 2003.

Burlingame, Lori. "Empowerment through 'Retroactive Prophecy' in D'Arcy McNickle's *Runner in the Sun: A Story of Indian Maize*, James Welch's *Fools Crow*, and Leslie Marmon Silko's *Ceremony*." *American Indian Quarterly* 24:1 (Winter 2000): 1–18.

Clifford, James. *The Predicament of Culture: Twentieth-Century Ethnography, Literature, and Art*. Cambridge, MA: Harvard University Press, 1988.

Cohen, Robin. "Of Apricot, Orchids, and Wovoka: An Interview with Leslie Marmon Silko." *Leslie Marmon Silko's* Ceremony: A Casebook. Ed. Allan Chavkin. Oxford: Oxford University Press, 2002. 257–63.

Coltelli, Laura. "Leslie Marmon Silko." *Leslie Marmon Silko's* Ceremony: A Casebook. Ed. Allan Chavkin. Oxford: Oxford University Press, 2002. 241–55.

——. *Winged Words: American Indian Writers Speak*. Lincoln, NE: University of Nebraska Press, 1990.

Cook, Barbara. "Introduction." *From the Center of Tradition: Critical Perspectives on Linda Hogan*. Boulder: University Press of Colorado, 2003. 1–10.

Cook-Lynn, Elizabeth. "American Indian Intellectualism and the New Indian Story." *Natives and Academics: Researching and Writing about American Indians*. Ed. Devon A. Mihesuah. Lincoln, NE: University of Nebraska Press, 1998. 111–38.

——. "The American Indian Fiction Writers: Cosmopolitanism, Nationalism, the Third World, and First Nation Sovereignty." *Nothing But The Truth: An Anthology of Native American Literature*. Eds John Purdy, James Ruppert. Upper Saddle River, NJ: Prentice Hall, 2001. 23–38.

Coulombe, Joseph L. "The Approximate Size of His Favorite Humor: Sherman Alexie's Comic Connections and Disconnections in *The Lone Ranger and Tonto Fistfight in Heaven*." *American Indian Quarterly* 26:1 (Winter 2002): 94–115.

Cox, James H. *Muting White Noise: Native American and European American Novel Traditions*. Norman, OK: University of Oklahoma Press, 2006.

——. "Muting White Noise: The Subversion of Popular Culture Narratives of Conquest in Sherman Alexie's Fiction." *Studies in American Indian Literatures* 9.4 (Winter 1997): 52–70.

Cruikshank, Julie. "Oral History, Narrative Strategies, and Native American Historiography: Perspectives from the Yukon Territory, Canada." *Clearing a Path: Theorizing the Past in Native American Studies*. Ed. Nancy Shoemaker. New York: Routledge, 2002. 3–28.

Deloria, Phillip. *Playing Indian*. New Haven, CT: Yale University Press, 1998.

Deloria, Vine Jr. *Custer Died For Your Sins: An Indian Manifesto*. London: Macmillan Co.: 1969.

——. "Preface." In *Earth's Mind: Essays in Native Literature*. Roger Dunsmore. Albuquerque, NM: University of New Mexico Press, 1977.

DiNova, Joanne R. *Spiraling Webs of Relations: Movement Toward an Indigenist Criticism*. New York: Routledge, 2005.

Donovan, Kathleen M. *Feminist Readings of Native American Literature: Coming to Voice*. Tucson, AZ: University of Arizona Press, 1998.

Eastman, Charles. *From The Deep Woods to Civilization: Chapters in the Autobiography of an Indian*. Boston, MA: Little, Brown, and Company, 1920.

Erdoes, Richard, and Alfonso Ortiz. "Introduction." *American Indian Trickster Tales*. New York: Viking, 1998. xiii–xxi.

Erdrich, Louise. *Tracks*. New York: HarperFlamingo, 1888.

Evans, Stephen F. "'Open Containers:' Sherman Alexie's Drunken Indians." *American Indian Quarterly* 25.1 (2001): 46–72.

Evers, Lawrence J. "Words and Place: A Reading of *House Made of Dawn*." In *Native-American Writers*. Ed. Harold Bloom. Philadephia, PA: Chelsea House Publishers, 1998.

Farr, William. *The Reservation Blackfeet, 1882–1945: A Photographic History of Cultural Survival*. Foreword by James Welch. Seattle, WA: University of Washington Press, 1984.

Fields, Gregory. "*Inipi*, the Purification Rite (Sweat Lodge), and Black Elk's Account in *The Sacred Pipe*." *The Black Elk Reader*. Ed. Clyde Holler. Syracuse, NY: Syracuse University Press, 2000: 169–97.

Fish, Stanley. "Literature in the Reader: Affective Stylistics." *Reader Response Criticism: From Formalism to Post-Structuralism*. Ed. Jane P. Thompkins. Baltimore, MD: Johns Hopkins University Press, 1980. 70–99.

Fixico, Donald. *American Indians in a Modern World*. New York: AltaMira Press, 2008.

García, Jule Gómez de, Melissa Axelrod, and Jordan Lachler. "English is the Dead Language: Native Perspectives on Bilingualism." *Native American Language Ideologies: Beliefs, Practices, and Struggles in Indian Country*. Eds. Paul V. Kroskrity and Margaret C. Field. Tucson, AZ: The University of Arizona Press, 2009. 99–122.

Gish, Robert Franklin. *Beyond Bounds: Cross-Cultural Essays on Anglo, American Indian, and Chicano Literature*. Albuquerque, NM: University of New Mexico Press, 1996.

Green, Rayna (ed). *The British Museum Encyclopedia of Native North America*. Bloomington, IN: Indiana University Press, 1999.

Greene, Jerome A. *Washita: The U.S. Army and the Southern Cheyennes, 1867–1869*. Norman, OK: University of Oklahoma Press, 2004.

Gross, Lawrence W. "The Comic Vision of Anishinaabe Culture and Religion." *American Indian Quarterly*. Summer 2002 (26: 3): 436–59.

Hafen, P. Jane. "Rock and Roll, Redskins, and Blues in Sherman Alexie's Work." *Studies in American Indian Literatures* 9.4 (Winter 1997): 71–78.

Hardin, Michael. "Standing Naked Before the Storm: Linda Hogan's *Power* and the Critique of Apocalyptic Narrative." In *From the Center of Tradition: Critical Perspectives on Linda Hogan*. Ed. Barbara Cook. Boulder, CO: University Press of Colorado, 2003. 135–55.

Harjo, Joy, and Gloria Bird, eds. *Reinventing the Enemy's Language: Contemporary Native Women's Writings of North America*. New York: Norton, 1998.

Himmelsbach, Erik. "The Reluctant Spokesman." *Los Angeles Times* (17 December 1996): http://www.fallsapart.com/art-lat.html (accessed on August 27, 2010).

Hobson, Geary. *The Last of the Ofos*. Tucson, AZ: The University of Arizona Press, 2000.

Hogan, Linda. *Dwellings: A Spiritual History of the Living World*. Greenfield Center, NY: Greenfield Review Press, 1991.

——. "Interview." 16 September 2003. http://www.amazon.com/exec/obidos/tg/feature/-/5195/002-1087688-5836826 (accessed on August 25, 2010).

——. "NEH Presentation." Olympia, WA. Summer, 2003.

——. *Power*. New York: W. W. Norton, 1998.

——. *The Woman Who Watches Over the World: A Native Memoir*. New York: W. W. Norton, 2001.

Horne, Dee. *Contemporary American Indian Writers: Unsettling Literature*. New York: Peter Lang, 1999.

Howe, LeAnne. "Blind Bread and the Business of Theory Making, by Embarrassed Grief." *Reasoning Together: The Native Critics Collective*. Eds. Craig S. Womack, Daniel Heath Justice, and Christopher B. Teuton. Norman, OK: University of Oklahoma Press, 2008. 325–39.

Iser, Wolfgang. "The Reading Process: A Phenomenological Approach." *Reader Response Criticism: From Formalism to Post-Structuralism*. Ed. Jane P. Thompkins. Baltimore, MD: Johns Hopkins University Press, 1980. 50–69.

Isernhagen, Hartwig. *Momaday, Vizenor, Armstrong: Conversations on American Indian Writing*. Norman, OK: University of Oklahoma Press, 1999.

Jaffe, Dan. "Gwendolyn Brooks: An Appreciation from the White Suburbs." In *The Black American Writer: Volume II, Poetry and Drama*. Ed. C.W.E. Bigsby. Deland, FL: Everett/Edwards, Inc., 1969. 89–98.

Jahner, Elaine. "An Act of Attention: Event Structure in *Ceremony*." *Leslie Marmon Silko's* Ceremony: *A Casebook*. Ed. Allan Chavkin. Oxford: Oxford University Press, 2002. 41–50.

——. "Trickster Discourse and Postmodern Strategies." *Loosening the Seams: Interpretations of Gerald Vizenor*. Ed. A. Robert Lee. Bowling Green, OH: Bowling Green State University Popular Press, 2000. 38–58.

Jalalzai, Zubeda. "Tricksters, Captives, and Conjurers: The 'Roots' of Liminality and Gerald Vizenor's *Bearheart*." *American Indian Quarterly* 23:1 (Winter 1999): 25–44.

Janke, Ronal A. "Population, Reservations, and Federal Indian Policy". *Handbook of Native American Literature*. Ed. Andrew Wiget. New York: Garland Publishing, 1996: 155–74.

Johansen, Bruce E. *The Praeger Handbook on Contemporary Issues in Native America: Volume 1 – Linguistic, Ethnic, and Economic Revival*. Westport, CT: Praeger Publishers, 2007.

Justice, Daniel Heath. "'Go Away, Water!': Kinship Criticism and the Decolonization Imperative." *Reasoning Together: The Native Critics Collective*. Eds. Craig S. Womack, Daniel Heath Justice, Christopher B. Teuton. Norman, OK: University of Oklahoma Press, 2008. 147–68.

——. "Seeing (and Reading) Red: Indian Outlaws in the Ivory Tower." *Indigenizing the Academy: Transforming Scholarship and Empowering Communities*. Eds. Devon Abbott Mihesuah, Angela Cavender Wilson. Lincoln, NE: University of Nebraska Press, 2004. 100–123.

Kaye, Frances W. "Just What is Cultural Appropriation, Anyway? The Ethics of Reading *Black Elk Speaks*." *The Black Elk Reader*. Ed. Clyde Holler. Syracuse, NY: Syracuse University Press, 2000: 165.

Kilcup, Karen L. "Introduction." *Native American Women's Writing, 1800–1924: An Anthology*. Oxford: Blackwell Publishers, 2000.

Krumholz, Linda. "Native Designs: Silko's *Storyteller* and the Reader's Initiation." *Leslie Marmon Silko: A Collection of Critical Essays*. Eds. Louise K. Barnett, James L. Hobson. Albuquerque, NM: University of New Mexico Press, 1999. 63–86.

Krupat, Arnold. *The Turn to the Native: Studies in Criticism and Culture*. Lincoln, NE: University of Nebraska Press, 1996.

——. *The Voice in the Margin: Native American Literature and the Canon*. Berkeley, CA: University of California Press, 1989.

Larson, Sidner. *Captured in the Middle: Tradition and Experience in Contemporary Native American Writing*. Seattle, WA: University of Washington Press, 2000.

Lee, A. Robert. *Loosening the Seams: Interpretations of Gerald Vizenor*. Bowling Green State University Press: Bowling Green, OH, 2000.

Lincoln, Kenneth. *Indi'n Humor: Bicultural Play in Native America*. New York: Oxford University Press, 1993.

——. *Native American Renaissance*. Berkeley, CA: University of California Press, 1983.

Loewen, James W. *Lies My Teacher Told Me: Everything Your American History Textbook Got Wrong*. New York: Simon, 1995.

Loxley, James. *Performativity*. New York: Routledge, 2007.

Lynch, Tom. "To Honor Impermanence: The Haiku and Other Poems of Gerald Vizenor." *Loosening the Seams: Interpretations of Gerald Vizenor*. Ed. A. Robert Lee. Bowling Green, OH: Bowling Green State University Popular Press, 2000. 203–24.

McFarland, Ron, Ed. *James Welch*. Lewiston, ID: Confluence, 1986.

——. "Sherman Alexie's Polemical Stories." *Studies in American Indian Literatures* 9.4 (Winter 1997): 27–38.

McKnickle, D'Arcy. *The Surrounded*. New York: Dodd, Mead, Company, 1936.

Mihesuah, Devon Abbott, Ed. *Natives and Academics: Researching and Writing about American Indians*. Lincoln, NE: University of Nebraska Press, 1998.

Mihesuah, Devon Abbott and Angela Cavender Wilson, Eds. *Indigenizing the Academy: Transforming Scholarship and Empowering Communities*. Lincoln, NE: University of Nebraska Press, 2004.

Miller, J. Hillis. *Speech Acts in Literature*. Stanford, CA: Stanford University Press, 2001.

Momaday, N. Scott. *House Made of Dawn*. New York: HarperCollins, 1968.

———. *The Man Made of Words: Essays, Stories, Passages*. New York: St. Martin's Press, 1997.

———. *The Way to Rainy Mountain*. Albuquerque, NM: University of New Mexico Press, 1969.

Murphree, Bruce. "Welch's *Fools Crow*." *Explicator* 52:3 (Spring 1994): 186–87.

Murray, David. "Crossblood Strategies in the Writings of Gerald Vizenor." *Loosening the Seams: Interpretations of Gerald Vizenor*. Ed. A. Robert Lee. Bowling Green, OH: Bowling Green State University Popular Press, 2000. 20–37.

———. "Representation and Cultural Sovereignty: Some Case Studies." *Native American Representations: First Encounters, Distorted Images, and Literary Appropriations*. Ed. Gretchen M. Bataille. Lincoln, NE: University of Nebraska Press, 2001. 80–97.

Nabokov, Peter (ed). *Native American Testimony: A Chronicle of Indian-White Relations from Prophecy to the Present, 1492–1992*. New York: Penguin, 1991 (expanded edition).

Nagel, Joane. *American Indian Ethnic Renewal: Red Power and the Resurgence of Identity and Culture*. New York: Oxford University Press, 1997.

Nelson, Robert M. "Rewriting Ethnography: The Embedded Texts in Leslie Silko's *Ceremony*." *Telling the Stories: Essays on American Indian Literatures and Cultures*. Eds. Elizabeth Hoffman Nelson, Malcolm Nelson. New York: Peter Lang, 2001. 47–58.

Occom, Samson. *The Collected Writings of Samson Occom, Mohegan*. New York: Oxford University Press, 2006.

Opitz, Andrea. "James Welch's *Fools Crow* and the Imagination of Pre-Colonial Space." *American Indian Quarterly* 24:1 (Winter 2000): 126–40.

Ortiz, Alfonso. *The Tewa World: Space, Time, Being and Becoming in a Pueblo Society*. Chicago: University of Chicago Press, 1969.

Ortiz, Simon. "Empowerment." *American Indian Quarterly* 28.1&2 (2004): 112–14.

Owens, Louis. "Afterword." *Bearheart: The Heirship Chronicles*. Minneapolis, MN: University of Minnesota Press, 1978. Republished 1990. 247–54.

———. "As If an Indian Were Really an Indian: Native American Voices and Postcolonial Theory." *Native American Representations: First Encounters, Distorted Images, and Literary Appropriations*. Ed. Gretchen M. Bataille. Lincoln, NE: University of Nebraska Press, 2001. 11–25.

——. "'Ecstatic Strategies': Gerald Vizenor's *Darkness in Saint Louis Bear-heart*." *Narrative Chance: Postmodern Discourse on Native American Indian Literatures*. Ed. Gerald Vizenor. Norman, OK: University of Oklahoma Press, 1993. 141–54.

——. *Mixedblood Messages: Literature, Film, Family, Place*. Norman, OK: University of Oklahoma Press, 1998.

——. *Other Destinies: Understanding the American Indian Novel*. Norman, OK: University of Oklahoma Press, 1992.

——. "The Last Man of the Stone Age: Gerald Vizenor's *Ishi and The Wood Ducks*." *Loosening the Seams: Interpretations of Gerald Vizenor*. Ed. A. Robert Lee. Bowling Green, OH: Bowling Green State University Popular Press, 2000. 233–45.

——. "'The Very Essence of Our Lives': Leslie Silko's Webs of Identity." *Leslie Marmon Silko's* Ceremony: *A Casebook*. Ed. Allan Chavkin. Oxford: Oxford University Press, 2002. 91–116.

Parker, Andrew, and Eve Kosofsky Sedgwick. "Introduction." *Performativity and Performance*. New York: Routledge, 1995. 1–18.

Parker, Robert Dale. *The Invention of Native American Literature*. Ithaca, NY: Cornell University Press, 2003.

Parsons, Elsie Clews. *Tewa Tales*. (Originally published: 1926.) Tucson, AZ: University of Arizona Press, 1994.

Petalesharo. "Speech of the Pawnee Chief." *Norton Anthology of American Literature: Shorter Seventh Edition*. Ed. Nina Baym. New York: W. W. Norton, 2008. 575–77. [originally published in Buchanan's *Sketches of the North American Indians* (1824)].

Peterson, Nancy J. "Introduction: Native American Literature – From the Margins to the Mainstream." *Modern Fiction Studies* 45.1 (1999): 1–9.

Petry, Sandy. *Speech Acts and Literary Theory*. New York: Routledge, 1990.

Peyer, Bernd. "Introduction." *American Indian Non-Fiction: An Anthology of Writings, 1760s–1930s*. Norman, OK: University of Oklahoma Press, 2007.

Piper, Karen. "Police Zones: Territory and Identity in Leslie Marmon Silko's *Ceremony*." *American Indian Quarterly* 21:3 (Summer 1997): 483–97.

Pratt, Richard. "The Advantages of Mingling Indians with Whites." *Americanizing the American Indians: Writings by the "Friends of the Indian" 1880–1900*. Cambridge, MA: Harvard University Press, 1973. 260–71.

Purdy, John. "Crossroads: A Conversation with Sherman Alexie." *Studies in American Indian Literatures* 9.4 (Winter 1997): 1–18.

——. "The Transformation: Tayo's Genealogy in *Ceremony*." *Leslie Marmon Silko's* Ceremony: *A Casebook*. Ed. Allan Chavkin. Oxford: Oxford University Press, 2002. 63–70.

——. *Writing Indian, Native Conversations*. Lincoln, NE: University of Nebraska Press, 2009.

Rainwater, Catherine. *Dreams of Fiery Stars: The Transformations of Native American Fiction*. Philadelphia, PA: University of Pennsylvania Press, 1999.

Reyhner, Jon Allan. *Education and Language Restoration*. Philadelphia, PA: Chelsea House, 2006.

Rice, David A. "Witchery, Indigenous Resistance, and Urban Space in Leslie Marmon Silko's *Ceremony*." *Studies in American Indian Literatures* 17. 4 (Winter 2005): 114–43.

Rice, Julian. "Black Elk." *Handbook of Native American Literature*. Ed. Andrew Wiget. New York: Garland Publishing, 1996. 211–16.

Richardson, Janine. "Magic and Memory in Sherman Alexie's *Reservation Blues*." *Studies in American Indian Literatures* 9.4 (Winter 1997): 37–51.

Ridge, John Rollin (aka Yellow Bird). *Life and Legend of Joaquín Murieta: The Celebrated California Bandit*. Norman, OK: University of Oklahoma Press, 1955.

Roemer, Kenneth M. "Silko's Arroyos as Mainstream: Processes and Implications of Canonical Identity." *Modern Fiction Studies* 45:1 (Spring 1999): 10–37.

Roppolo, Kimberly. "Samson Occom as Writing Instructor: The Search for an Intertribal Rhetoric." In *Reasoning Together: The Native Critics Collective*. Eds. Craig S. Womack, Daniel Heath Justice, and Christopher B. Teuton. Norman, OK: University of Oklahoma Press, 2008. 303–24.

Ruoff, LaVonne Brown. "Native American Writings: Beginnings to 1967." *Handbook of Native American Literature*. Ed. Andrew Wiget. New York: Garland Publishing, 1996. 145–55.

Ruppert, James. *Mediation in Contemporary Native American Fiction*. Norman, OK: University of Oklahoma Press, 1995.

——. "The Reader's Lessons in *Ceremony*." *Arizona Quarterly* 44:1 (Spring 1988): 78–85.

Sarris, Greg. *Keeping Slug Woman Alive: A Holistic Approach to American Indian Texts*. Berkeley, CA: University of California Press, 1993.

Scarberry-García, Susan. *Landmarks of Healing: A Study of House Made of Dawn*. Albuquerque, NM: University of New Mexico Press, 1990.

Schorcht, Blanca. *Storied Voices in Native American Texts: Harry Robinson, Thomas King, James Welch, and Leslie Marmon Silko*. New York: Routledge, 2003.

Schweninger, Lee. *Listening to the Land: Native American Literary Responses to the Landscape*. Athens, GA: University of Georgia Press, 2008.

Selinger, Bernard. "*House Made of Dawn*: A Positively Ambivalent Bildungs-roman." *Modern Fiction Studies* 45.1 (1999): 38–68.

Senier, Siobhan. "Allotment Protest and Tribal Discourse: Reading *Wynema's* Successes and Shortcomings." *American Indian Quarterly* 24.3 (2000): 420–40.

Sequoya-Magdaleno, Jana. "Telling the *différence*: Representations of Identity in the Discourse of Indianness." *The Ethnic Canon: Histories, Institutions, and Interventions*. Ed David Palumbo-Liu. Minneapolis, MN: University of Minnesota Press, 1995.

Shanley, Kathryn. "Lady Luck or Mother Earth? Gaming as a Trope in Plains Indian Cultural Traditions." *Wicazo Sa Review: A Journal of Native American Studies* 15:2 (2000): 93–101.

——. "Metacritical Frames of Reference in Studying American Indian Litera-ture: An Afterword." *Native American Representations: First Encounters, Distorted Images, and Literary Appropriations*. Ed. Gretchen M. Bataille. Lincoln, NE: University of Nebraska Press, 2001. 224–26.

——. "The Indians America Loves to Love and Read: American Indian Identity and Cultural Appropriation." *Native American Representations: First Encounters, Distorted Images, and Literary Appropriations*. Ed. Gretchen M. Bataille. Lincoln, NE: University of Nebraska Press, 2001. 26–49.

Silko, Leslie Marmon. *Almanac of the Dead*. New York: Simon and Schuster, 1991.

——. *Ceremony*. New York: Penguin, 1977.

——. *Conversations with Leslie Marmon Silko*. Ed. Ellen Arnold. Jackson, MS: University Press of Mississippi, 2000.

——. *Gardens in the Dunes*. New York: Simon & Schuster, 1999.

——. "Interior and Exterior Landscapes: The Pueblo Migration Stories." *Yellow Woman and A Beauty of the Spirit: Essays on Native American Life Today*. New York: Simon & Schuster, 1996.

——. "Language and Literature from a Pueblo Indian Perspective." *Yellow Woman and A Beauty of the Spirit: Essays on Native American Life Today*. New York: Simon & Schuster, 1996.

Smith, Linda Tuhiwai. *Decolonizing Methodologies: Research and Indigenous Peoples*. New York: St. Martin's Press, 1999.

Snipp, C. Matthew. "Population Size, Nadir to 2000." *Handbook of Native American Indians, Volume 3; Environment, Origins, and Population*. Washington, D.C.: Smithsonian Institution, 2006.

Standing Bear, Luther. *My People, The Sioux*. Lincoln, NE: University of Nebraska Press, 1975.

Stratton, Billy J. and Frances Washburn. "The Peoplehood Matrix: A New Theory for American Indian Literature." *Wicazo Sa Review* 23.1 (2008): 51–72.

Tapahonso, Luci. *Sáanii Dahataał: The Women Are Singing*. Tucson, AZ: University of Arizona, 1993.

Taylor, Alan. *American Colonies: Volume 1 of The Penguin History of the United States*. New York: Penguin, 2002.

Taylor, Paul Beekman. "Silko's Reappropriation of Secrecy." *Leslie Marmon Silko: A Collection of Critical Essays*. Eds. Louis K Barnett and James L Thorson. Albuquerque, NM: University of New Mexico Press, 1999. 23–62.

Teuton, Christopher B. "Theorizing American Indian Literature: Applying Oral Concepts to Written Traditions." *Reasoning Together: The Native Critics Collective*. Eds. Craig S. Womack, Daniel Heath Justice, and Christopher B. Teuton. Norman, OK: University of Oklahoma Press, 2008. 193–215.

Teuton, Sean Kicummah. *Red Land, Red Power: Grounding Knowledge in the American Indian Novel*. Durham, NC: Duke University Press, 2008.

Tohe, Laura. *No Parole Today*. Albuquerque, NM: West End Press, 1999.

Velie, Alan. "The Indian Historical Novel." *Native-American Writers*. Ed. Harold Bloom. Philadelphia, PA: Chelsea House, 1998. 195–209.

Vizenor, Gerald. *Bearheart: The Heirship Chronicles*. Minneapolis, MN: University of Minnesota Press, 1978. Republished 1990.

——. *Narrative Chance: Postmodern Discourse on Native American Indian Literatures*. Ed. Gerald Vizenor. Norman, OK: University of Oklahoma Press, 1993.

——. *The Heirs of Columbus*. Hanover, NH: The University Press of New England, 1991.

——. *The People Named the Chippewa: Narrative Histories*. Minneapolis, MN: University of Minnesota Press, 1984.

Walter, Roland. "Pan-American (Re)Visions: Magical Realism and Amerindian Cultures in Susan Power's *The Grass Dancer*, Gioconda Belli's *La Mujer Habitada*, Linda Hogan's *Power*, and Mario Vargas Llosa's *El Hablador*." *American Studies International* 37: 3 (October 1999): 63–80.

Warrior, Robert Allen. *American Indian Literary Nationalism*. With Weaver and Womack. Albuquerque, NM: University of New Mexico Press, 2006.

——. *Tribal Secrets: Recovering American Indian Intellectual Traditions*. Minneapolis, MN: University of Minnesota Press, 1995.

Weaver, Jace. *American Indian Literary Nationalism*. With Warrior and Womack. Albuquerque, NM: University of New Mexico Press, 2006.

——. "More Light Than Heat: The Current State of Native American Studies." *American Indian Quarterly* 31.2 (2007): 233–55.

Welch, James. *Fools Crow*. New York: Penguin, 1986.

——. with Paul Stekler. *Killing Custer*. New York: Norton, 1994.

——. *The Heartsong of Charging Elk*. New York: Doubleday, 2000.

Wiget, Andrew. *Handbook of Native American Literature*. New York: Garland Publishing, 1996.

Wilson, Terry P. "John Joseph Matthews." *Handbook of Native American Literature*. Ed. Andrew Wiget. New York: Garland Publishing, 1996. 245–50.

Winnemucca (Hopkins), Sarah. *Life among the Piutes: Their Wrongs and Claims*. Reno, NV: University of Nevada Press, 1994.

Wise, R. Todd. "The Great Vision of Black Elk as Literary Ritual." *The Black Elk Reader*. Ed. Clyde Holler. Syracuse, NY: Syracuse University Press, 2000: 241–61.

Womack, Craig S. *American Indian Literary Nationalism*. With Warrior and Weaver. Albuquerque, NM: University of New Mexico Press, 2006.

——. "A Single Decade: Book-Length Native Literary Criticism between 1986 and 1997." *Reasoning Together: The Native Critics Collective*. Eds. Craig S. Womack, Daniel Heath Justice, and Christopher B. Teuton. Norman, OK: University of Oklahoma Press, 2008. 3–104.

——. *Red on Red: Native American Literary Separatism*. Minneapolis, MN: University of Minnesota Press, 1999.

Wright, Anne, Ed. *The Delicacy and Strength of Lace: Letters Between Leslie Marmon Silko and James Wright*. Saint Paul, MN: Graywolf Press, 1986.

Zitkala-Sa. *American Indian Stories*. Washington, D.C.: Hayworth Publishing House, 1921.

INDEX